Beginning Office 365 Collaboration Apps

Working in the Microsoft Cloud

Ralph Mercurio

Apress®

Beginning Office 365 Collaboration Apps

Ralph Mercurio
Clayton, North Carolina, USA

ISBN-13 (pbk): 978-1-4842-3848-6   ISBN-13 (electronic): 978-1-4842-3849-3
https://doi.org/10.1007/978-1-4842-3849-3

Library of Congress Control Number: 2018955066

Managing Director, Apress Media LLC: Welmoed Spahr
Acquisitions Editor: Joan Murray
Development Editor: Laura Berendson
Coordinating Editor: Nancy Chen

Cover designed by eStudioCalamar

Cover image designed by Freepik (www.freepik.com)

Distributed to the book trade worldwide by Springer Science+Business Media New York, 233 Spring Street, 6th Floor, New York, NY 10013. Phone 1-800-SPRINGER, fax (201) 348-4505, e-mail orders-ny@springer-sbm.com, or visit www.springeronline.com. Apress Media, LLC is a California LLC and the sole member (owner) is Springer Science + Business Media Finance Inc (SSBM Finance Inc). SSBM Finance Inc is a **Delaware** corporation.

For information on translations, please e-mail rights@apress.com, or visit www.apress.com/rights-permissions.

Apress titles may be purchased in bulk for academic, corporate, or promotional use. eBook versions and licenses are also available for most titles. For more information, reference our Print and eBook Bulk Sales web page at www.apress.com/bulk-sales.

Any source code or other supplementary material referenced by the author in this book is available to readers on GitHub via the book's product page, located at www.apress.com/9781484238486. For more detailed information, please visit www.apress.com/source-code.

To my wife, Sarah; son, Bobby; and daughter, Julia:
Thank you for letting me take the time to write this book.
It was difficult not spending time with you during this project, and
I couldn't be more grateful to call you my family. I love you all.

To my parents: Thank you for always supporting my
endeavors and giving me the courage to take this journey no matter
where I end up. I love you.

Table of Contents

About the Author

 **Ralph Mercurio** is an IT pro with 15 years of experience. He is currently working for the City of Durham in North Carolina, focusing his efforts on providing collaborative solutions to the city's many departments. Ralph has held various roles in the technology field, including as a SharePoint Infrastructure Architect consulting for various companies in the NY Metro Area.

Ralph also has experience architecting and deploying solutions that leverage the best features of SharePoint/ Office 365 and provide real business value while solving the user experience. He has seen many technology changes throughout the years and he discovered a passion for helping users find ways to leverage what they know to learn a new technology. With Office 365, he has made it his goal to help readers realize the potential of this powerful platform in order to get the most out of these ever-changing applications.

You can find more information about Ralph as well as an Office 365 blog and Office 365 consulting services at `www.capelesssolutions.com`.

About the Technical Reviewer

Massimo Nardone has more than 22 years of experience in security, web/mobile development, and cloud and IT architecture. His true IT passions are security and Android.

He has been programming and teaching how to program with Android, Perl, PHP, Java, VB, Python, C/C++, and MySQL for more than 20 years.

He holds a Master of Science degree in Computing Science from the University of Salerno, Italy. He has worked as a Project Manager, Software Engineer, Research Engineer, Chief Security Architect, Information Security Manager, PCI/SCADA Auditor, and Senior Lead IT Security/Cloud/SCADA Architect for many years.

Technical skills include security, Android, cloud, Java, MySQL, Drupal, Cobol, Perl, web and mobile development, MongoDB, D3, Joomla, Couchbase, C/C++, WebGL, Python, Pro Rails, Django CMS, Jekyll, Scratch, etc.

He currently works as Chief Information Security Office (CISO) for Cargotec Oyj. He worked as visiting lecturer and supervisor for exercises at the Networking Laboratory of the Helsinki University of Technology (Aalto University). He holds four international patents (PKI, SIP, SAML, and Proxy areas).

Massimo has reviewed more than 40 IT books for different publishing companies and he is the coauthor of *Pro Android Games* (Apress, 2015).

Acknowledgments

Thank you to Nancy Chen, Joan Murray, Laura Berendson, and the rest of the team at Apress for your continued guidance throughout the writing of this book. This was a daunting first experience and it would have not been possible without you.

I want to take a moment to mention Tony Smith for his support throughout the years both personally and work-related. Even though we no longer work for the same employer, thank you for your friendship and encouragement; I truly value it.

I would also like to thank the technical reviewer, Massimo Nardone, for his work reviewing the book to help ensure its accuracy.

Introduction

Office 365 is Microsoft's SaaS (Software as a Service) platform. It offers Outlook, SharePoint, OneDrive, Office, and other collaboration applications to help businesses and other entities use the cloud to provide these applications to their users.

By utilizing Office 365, entities can offer low-cost access and reduce the administrative and IT overhead associated with providing these services. By doing so, end users gain access to updated applications without having to wait and can utilize these new features or applications once Microsoft releases them. However, many users are not adequately trained in using these applications, and without a foundational understanding of them, these applications can be overwhelming. Because of this ever-increasing issue, this book attempts to bridge the gap for end users new to the Office 365 platform as well as for more advanced users by providing a functional understanding of each application in the Office 365 suite.

As Office 365 evolves and Microsoft releases new features or applications, I will maintain a "Beginning Office 365 Collaboration Apps" blog where I will post updates to accompany this book; go to `www.capelesssolutions.com`. If you encounter any issues, comments, or questions, please feel free to reach out to `ralph@capelesssolutions.com` and I will respond as soon I can.

Whom This Book Is For

The goal and purpose of this book is to provide the knowledge to use Office 365, particularly around the collaboration apps described below. These applications form the foundation of Office 365, and each chapter guides you through the basics of them via text and images.

This book also serves as a resource to users who have been introduced to Office 365 but are still unfamiliar with many of the applications. This book does not require a subscription to Office 365 but having one will allow you to follow along as we dive into each collaboration application.

How This Book Is Structured

This book is organized by chapters, with each chapter introducing a particular collaboration app in Office 365. This was done on purpose because it will allow you to read the chapters that interest you most or that cover the application you are currently using—without the need to read the entire book cover to cover. This book includes step-by-step instructions, images, tables, and examples detailing the features of each application.

Chapter 1: Introduction to Office 365

This chapter introduces you to the concept of Office 365 and SaaS. It also guides you through creating an Office 365 Trial account if needed.

Chapter 2: SharePoint

This chapter provides an overview of creating lists, libraries, and sites. It also introduces some of the basic principles such as list/library columns, metadata, views, and the available templates to use.

Chapter 3: OneDrive

This chapter covers OneDrive and how to navigate around OneDrive and use it effectively to manage your files. This chapter also shows how to create Office files within OneDrive and how to share files with users.

Chapter 4: Office 365 Groups

This chapter discusses the components of an Office 365 group as well as how to create and maintain a group. It also shows you how to manage users and invite external users.

Chapter 5: Teams

This chapter introduces Teams and provides a functional understanding of the application. You learn how to navigate within Teams and understand the interface. This chapter also discusses creating teams, channels, and using some of the basic functions included in Teams.

Chapter 6: Yammer

This chapter details using Yammer within an enterprise environment. It discusses the Yammer interface and creating posts that can be shared with users.

Chapter 7: Office

This chapter introduces Office and Office Online. It discusses some of the similarities and differences between the versions. It also demonstrates some of the advanced capabilities of the platform including real-time coauthoring.

Chapter 8: Planner

This chapter introduces Microsoft Planner and is concerned with task management. It covers the basic of Planner, including creating tasks, editing tasks, deleting tasks, and reporting of task statuses.

Chapter 9: Stream

This chapter introduces Microsoft Stream, an enterprise-capable video platform, and some of the basic functions within Stream. This chapter also discusses some of the advanced features of Stream and how to access them.

Chapter 10: Forms

This chapter introduces Microsoft Forms, an application to create a variety of browser and mobile-ready forms. You can create forms, surveys, and a quizzes. You also learn about some of the features within the application such as data types, reporting, and grading.

Chapter 11: Flow

This chapter demonstrates Microsoft Flow from a simple flow to a complex flow. It will guide you through creating a flow. You will create an approval flow and a flow that incorporates a third-party service for electronic signatures.

Chapter 12: Putting It All Together

This chapter serves as a summary chapter, highlighting each application and its intended purpose within Office 365.

CHAPTER 1

Welcome to Office 365

Welcome to *Beginning Office 365 Collaboration Apps*. My intention with this book is to introduce the concepts behind Office 365, how it works, and what it can offer you regarding functionality, collaboration, and ease of use. There are many applications within Office 365, and I will focus on the specific applications that foster collaboration, dedicating a chapter to each.

In this book, I will discuss SharePoint, OneDrive, Teams, Office, and a few other applications which make up Office 365. I will also introduce two relatively new applications from Microsoft: Stream and Flow. Microsoft Stream is a video sharing and collaboration application; Flow connects workflow actions across a majority of Office 365 and external applications.

In this chapter, I will approach Office 365 from a very high level, including a perspective on collaboration and how it has evolved throughout the years. It is important to understand and acknowledge the past and present as Office 365 lays the foundation for collaboration in the future. I will also discuss how to set up an Office 365 account so that you can experiment and follow along. I am a firm believer in doing as opposed to reading because it reinforces the content and allows you to become familiar and confident in the interface and nuances of Office 365.

Collaboration in the Workplace

Collaboration has changed over the years from a rigid structure to a more flexible model that embraces technology and allows information workers to have more freedom and control over getting their work completed. Microsoft classifies information workers as employees who consume and create content. This includes nearly every department of an organization; some examples of content are budgets, employee records, project documents, technical guides, and forms. With that, not all companies embrace the model and prefer (sometimes strongly) that employees report to a company office location to perform their duties.

1

© Ralph Mercurio 2018
R. Mercurio, *Beginning Office 365 Collaboration Apps*, https://doi.org/10.1007/978-1-4842-3849-3_1

Technology is supposed to make our lives easier and allow us to spend more time on the things we want to do. If you look around, there are apps and services that accomplish this goal, from Amazon Prime to Netflix to Uber to being able to scan your boarding passes at your departure gate. These applications save you money, allow you to consume video content on demand, and let you order a car service and know the cost and route ahead of time. These applications didn't exist years ago, so you would have ordered from a catalog, watched whatever movie HBO was showing on Saturday night, and waited without much luck for a taxi in New York City.

As technology has evolved outside the workplace and made our lives arguably easier, technology has also evolved inside the workplace. In today's workplace, you can have a video conference with someone halfway around the world and see and hear them in high definition. You can also search and retrieve email messages from years ago or get your mail on your mobile device with all the bells and whistles you expect.

Part of the allure of Office 365 is that the content you are interested in is searchable and relevant. Think back 20 years ago and how you found information before the introduction of search engines, notably Google. To think I once used Microsoft Encarta or asked for a ride to the library to access their collection of Encyclopedia Britannica volumes, it boggles my mind to this day. Now Office 365 is capable of searching across e-mail, SharePoint, OneDrive and the other applications to ensure you find the relevant item; it is even capable of searching within the document to improve its relevancy.

As with anything, there is always a downside. Take a look at your phone. How many apps are on there that you haven't used in a while? How many apps have not worked as claimed or have some limitations? How many apps have failed or stopped working entirely because you upgraded the OS of the phone?

In some cases, a VPN is still required to access large systems such as an ERP system, billing system, and custom-built applications that aren't exposed outside of the company through a proxy or some other means. I won't touch base on Azure, which is another Microsoft Offering for companies looking to use IaaS (Infrastructure as a Service). Azure has the ability expose internal URLs to the outside in a safe way without exposing the company to vulnerabilities.

Today's collaboration tools allow for sharing of information, which ultimately improves processes, boosts the bottom line, and delivers well-executed projects. Individuals working in a silo can't bounce ideas off each other or seek out other experienced individuals and so must bear the cost of a poorly executed project.

An excellent example of how collaboration works is to think of group of university professors aligning their resources and experiences to deliver a well-received article or a world-changing vaccine. If they worked in their own isolated environments, their outcomes and innovations might be much less impactful.

In the business world, teams collaborate around the launch of a new product, which involves teams from marketing, technology, sales, and leadership. This type of activity may include geographically dispersed teams or team members in other offices around the world. Technology must bring them all together so the objectives can be met and the product gets to market.

Part of the design and success of Office 365 is that it allows companies to have a digital workplace. It allows companies and employees to have the tools to not only collaborate but get work done on their time on a cloud-based platform supported by Microsoft. It provides applications around the way people need to work, whether that is document-based, e-mail, chat, or video collaboration; Office 365 moves the common applications we use on a daily basis to the cloud and allows us to use the tools and applications we need to get our job done.

Let's dig into Office 365 and discuss the elements of Office 365 and why it makes business sense to move to it.

What Is Office 365?

Office 365 is Microsoft's SaaS offering for email, collaboration applications, and Office 2016. SaaS stands for Software as a Service. The easiest way to understand the concept is that you simply sign into a website and access the software instead of installing it locally on your PC or Apple device. Popular examples of SaaS are not only Office 365 but QuickBooks or Salesforce.

With SaaS there generally is no software to install; the vendor maintains and supplies the software, updates, and hardware needed to run the software. In turn, you simply pay a monthly fee and you have access to the software or platform.

Office 365 is Microsoft's biggest software endeavor yet and has been years in the making. For over 25 years Microsoft has been developing software to be installed on a company's servers within a company's data center. This includes not only Microsoft Exchange (e-mail) but also products like Microsoft SharePoint, which was first released in the early 2000s. This approach required companies to buy and maintain expensive server equipment and needed the appropriate technical staff to support the systems.

Office 365 changes the game by removing the need to buy expensive servers or ensure that the IT staff is trained to administer and support the software. By transitioning to Office 365, IT departments and personnel can now focus on providing solutions that can help a business grow instead of managing software and infrastructure.

How Does It Work?

Microsoft maintains data centers around the world in many different regions to be able to offer this service. Each data center contains thousands of servers in perfectly stacked arrays with multiple electrical connections, cooling equipment, on-site support, and all in a highly secure facility with multiple levels of protection. Because Microsoft provides all the hardware, it also maintains an extensive disaster recovery plan. If one of the data centers were to experience an outage or catastrophic event, Office 365 and its users would see minimum disruption and very little downtime, if any. This model is also supported by a financially backed service level agreement (SLA), ensuring that if Microsoft doesn't maintain its agreed SLA, there is a financial penalty for the company.

But all of this doesn't matter because of the beauty of all it is that you simply go to Office365.com from any major supported web browser and log in with your credentials. Once authenticated, you will be presented with a variety of applications to choose from. From an end-user perspective, that is 100% correct but let's take a brief look at what must happen first to make it a seamless experience for the end user.

In most cases, your company's IT department has already done the heavy lifting. This includes signing up for Office 365, configuring the service, and licensing the end users so they can access the appropriate applications. I do want to touch upon a few key points that can affect the Office 365 experience.

- Office 365 comes in a variety of license levels, each with a different per-user cost. This book will focus on Office 365 for Business and Office 365 for Enterprise; some applications will not be available for education, government, and non-profit license levels. This is relevant because if an application we are discussing is not available to you, it could be because of the plan your company has subscribed to or a licensing issue.

- Some applications or features discussed in this book may not be visible to you because you may not have an appropriate license assigned to you to use the application. If an application is not visible, your IT department may need to assign a license to you to use it.

- Companies have the option to determine when updates and new functionality get released to their respective tenants. This is known as the release preferences. By default, Microsoft sets all tenants to "standard release." This means that updates and applications are deployed when they are publicly available and not in beta. Companies have the option to set the Office 365 tenant to "targeted release for everyone" and "targeted release for selected users." "Targeted release for everyone" means that everyone who is using Office 365 in your organization will get Office 365 updates during the first phase of deployment. This will introduce functionality and features before the majority of Office 365 tenants get the updates. "Targeted release for selected users" allows updates and features to be deployed to a specific set of selected users. This is useful to test and review updates before they are deployed to everyone. Keep in mind that some updates only get deployed to the entire organization. The interesting part of this feature is that it allows Microsoft to be agile by monitoring support tickets and fixing issues before the update is deployed to everyone using Office 365.

- If you do not have access to Office 365 or if your company will not license the appropriate applications to you, Microsoft will allow a 30-day trial to be created, and you will have access to the applications discussed in this book. After 30 days, your account will be deactivated by Microsoft. You also will be able to purchase a single license monthly if you want to experiment for a longer period.

Why Should You Choose Office 365?

Office 365 combines the best of the Microsoft products with an amazing, proven infrastructure platform all for a price that makes it attractive to businesses. And because it is SaaS, the service is continually updated and made better each day. These new additions can be taken advantage of on day one without the typical installation and planning that traditional software requires.

> **Note**   If you already have access to Office 365 and the related applications, feel free to skip to the next section. This next section is intended for users who do not have access to an Office 365 tenant or wish to create one simply as an exercise in conjunction with this book.

Creating the Office 365 Trial Tenant

Open your favorite web browser and navigate to `www.office365.com`. For the purposes of this book, you will create a trial Office 365 Business Premium Account. On the `Office365.com` website, select Products ➤ For business ➤ Plans & pricing. See Figure 1-1.

Figure 1-1.   *Creating the trial account for Office 365*

Scroll to the bottom of the page and expand the Office 365 Business Premium column by selecting "More Details." On the bottom of the column, click the "Try for free" button. Fill out the form, substituting your information instead of my information. See Figure 1-2.

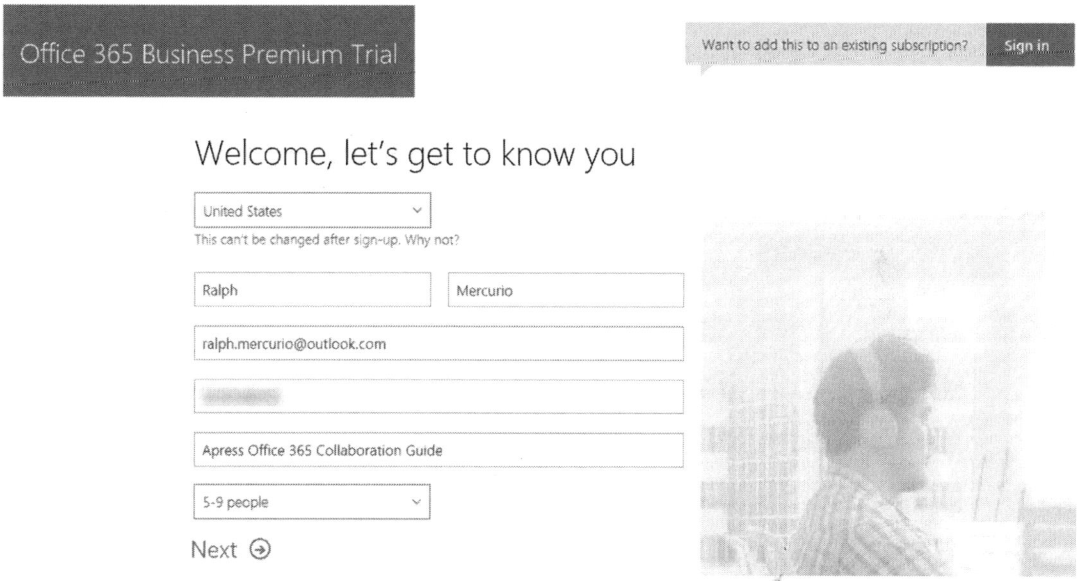

Figure 1-2. Entering account details to create the Office 365 account

Click "Next" when you're ready to move to the next screen. On the "Create your user ID" screen, enter a user name and unique company name. Your company name cannot be your current employer because that name may be reserved or already used. Make up your own company name. Enter a strong password and click the "Create my account" link. See Figure 1-3.

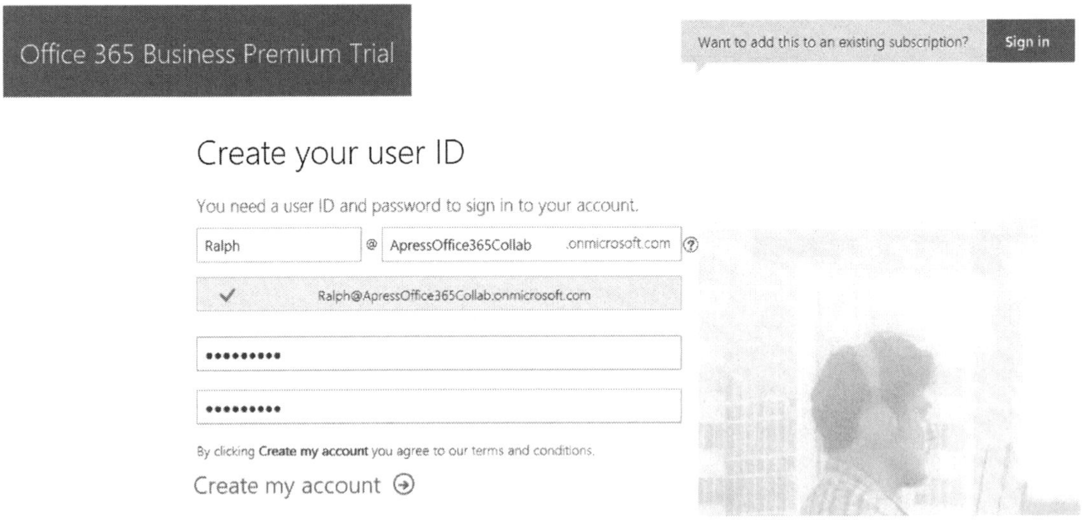

Figure 1-3. *Create your user ID for Office 365*

Enter your valid mobile number. The Microsoft service will call to verify the tenant requested is actually being created by a person and not a robot. See Figure 1-4.

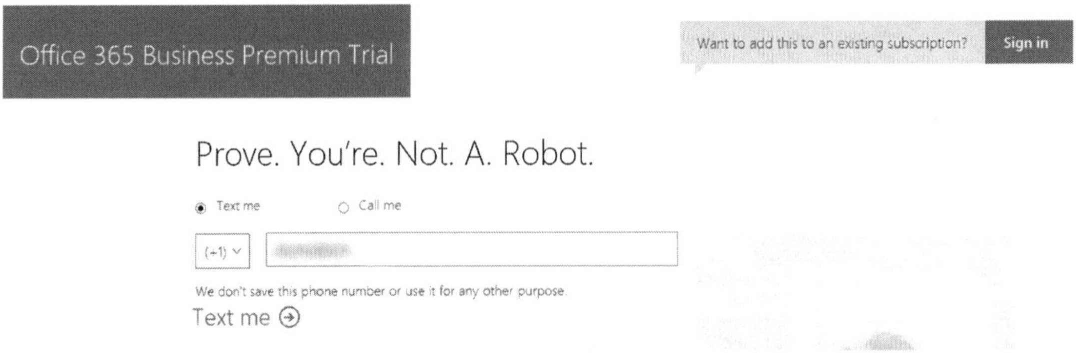

Figure 1-4. *Proving you are a real person*

It could take a few seconds for Microsoft to send the validation code. Just be sure you entered the correct phone number to authenticate against. Once you receive your code, enter it on the following screen. See Figure 1-5.

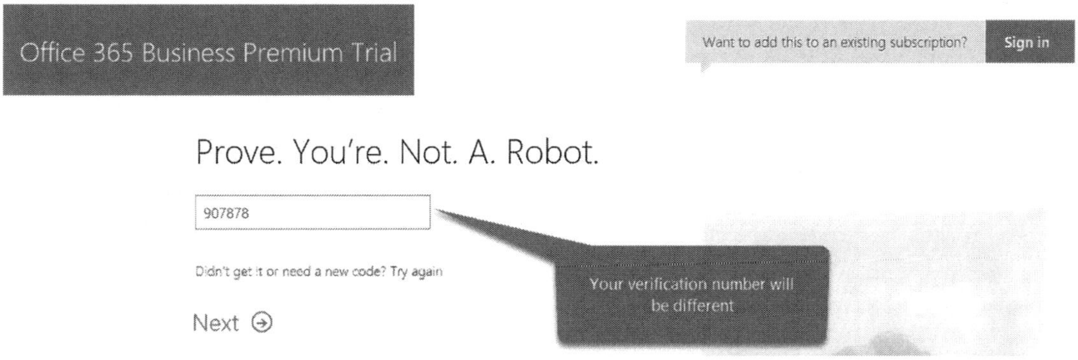

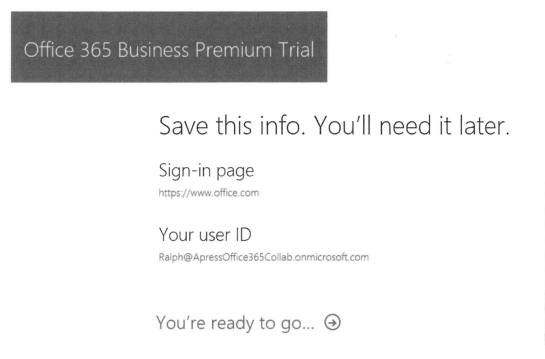

Office 365 Business Premium Trial

Want to add this to an existing subscription? | Sign in

Prove. You're. Not. A. Robot.

907878

Didn't get it or need a new code? Try again

Next ⊕

Your verification number will be different

Figure 1-5. Providing the Microsoft verification number

Click "Next" and wait a minute. Voila! You just created a 30-day Microsoft Office 365 Business Premium tenant. Before you get too excited, take a moment to write down your login information and the password you created earlier. The user ID is your login to gain access to all of Office 365. See Figure 1-6. Once you have the information written down, click the "You're ready to go" link.

Office 365 Business Premium Trial

Save this info. You'll need it later.

Sign-in page
https://www.office.com

Your user ID
Ralph@ApressOffice365Collab.onmicrosoft.com

You're ready to go... ⊖

Figure 1-6. Office 365 account details

You'll be redirected to the Office 365 home screen where after a few moments you will have access to all the applications you need. It does take Microsoft time to set up and configure the Office 365 tenant as well as the associated applications. If you don't see everything the first time after logging in, just be patient. Try closing your Internet browser and opening a new one; this will ensure a seamless experience moving forward.

Logging into Office 365 for the First Time!

Ready, set, go! Navigate to your favorite supported web browser to www.office365.com and select the "Sign in" link located in the upper right corner. If you already have access to a tenant and feel comfortable using it, enter the appropriate credentials. If you created a trial tenant as described, enter the email and password that was used during the creation of the subscription. Choose a work or school account in this instance and enter your email and password.

Once you are authenticated, you will be presented with the Office 365 Home screen. This screen contains some of the applications (see Figure 1-7) you are licensed to use, a document rollup (see Figure 1-8) of documents you recently accessed, and a list of SharePoint sites you recently accessed (see Figure 1-9).

Note   Great care has been taken to ensure that the images are correct. However, with any SaaS offering, the product can be changed by the vendor at any time. Even though the product may change, the information will still be relevant.

Figure 1-7. *Office 365 home screen*

The Documents panel keeps track of recent or shared documents so you can quickly see what you might have been working on. See Figure 1-8.

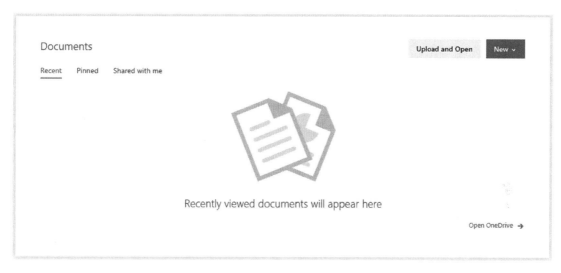

Figure 1-8. *Recently viewed documents*

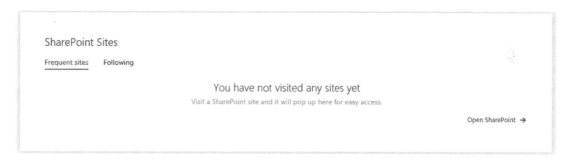

Figure 1-9. *SharePoint sites you recently visited*

The home screen contains a few key areas that you can use to find applications and change your settings or Office 365 experience.

App Launcher (The Waffle)

The app launcher (or waffle) holds all the applications you can access and will be on every Office 365 screen regardless of which application you might be using. See Figure 1-10.

Figure 1-10. *The Office 365 app launcher*

The app launcher is always available in the upper right corner of Office 365 and any application you are using. It provides links to launch the applications we will be discussing and it provides an admin interface for Office 365 administrators.

Cog

The cog or settings menu (Figure 1-11) allows some settings to be changed. Some of the settings that can be changed include the theme, Start page, password, and notifications.

Figure 1-11. *The Office 365 cog*

My Accounts

The My Accounts menu allows you to manage your profile and account or to sign out of Office 365 completely. See Figure 1-12. When you click on My profile, it takes you to the Microsoft Delve page, which is a site where you can update your profile including but not limited to birthday, contact numbers, About Me, projects, skills, expertise, schools, education, interests, and hobbies. The more you fill out, the better profile you create and the easier it is for Delve to begin to catalog documents that you might want to see. A word to the wise: only include personal information (birthday, etc.) if you feel comfortable sharing that information. I will discuss Delve in a later chapter.

Figure 1-12. *My Accounts menu*

The My Accounts settings related to your account are Office 2016 installs and which computer they have been installed on, personal info, and which licenses you are personally assigned.

The apps (Figure 1-13) collectively make up the collaboration applications of Office 365. Yes, some are new and some are powerful, but as I go through them you will see that they need each other to either generate content or consume content. They can be accessed by clicking on the app launcher shown in Figure 1-10.

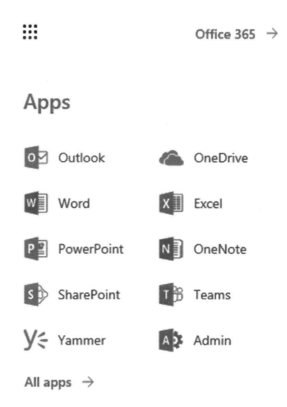

Figure 1-13. *The collaboration apps of Office 365 via the app launcher*

Some of the applications aren't shown in the app launcher and are available by clicking on the "All apps" link located below the Yammer application. Clicking this link shows every application, including some that are not discussed in this book.

Office 365 Collaboration Applications

Now that I have discussed Office 365 and you feel comfortable with what it is, how it works, and why you should use it, let me introduce each of the applications I will be discussing in the book.

Outlook

Outlook includes the following components:

- **Mail**: This application is your inbox for e-mail communication. You can send/receive emails to anyone just as you do now.

- **People**: This is your standard Outlook address book but with some extended features, which I will discuss in a later chapter.

- **Calendar**: Just like the Outlook Calendar you may have been using for years. Use it to schedule meetings with other people, days you might not be in the office, etc.

- **Tasks**: This application contains all the tasks from Outlook that you have created or the application has created on your behalf.

This version of Outlook is commonly referred to as webmail.

Office 2016

The newest version of the familiar Office tools you have been using has been upgraded to Office 2016 and eventually will be Office 2019. There are two flavors available to you as a subscriber to Office 365. You can download and install the applications or use them through the web browser. In this book, I will refer to Office Online as the web version of Office while client apps will be the version you download and use locally on your device.

- **Word**: Arguably the world's most widely used word processing program. Create documents, resumes, and other content using one of the world's most popular word processing programs.

- **Excel**: Create powerful spreadsheets, charts, and insights. A workhorse of the Office Platform for years.

- **PowerPoint**: Create engaging presentations for meetings. Just don't make them too long.

- **OneNote**: Excellent application for taking notes, I use it almost every day and it has replaced my little treasure trove of Post-It notes all over my desk.

- **Sway**: Create newsletters and other documents and share them easily.

- **Outlook**: Similar to Outlook in terms of functionality but this version is installed on your device.

OneDrive

OneDrive allows you to store files in the cloud and access them from anywhere and on nearly every type of device. Items can be shared with users internally and externally; you can also view and edit documents in Office Online or the client apps of Office 2016.

SharePoint

One of the core pillars of collaboration in Office 365, SharePoint offers document management, sites, and collaboration tools, and it integrates with Office 2016.

Delve

Delve is your personal site in Office 365. It contains documents that are relevant to you and people with whom you have everyday contact; it tries to create a site where the data you are looking for is at your fingertips. I will not be discussing this application in this book but feel free to explore it.

Teams

A new offering from Microsoft, Teams enables teams or smaller groups to work together in one application instead of working in different applications and then using a common application to collaborate. This differs from most applications because it is based the concept of chat, not email.

Yammer

Similar to Teams, Yammer is designed to foster communication and disseminate information to the entire organization, ideally replacing e-mail as the primary method. Employees can subscribe to groups and interact with other employees across the organization.

Flow

Flow allows users to create no-code workflows that can be used with the Office 365 Platform or as a connector to other external systems. This new application blurs the line and works across many applications.

Planner

Planner offers "light" project management via the ability to keep track of tasks and resources for small projects that don't require a project manager to manage the project.

Forms

Microsoft's form offering to tackle the issue of collecting information from end users, Forms gives you the ability create forms and surveys and then view the results within an easy-to-use dashboard.

PowerApps

PowerApps allows for application development that works across multiple device platforms and easily connects to your data sources. Examples include an organization browser or address book, or capturing meeting minutes. PowerApps includes templates and connectors to streamline development of these applications. It's not discussed in the book, but it's a ground-breaking application from Microsoft and can be used to easily deploy an application to solve a particular business issue.

Stream

Microsoft Stream provides a rich collaborative platform for video sharing in a secure manner. This platform allows video content to be published and searchable; it gives everyone in the organization the ability to create video content.

Summary

Microsoft has gone to great lengths in investing and creating Office 365. From the stability of the infrastructure, the disaster recovery planning perspective, and the affordable pricing structure, Office 365 is a great tool to increase productivity, reduce administrative overhead, and empower users with the tools necessary to make their work successful.

If you are already using Office 365 in your organization, then you are well on your way to understanding the collaboration apps mention earlier in this chapter. If not, I hope the walkthrough of setting up a trial account was successful and now you are ready to explore the basics of the Office 365 collaboration apps.

In the next chapter, you will explore SharePoint Online, a document-centric application that allows users to create and view SharePoint Online sites, manage documents, and create a collaborative document environment.

CHAPTER 2

SharePoint Online

In the last chapter, you created the Office 365 environment to begin your journey through the collaboration apps. The first app I will discuss is SharePoint, which has gone through a few iterations and with each release gets better and better. SharePoint is Microsoft's answer to document management, sites, and collaboration; it serves as an integration backbone for many of Microsoft's other products, such as OneDrive and Flow.

Microsoft offers two flavors of SharePoint: SharePoint Online and SharePoint on-premises. In this book, we will focus on SharePoint Online, which is included with an Office 365 subscription. SharePoint Online differs from SharePoint on-premises with regards to capabilities, but the foundation of both products is nearly identical from an end-user perspective.

© Ralph Mercurio 2018
R. Mercurio, *Beginning Office 365 Collaboration Apps*, https://doi.org/10.1007/978-1-4842-3849-3_2

The Starting Line

SharePoint Online is accessible via the app launcher located in the upper left of the Office 365 site, as shown in Figure 2-1.

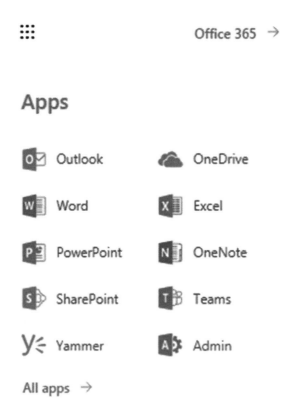

Figure 2-1. *Accessing the SharePoint Online icon from the Office 365 app launcher*

Clicking the SharePoint icon opens a SharePoint Site, which presents a single view of your particular SharePoint activity (Figure 2-2).

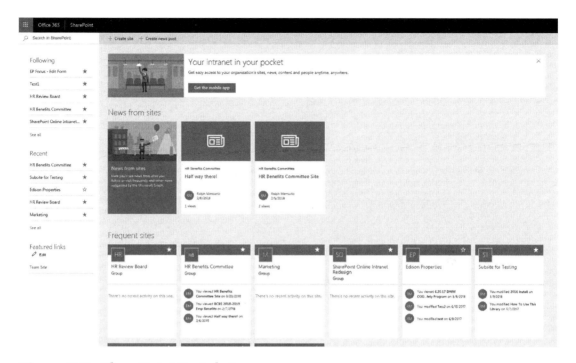

Figure 2-2. *SharePoint Portal site*

This site contains sites that you are following, recently visited sites, and a roll-up of news articles from all the sites you access. All of this requires very little intervention on your part because the Office 365 service aggregates and catalogs the activity for you seamlessly.

This view also contains Office 365 Groups, which are discussed in Chapter 4. SharePoint sites and Office 365 groups are closely related and share many of the same features and functionality.

Sites

The building blocks of SharePoint Online are sites. Sites allow users to create workspaces, which are used to organize content, disseminate information, or track projects. Sites can be created from various templates, each with a slightly different purpose or a way to convey information.

Team Site

The most widely used template available is a team site, which contains default document libraries, default lists, and default page templates for users to use to collaborate and share information. Later in the chapter, I will discuss each of the site components more in-depth.

Team sites come in two flavors: classic and modern. A classic team site (Figure 2-3) looks like SharePoint 2010, 2013, and 2016 team site.

Figure 2-3. *SharePoint classic team site*

A modern team site contains many of the same components as a classic team site, but the look is different, as you can see in Figure 2-4.

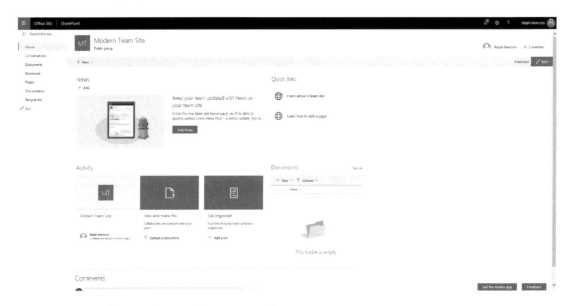

Figure 2-4. *SharePoint modern team site*

While the look is different, they share the same set of lists and libraries but with a few added features. The first change from all previous versions of SharePoint is that a modern team site also will have a corresponding Office 365 group (Chapter 4) created as well. With the addition of the Office 365 group, modern team sites also gain the conversation stream as well as an updated calendar feature. The second change is that Office 365 groups are accessible two ways: either via Outlook 2016 or Office 365 Outlook and the SharePoint portal site.

Now that I have addressed the two available team site templates (classic experience and modern), let's discuss the rest of the available site templates before you actually create your first site. SharePoint Online includes the templates covered in the following sections.

Communication Site

A communication site (Figure 2-5) is a new site template available in SharePoint Online only and cannot be created as subsites like the rest of the available templates.

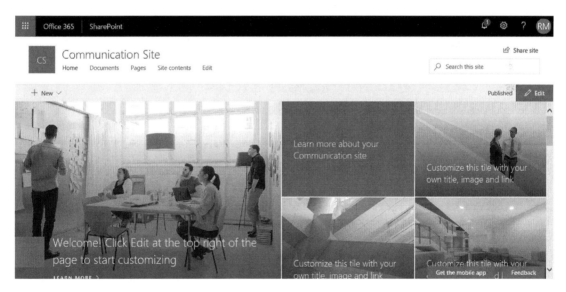

Figure 2-5. *Communication site*

This site template aims to foster communication by providing three different designs, which are also designed for the mobile experience. The three designs are

- **Topic**: Used primarily to share information

- **Showcase**: Used to share information and highlight a product or company event

- **Blank**: A blank site which can then be customized

Blog

A blog site (Figure 2-6) is used to convey ideas, conversations, and posts about a particular subject. Visitors can also post comments on any of the blog posts.

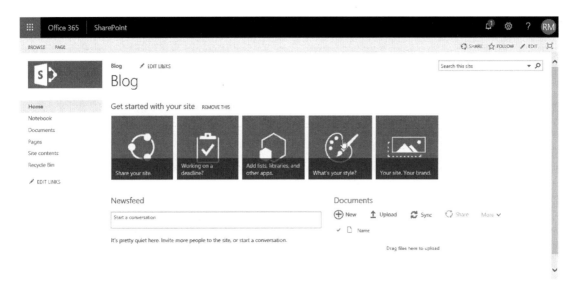

Figure 2-6. *A blog site*

The blog site can be selected in the Collaboration tab of Template section when creating a new site.

Project Site

A project site (Figure 2-7) contains components that are helpful in managing a project in a concise site. The Project site template can be selected from the Collaboration tab of Template section when creating a new site.

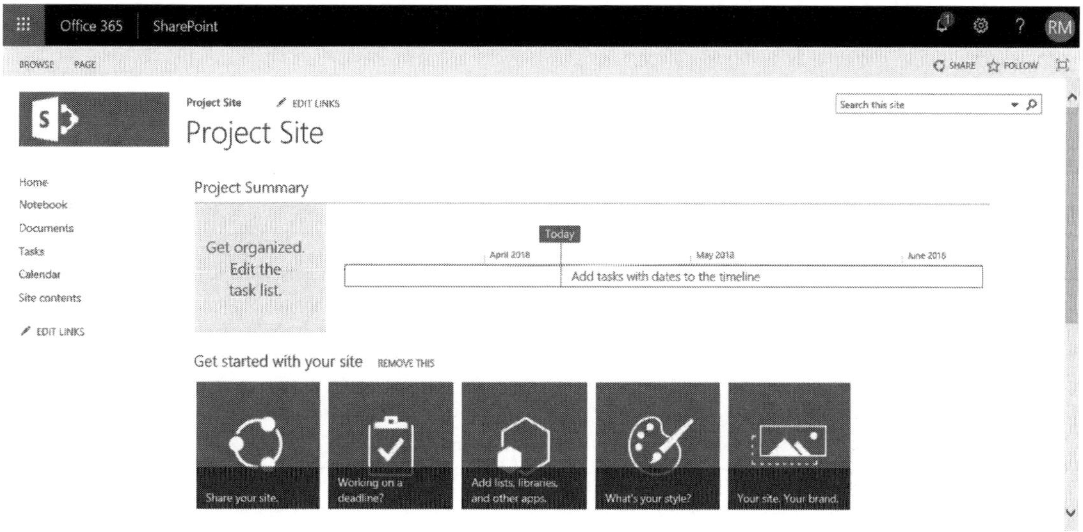

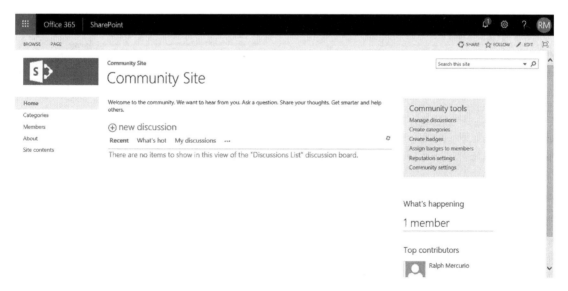

Figure 2-7. *A project site*

Community Site

A community site (Figure 2-8) allows members of the site to discuss and comment on interests. It primarily works around the ideas of discussions and liking or rating discussion posts. This site template is accessible under the Collaboration tab of the Template section when creating a new site.

Figure 2-8. *A community site*

This site can only be created when the parent site is a classic team site. This template is not available for modern team sites.

Document Center

A document center site (Figure 2-9) allows for a location to centrally manage documents. The document center site is available in the Enterprise tab within the Template section when creating a new site.

Figure 2-9. *Document center site*

Records Center

A Records Center site (Figure 2-10) is used to manage records, which are permanent artifacts and have a retention period and cannot be modified once the document becomes a record.

Figure 2-10. *A Records Center site*

Records Center sites also have specific rules that must be configured to ensure adherence to a specific record policy.

Business Intelligence Center

The Business Intelligence Center site (Figure 2-11) allows for the displaying of BI content within SharePoint. The site template can be selected from the Enterprise tab within Template section when creating a new site.

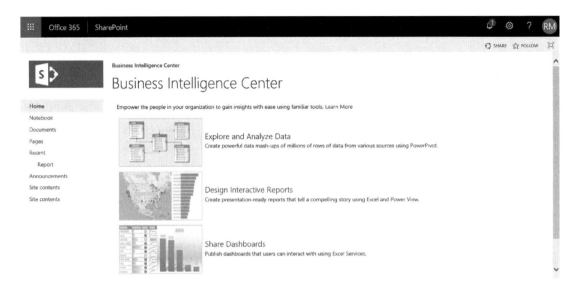

Figure 2-11. *Business Intelligence Center site*

This includes the ability to upload reports and leverage Excel services. This template does not provide BI dashboarding capabilities.

Basic Search

A basic search site (Figure 2-12) provides a central site to execute searches from. It includes an Advanced Search page in addition to the basic Search page. The site template can be selected from the Enterprise tab within Template section when creating a new site.

Figure 2-12. *Basic Search site*

This site does not have any associated lists and libraries with it because it is not meant for collaboration but rather to provide a basic search experience regardless of what SharePoint site the user is currently on.

Enterprise Search Center

The Enterprise Search site (Figure 2-13) provides an intranet approach to searching. Not only can it search for the same content as the basic Search but it also provides specific searching for people, conversations, and videos. The site template can be selected from the Enterprise tab within Template section when creating a new site.

Figure 2-13. Enterprise Search site

On the surface, it looks like a basic Search site, but after a search term is entered, the Enterprise Search site will allow the search term to be refined through people, conversations, or videos, as shown in Figure 2-14.

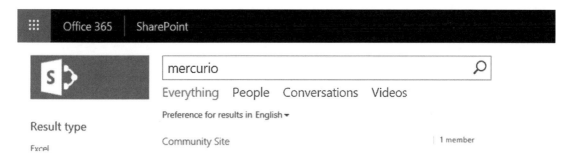

Figure 2-14. Enterprise search term refiners

This site does not have any associated lists and libraries with it because it is not meant for collaboration but rather to provide an enterprise search experience regardless of what SharePoint site the user is currently on. This site can only be created when the parent site is a classic team site. This template is not available for modern team sites.

Visio Process Repository

A Visio Process Repository (Figure 2-15) is a site where Visio documents are stored. This site template can be created by selecting "Visio Process Repository" from the Enterprise tab when creating a new site. The site template can be selected from the Enterprise tab within Template section when creating a new site.

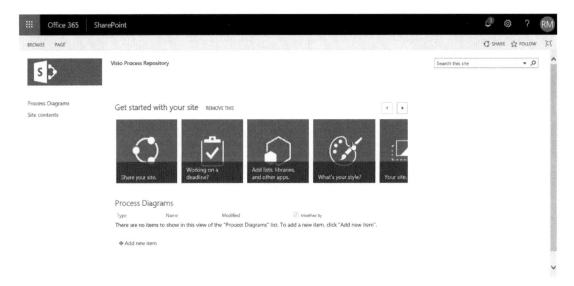

Figure 2-15. *Visio Process Repository site*

Publishing Site

The publishing site template (Figure 2-16) allows for content creators to create and edit pages in draft mode and publish them when ready for general consumption. The site template can be selected from the Publishing tab within the Template section when creating a new site.

Figure 2-16. *A publishing site*

This site can only be created when the parent site is a classic team site. This template is not available from modern team sites.

Publishing Site with Workflow

A publishing site with workflow (Figure 2-17) is similar to a publishing site; the only real difference is that pages can be scheduled for publishing by leveraging an approval workflow.

Figure 2-17. *Publishing site with workflow*

The site template can be selected from the Publishing tab within the Template section when creating a new site. This site can only be created when the parent site is a classic team site. This template is not available for modern team sites.

Enterprise Wiki

The enterprise wiki site (Figure 2-18) is used to create an enterprise repository of information in a wiki-style format. It allows content to be put into defined categories and page content to be rated.

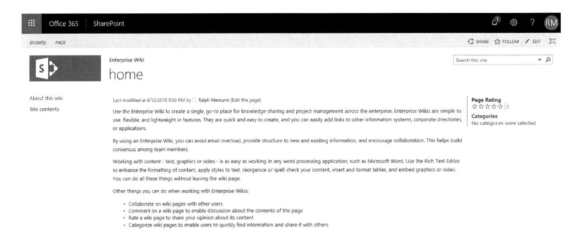

Figure 2-18. *Enterprise wiki site*

The site has limited lists and libraries because the most of the content are pages. This site can only be created when the parent site is a classic team site. This template is not available for modern team sites.

SAP Workflow Site

The SAP workflow site template (Figure 2-19) is, in my opinion, is the least site template used out of all of them. It does require a SAP Duet subscription and allows SAP workflow steps to be disseminated from SharePoint.

Figure 2-19. *A SAP workflow site*

The site template provides an interface for tasks through SharePoint, and the user works on the SharePoint site. This integration is useful if Duet exists and the associated business logic of documents that go along with the workflow tasks.

Creating a Site

Before creating any sites, try to envision what your site hierarchy will look like and how you want to the site to function. A bit of planning around site structure will alleviate site sprawl, create a logical hierarchy, and allow for specific sites to be located in particular site collections.

Creating sites is a simple process in SharePoint Online as long the user has the correct rights assigned to create sites. As you progress through this book, you'll create a modern team site; an Office 365 group (Chapter 4) will also be created. This means that, since Office 365 groups are created within Outlook, they will also create a corresponding SharePoint site. I know it's a little confusing but remember that planning is the key to ensuring that sites are not duplicated.

Communication Site

To create a communication site, select "+ Create Site," near the top of the SharePoint Portal site, as depicted in Figure 2-20. You can access this site by clicking SharePoint in the app launcher.

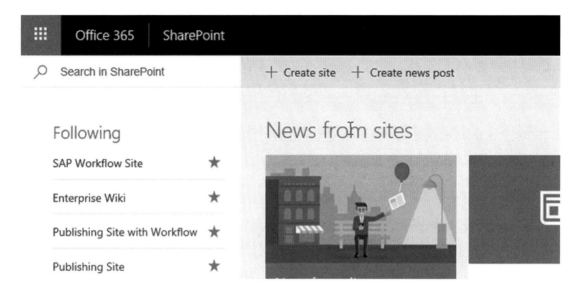

Figure 2-20. *SharePoint creation interface from the SharePoint portal site*

Clicking the link opens the creation interface and presents you with two options: team site and communication site. Select communication site by clicking the image.

1. Choose a design based on your specific requirements. You can choose from the following layouts: topic, showcase, and blank.

    Enter a site name within the Site Name text box. As you type the site name, SharePoint will fill out the Site Address field, removing spaces or special characters. If you do not want the generated site name, click the pencil and edit accordingly.

2. Enter a site description if desired; it is not a required field.

3. Press the Finish button, and the site will be created in the background.

4. Once the site is created, you will be automatically navigated to the site.

Modern Team Site

Creating a modern team site is a nearly identical process to a communication site. To create a modern team site, select "+ Create Site" near the top of the SharePoint site, as shown in Figure 2-19, and select team site by clicking the corresponding image.

1. Enter a site name within the Site Name text box.

2. As you type the site name, SharePoint will fill out the Group email address field, removing spaces or special characters. If you do not want the generated site name, click the pencil and edit accordingly.

3. Enter a site description if desired; it is not a required field.

4. Choose a privacy setting, either public or private.

    • **Public**: Anyone in the organization can view the site.

    • **Private**: Only a select group of specified individuals can view the site.

5. Press the Finish button, and the site will be created in the background.

During the creation process, you also have the ability to add additional owners and additional members. I will discuss basic permissions later in this chapter. Once the site is created, you will be automatically navigated to the site.

Classic Experience Team Site

Classic experience team sites are slowly being phased out of SharePoint Online. Classic experience team sites will slowly be transitioned to modern team sites, and eventually, only modern team sites will be able to be created. Classic experience team sites have been around for quite a while and hence have quite the following from the community and SharePoint users. Classic experience team sites can be created either as a subsite of a modern team site or as a subsite of the SharePoint aggregate site, as depicted in Figure 2-2. The process is the same for creating classic team sites and begins by selecting the cog (gear) in the upper right corner.

1. Choose Site Contents from the cog menu.

2. Select the "+ New" drop-down menu below the title of the site, as seen in Figure 2-21.

Figure 2-21. *Creating a new subsite*

3. The New SharePoint Site form will open. Fill out the details as needed.

    a.   **Title and Description**: Give your site a title and description.

    b.   **Web Site Address**: Unlike when creating modern or communication sites, you must specify the address here. You can't change the beginning of the URL. Avoid spaces or special characters here.

    c.   **Template Selection**: Choose the Team Site (Classic Experience).

    d.   **Permissions**: You have the ability to inherit permissions or create new permission groups for your users. I will discuss permissions later in this chapter.

    e.   **Navigation Inheritance**: You can choose to use the same global navigation as the parent site or not.

4. Once you have filled in the form, click the Create button.

Creating Non-Team Sites

As you can see, creating sites is a pretty straightforward and simple process. The only gotcha is that specific site templates can only be used when the parent site is a classic team site. To make a non-team site, follow these instructions:

1. Choose Site Contents from the cog (gear) menu in the upper right corner.

2. Select the "+ New" drop-down menu below the title of the site, as shown in Figure 2-20.

3. The New SharePoint Site form will open and you can proceed to fill out the details as needed.

   a. **Title and Description**: Give your site a title and description.

   b. **Web Site Address**: Unlike when creating Modern or Communication sites, you must specify the address here. You cannot change the beginning of the URL. Avoid spaces or special characters here.

   c. **Template Selection**: Choose the site template you want to use. An explanation of each of the templates is included earlier in this chapter.

   d. **Permissions**: You have the ability to inherit permissions or create new permission groups for your users. I will discuss permissions later in this chapter.

   e. **Navigation Inheritance**: You can choose to use the same global navigation as the parent site or not.

4. Once you have filled in the form, click the Create button.

Lists and Libraries

Now that I have covered sites and the different kinds of sites, let's discuss lists and libraries, which are the foundational building blocks of sites. Think of lists and libraries as the walls of a building and sites as the foundation upon which everything is built.

Lists

SharePoint Online offers 22 preconfigured lists or libraries. The following sections cover each of the available templates and a brief explanation of each list and library template.

Announcements

An announcement list is a predefined list that allows you to create an item and other types of news-related items. The announcement list is generally used to show announcements, which can be set to expire on a preselected date.

Calendar

The calendar list is a SharePoint calendar that can be used by the team to add events and schedule meetings within a SharePoint site. The calendar can also be connected to Outlook to enable seamless editing through Outlook.

Contacts

The contacts list is similar to an address book, and contacts can be added through Outlook. The contacts list can hold employees, vendors, or partners and keep their information centralized.

Custom List

A custom list is merely a list with minimal preconfigured columns. This is a blank list that can be configured in any way you see fit to support the business requirement.

Custom List in Datasheet

A custom list in a datasheet is the same as a custom list except you can edit the list in an Excel-like format, making data entry a lot easier.

Discussion Board

A discussion board is a preconfigured list template that supports discussions and conversations. The list can also be configured to require approval before any post becomes viewable by all.

External List

External lists are out of scope for this book but connect to external content types, which in turn connect to a SQL database, for example. They can present the SQL database view as a SharePoint list and allow data to be added, deleted, or modified records stored in a SQL database.

Import Spreadsheet

The import spreadsheet list template allows you to upload an Excel spreadsheet and use the headers of the sheet as column types. It imports the data from Excel and creates nearly identical columns.

Issue Tracking

An issue tracking list allows you to track issues that can be assigned to be prioritized and completed; you can also assign statuses.

Links

The links list template allows a list of links to be created. The links list contains a URL column where the website address is stored.

Promoted Links

Similar to a links list above, the promoted links list will display the links in a graphical tile-based format.

Survey

You can create a list of questions in a survey format. I discuss Microsoft Forms in Chapter 10, which provides a much better interface to create surveys and view responses.

Tasks

A task list allows tasks to be created plus details like whom the task is assigned to, a due date, progress, and a few other fields.

Libraries

Libraries act and share a lot of the same features as lists such as columns, views, and the ability to organize the data. The significant difference between lists and libraries is that libraries are geared toward containing some sort of content such as document, reports, or images. In the next few pages, I will list the available out-of-the-box library templates and provide a brief description of their purposes.

Asset Library

An asset library is similar to a picture library but is geared to manage assets such as images, audio, or video files.

Data Connection Library

Data connections are outside the scope of this book but are used to store connection files which can be used throughout SharePoint.

Document Library

A document library is a library with minimal preconfigured columns. This is a blank library which can be configured in any way you see fit to support the business requirement.

Form Templates

A form template library is a library that is used to store InfoPath forms, which could be employee forms, status reports, or business forms. With InfoPath being deprecated and the industry moving to Microsoft PowerApps to create forms, this library is slowing being phased out.

Picture Library

The picture library template contains columns that correspond to images and provide different views into the library. I will discuss views later in this chapter.

Report Library

A report library contains preconfigured columns that can be used to describe the status, category, and description of a report.

Site Mailbox

The site mailbox is a deprecated library template; it was used to connect an Exchange Mailbox to SharePoint. The recommendation is to use Office 365 Groups going forward.

Wiki Page Library

This library supports wiki pages and the ability to create a wiki using text and images.

List and Library Columns

Every list and library contains columns. These columns can be a variety of types and are used to store information about the item or content. For example, many lists and libraries contain Modified, Modified By, Created, and Created By columns, which are used to store details about the user and date of modification. In fact, these types of columns have been around for years because Windows uses them to store information. The only real difference is now they are more visible and are used more frequently in SharePoint and in every other Office 365 application such as OneDrive for Business.

Every list or library contains columns, which can be created from a wide variety of types. Different types of columns can be added to a list or library, and the column dictates what information it accepts. Table 2-1 contains a list of the available columns and their associated type.

Table 2-1. *SharePoint Columns by Type and Associated Data Type*

Type	Data Type	Notes
Single line of text	Text	Only accepts plain text
Multiple lines of text	Text	Accepts either plain or enhanced rich text
Choice (menu to choose from)	Text	Choose from drop-down, radio buttons, or checkboxes
Number (1, 1.0, 100)	Numeric	
Currency ($, ¥, €)	Currency	
Date and Time	Date and Time	
Lookup (information already on this site)	Text or Numeric	Only available on the current site, cannot look up information on other sites
Yes/No (check box)	Text	Can only be Yes/No, no other entries are allowed
Person or Group	Person	Finds a person in Active Directory or a SharePoint Group
Hyperlink or Picture	URL	
Calculated (calculation based on other columns)	Formula-based	
Task Outcome	Text	Can be a choice field or calculated value
External Data	External Content Types	
Managed Metadata	Term Set	

The majority of the columns also can be set to Required or to enforce unique values. To set one of these settings within the column, make sure to toggle the appropriate radio button when creating the column.

Creating Columns

To create a column in a list or library, open a list first. In this example, you are going to create a column in the documents library of a modern team site. If you didn't create a modern team site earlier in this chapter, please go ahead and do so now.

On the modern team site, click Documents in the left-hand navigation control (otherwise known as the quick launch). The window will refresh, and you will be presented with a view of the Documents library. In the main area, to the right of Modified By, click the + sign. You'll be presented with 10 frequently used field types ranging from a single line of text to a picture. If the field type you are interested in is not listed, click the More option.

Let's create a Choice field (you can select any column type) and create your first library column. Clicking "Choice" opens the "Create a column" form (Figure 2-22). Fill in the fields.

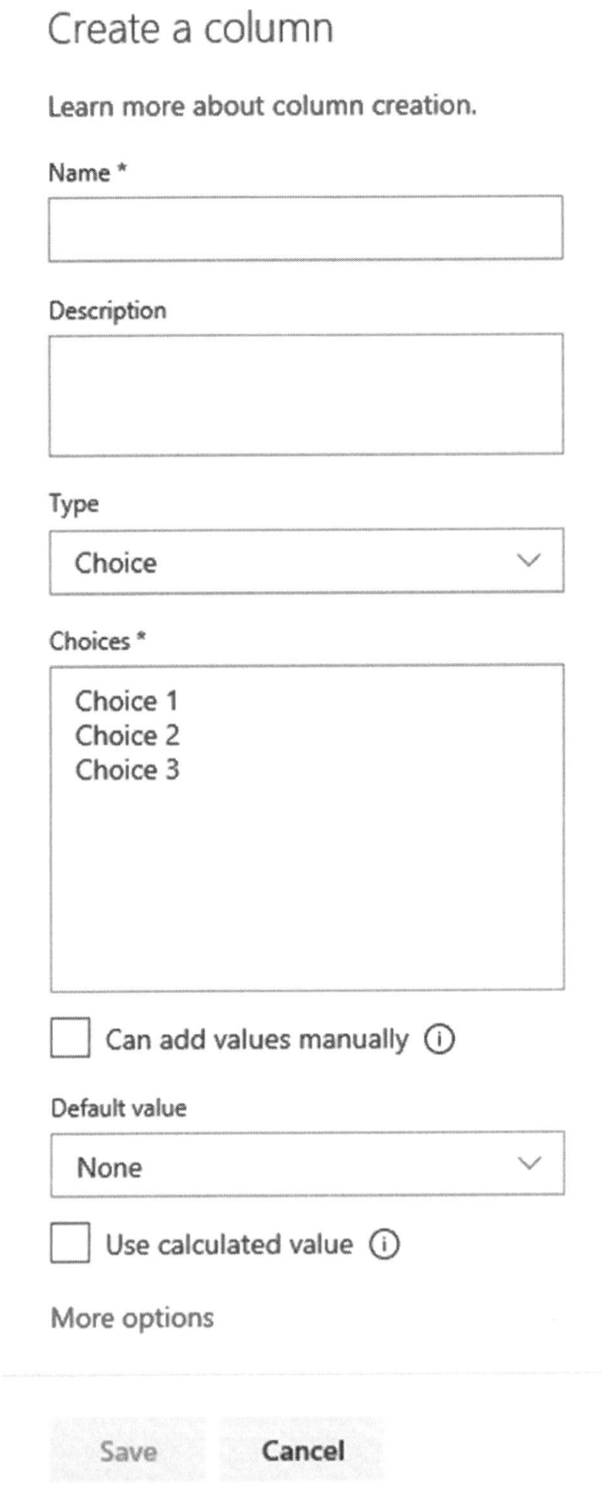

Create a column

Learn more about column creation.

Name *

Description

Type

Choice   ⌄

Choices *

Choice 1
Choice 2
Choice 3

☐ Can add values manually ⓘ

Default value

None   ⌄

☐ Use calculated value ⓘ

More options

Save   **Cancel**

Figure 2-22. *The "Create a column" form for a Choice column*

On the "Create a column" form, the name and choices text boxes are required, as denoted by the asterisk. The fields and their description are listed below:

- **Name**: Name of the column.

- **Description**: Enter a description of the purpose of the column.

- **Type**: Column type selected, remaining fields are based on the type field.

- **Choices**: Enter the choices for the column.

- **Can add values manually**: Allows a user to add a choice to the choices drop-down menu manually.

- **Default value**: Specify if you want the column to have a default value when a document is uploaded or created.

- **Use calculated value**: Allows a formula to compute the value for the column.

- **More options**

  - **Allow multiple selections**: Toggle if you want the user to be able to select more than one choice.

  - **Require that this column contains information**: Toggle if the field must be filled out for the document to be created or uploaded.

  - **Enforce unique values**: Toggle if you do not want multiple items to have the same value.

- **Column Validation**

  - **Formula**: Validate the choice selected by using a formula.

  - **User message**: Based on the formula, show a message.

I populated the form with the values shown in Figure 2-23.

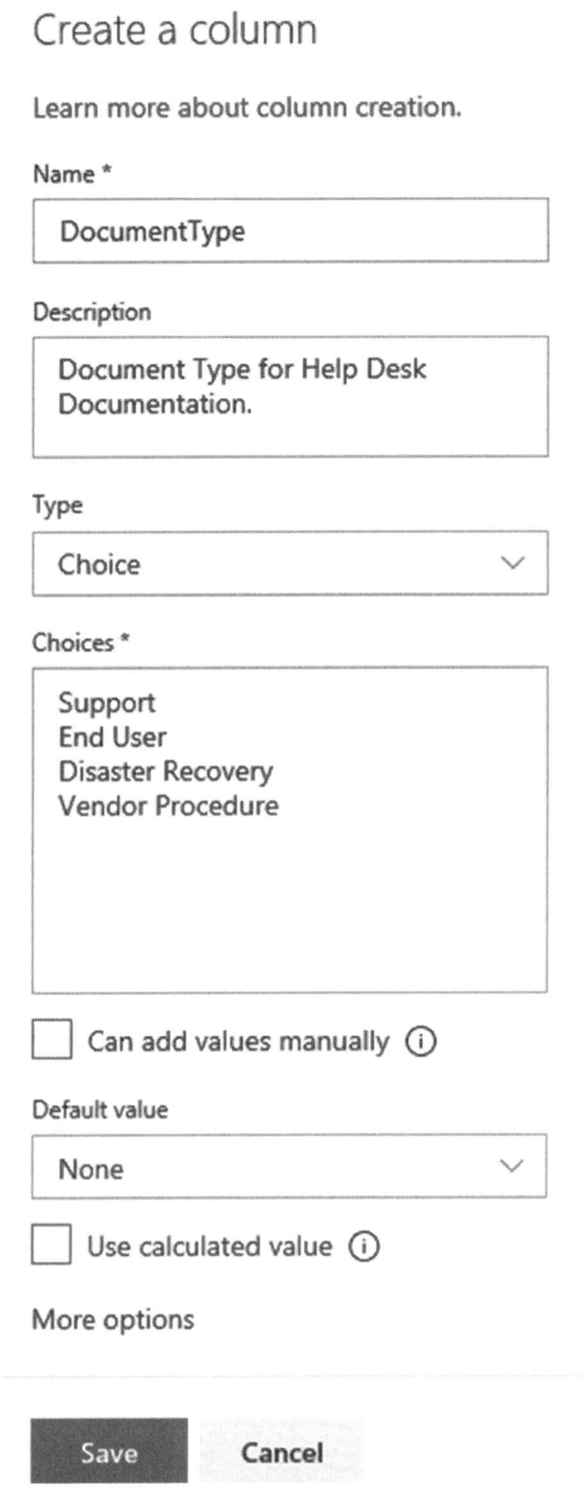

Create a column

Learn more about column creation.

Name *

DocumentType

Description

Document Type for Help Desk
Documentation.

Type

Choice   ⌄

Choices *

Support
End User
Disaster Recovery
Vendor Procedure

☐ Can add values manually ⓘ

Default value

None   ⌄

☐ Use calculated value ⓘ

More options

Save   Cancel

Figure 2-23. *Choice column form populated with values*

46

Click the Save button, and the column will be created and be added not only to the library but to the view as well. This process is the same for all column types regardless if they are lists or libraries. The procedure is slightly different for classic experience team sites and is covered next.

To create a column in the classic experience, follow these steps:

1. In the SharePoint ribbon, click the List or Library tab.

2. Click the Library Settings icon.

3. In the middle of the Settings page, click "Create column."

4. On the Create column page, fill out the fields as needed. They are the same as when creating a column in the modern interface.

5. Press the OK button to create the column.

Document Library Experience

As of now, I have covered the foundation elements of SharePoint Online: sites, lists, libraries, and columns. The next element is actual content (Office documents, images, and other files) and list items.

Uploading a document is one of the most common functions that we all do in SharePoint Online. For this example, let's upload a Word document to a Documents library on a modern team site. To do so, follow these steps:

1. On the modern team site, click the Upload button on the Documents web part, as depicted in Figure 2-24.

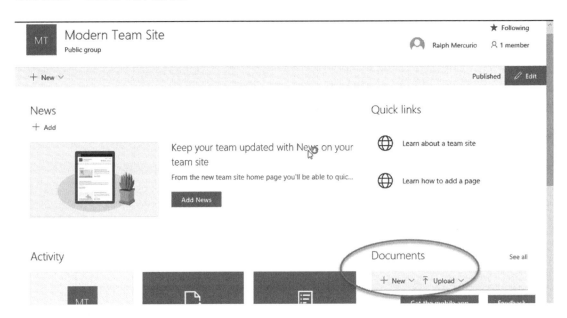

Figure 2-24. *The Upload button on a modern team site*

2. Select "Files" and browse to the location of the file you want to upload.

3. Select the file to upload and press the Open button.

4. The file will upload to the Documents library.

Now that a document has been uploaded to a document library, let's explore the available options not only at the library level but also at the document item level. A document library contains a few key areas, as shown in Figure 2-25.

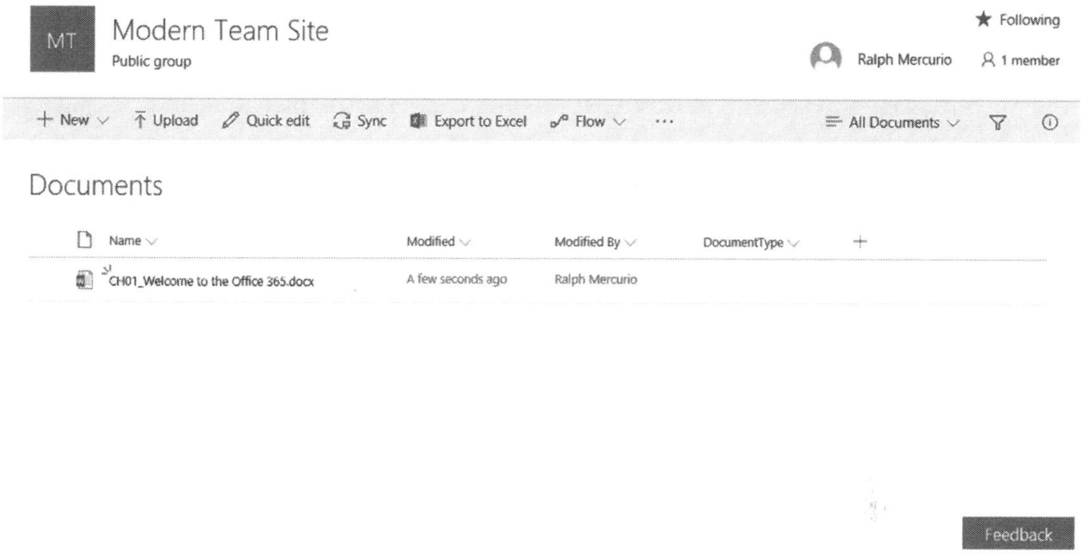

Figure 2-25. *A document library*

A document library contains a menu bar consisting of New, Upload, Quick edit, Sync, Export to Excel, Flow, and the ability to switch views and filter. The central area where documents are stored contains columns that describe the attributes of the file (metadata). The third area offers item functions, which are accessible from the three dots next to the file. Let's explore each of these areas a little more in-depth because they form a foundation for a lot of other Office 365 applications.

The first area to explore is the menu bar. This menu bar contains actions that allow you to do a variety of things and some actions can be performed on more than one file at a time. The following list offers a description of the available actions:

- **+ New**: Creates a new document. It integrates with Office Online to create documents inside the browser. I discuss Office Online in Chapter 7.

- **Upload**: Uploads an existing file to the document library from your device.

- **Quick Edit**: Allows you to edit the column values of documents to quickly change their metadata in bulk without having to edit each item individually.

- **Sync**: Allows OneDrive for Business (Chapter 3) to sync the contents of the library with your device.

- **Export to Excel**: Exports the library to Excel. This export does require Excel to be installed, and you can't import it back. It also will not download the documents; it just links back to the document library via a URL.

- **Flow**: New to Office 365, Flow allows workflows to be created and executed against content. I introduce Flow and the basic concepts in Chapter 11.

- **...**: Refer to the three dots as an ellipsis.

- **Alert me**: Sets up alerts on changes in the library. An e-mail will be sent with the subscribed changes.

- **Manage my alerts**: Allows you to add/edit/remove alerts that have been created by you.

- **All Documents**: The standard and default view on all document libraries. This view shows all documents and created columns. In the next section, I will discuss creating and using your own specified views.

- **Filters**: If filters are available on a particular view, you can filter the documents based on the parameters specified. The filters are denoted by the funnel icon.

- **Details**: Clicking the icon (question mark) shows a stream of recent activity. If a document is selected and details are selected, it shows details surrounding a file such as permissions and metadata.

The second area is where documents are stored. This area is where you create new columns, as described earlier in this chapter, and edit the associated metadata of documents by either selecting the item and editing the properties or using the Quick edit action in the document library menu bar.

The third area is where the core SharePoint actions are located and are used to manipulate the documents. Clicking the three dots next to the file (ellipsis) opens a new menu with a variety of options. Each one of these options has a unique purpose, and the easiest way to familiarize yourself with the options is to review the following list:

- **Open**: Opens the document. If it is a recognized file type, you will get the option to open in Office Online or locally installed Office.

- **Preview**: Previews the document in Office Online.

- **Share**: Allows sharing the document with users inside the organization, users with existing access, and specific people. You can also share the document with anonymous users if it has been configured by the SharePoint administrator to do so.

- **Copy link**: You can copy the link and then the link can be sent to a user via email or Skype.

- **Download**: Allows you to download the file to your local device. Once it is downloaded and you make changes to the item, they will not sync or be saved back.

- **Delete**: The document will be deleted and sent to the recycle bin.

- **Flow**: Allows you to start a Flow that has been already created. Flows can also integrate with other Office 365 applications.

- **Pin to top**: Pins the document to the top of the library, so it is always in the first position.

- **Move to**: Moves the document to another library on the site.

- **Copy to**: Makes a copy of the document and stores it in a different library on the site.

- **Rename**: Allows you to change the name of the file. Well-formed file names are crucial to finding your documents when searching for them.

- **Version history**: Shows a stream of changes in the document and can restore a previous version.

- **Alert me**: Sends an alert when there is a change, someone else changes a document, someone else changes a document created by you, and someone else changes a document last modified by you. The alert can be sent immediately, daily, or weekly. These alerts will also apply to the entire library.

- **More** >

  - **Properties**: Shows the properties of the file, including the default columns and columns created to support different metadata.

  - **Workflow**: Allows you to start a legacy workflow on the document. These workflows are slowly being replaced by Flow, but you can create workflows in SharePoint Designer 2013 until further notice. This is still available because Flow has not reached the same maturity as Workflow, which has been in existence for over 10 years.

  - **Compliance details**: Displays any compliance parameters around the document including if it is on legal hold or if it is in a different retention stage.

  - **Check out**: Sets the document to a status of checked out. While the document is in a checked out status, no other user can edit the file until it is checked back in. You must check in the document once you are done with your changes.

  - **Details**: Shows a stream of recent activity and details surrounding a file such as permissions and metadata.

List Experience

Lists and libraries are very similar; the only measurable difference, beyond some minor differences in actions, is that lists are used to store items and not content. Looking at a list in Figure 2-26 you can see that it looks very familiar to what I just discussed.

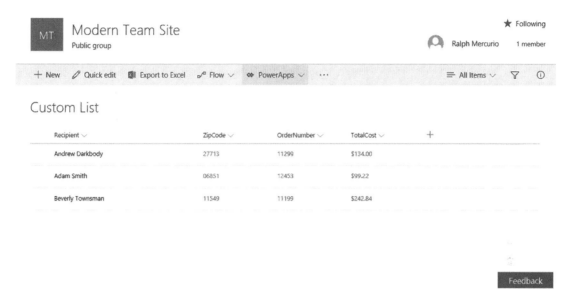

Figure 2-26. *A SharePoint Online list*

A list shares the same structures as a library, except you have the ability to utilize PowerApps in the menu bar. PowerApps allow you to customize the add item and edit item forms to provide a more robust business center form than the standard SharePoint forms. Another change is in the available actions when selecting the ellipsis next to a list item. The following list details the available actions and their intended purpose:

- **Open**: Opens the item in View mode. You are able then able to edit the values of the columns by clicking the corresponding text box.

- **Edit**: Opens the item in edit mode.

- **Share**: Allows the sharing of the item with users inside the organization, users with existing access, and specific people. You can also share the item with anonymous users if it has been configured by the SharePoint administrator to do so.

- **Copy link**: You can copy the link and then the link can be sent to a user via e-mail or Skype.

- **Copy field to clipboard**: Copies the fields of the item to the clipboard so that you can paste them into another document or application.

- **Delete**: The item will be deleted and sent to the recycle bin.

- **Flow**: Allows you to start a Flow that has been already created. Flows can also integrate with other Office 365 applications.

- **Alert me**: Sends an alert when there is a change, someone else changes an item, someone else changes an item created by you, and someone else changes an item last modified by you. The alert can be sent immediately, daily, or weekly. These alerts apply to the entire list.

- **More** >

  - **Workflow**: Allows you to start a legacy workflow on the item. These workflows are slowly being replaced by Flow, but you can create workflows in SharePoint Designer 2013 until further notice. This is still available because Flow has not reached the same maturity as Workflow, which has been in existence for over 10 years.

  - **Compliance Details**: Displays any compliance parameters around the document, including if it is on legal hold or if it is in a different retention stage.

  - **Details**: Shows a stream of recent activity and details surrounding a file such as permissions and metadata.

In summary, lists and libraries are very similar. The best way to gain an understanding of all the features, which are too many to cover in this introductory book, is to create them and explore them. If you have any questions, please feel free to e-mail me. I can't promise an immediate response but I will try to respond in a timely manner.

Views

Views allow us to manipulate data, whether in lists or libraries, to show or hide data that does not fit the story we are trying to tell. If you look any data, the data is rarely ever presented in a flat file. Usually, there is some grouping or filtering to show the data that we want to present. For example, if you have a list of orders for a product company, it might be best to show that data grouped by location and filtered above certain order cost. In this next section, you will explore the standard views of SharePoint and learn how to customize a view in a way to suit your needs.

The standard view that comes with a list is titled "All Items," and the standard view for document libraries is titled "All Documents." Both views function precisely the same way: they render all items or documents in a single view with no data logic applied. These views are great for when there is a limited number of items or documents, but once the content grows, these views become very useless unless you filter as described in the previous section.

Note   You can always sort the column values and filter when applicable to show different data in the standard view. However, a better practice is to create a set of views that support the business need of the list so they are always available and users do not need to spend time filtering a list manually.

Filtering on demand works well to quickly create a view of the data that you are interested in. Another approach is to create views that everyone is interested in. For example, for a helpdesk ticket list, the view could be open tickets, closed tickets, high priority tickets, and tickets not started. This allows anyone using the application to quickly switch between different views to find the data they need.

In this example, let's create a new list called "Shipping Orders". You will need to create the columns such as "Recipinet(Single line of text)", "ZipCode(Number)", OrderNumber(Number)", and "ToalCost(Currency)".

Once the list is and columns are created, populate it with a few dummy orders and create a view to show all orders grouped by ZIP code. To create the view, follow these steps:

1. In the list, click the down arrow next to "All Items."

2. Click "Save view as."

3. Save it as "Grouped by ZIP Code" and click the Save button.

4. Select the down arrow again, and the Grouped by ZIP Code view should have a checkmark next to it. If it doesn't, select the view you created in Step 3.

5. In the same drop-down menu, select "Edit current view."

6. The Edit view page allows you to configure the view on a variety of factors. In this example scroll, down to Group By and set the First group by the column to ZIP Code.

7. Scroll to the bottom of the Edit view page, and press the OK button.

When you look at the list again, you will notice that the items are grouped by ZIP code, and you can easily see how many orders are in which ZIP code. When creating the view, you may have noticed that there are many other options that can be used to configure a view. The available options are as follows:

Name:

- **View Name**: Specify the name of the view.

- **Web address of this view**: Specify the URL. If needed, SharePoint will create a default value.

- **Make this the default view**: Check the checkbox if you want this to be the default view that everyone user will see when they access the list. If not checked, the view will be available for a user to select.

- **Columns**: Select or deselect any columns you do not want to show in the view. At a minimum, one column must be checked.

- **Sort**: You can sort the list by two columns in either ascending or descending order. You cannot sort by more than two fields.

- **Filter**: Set a filter or multiple filters and use and/or logic to create a sophisticated filter. You can also use different mathematical equations such as "is equal to" or "less than or equal to."

- **Tabular View**: By default, this checkbox is checked and allows an item to be checked so that multiple items can be selected for bulk actions.

- **Group By**: Select at most two columns and group items by a column value. Each Group By field can also be sorted in either ascending or descending order. You can also set the groups to be collapsed or expanded when a user accesses the list and the associated view.

- **Totals**: In views, you can sum all the values of a column and have it displayed in the view. You can choose from Count, Sum, Average, Maximum, Minimum, Std Deviation, and Variance. The available options are based on column type and only not the default columns such as Created or Modified By.

- **Style**: With a view, you can apply a style to change the way the list or library looks. If there are a lot of columns in your view, the Shaded Style will make it easier to read.

- **Folders**: You can specify whether to show folders or not to show folders at all. This pertains more to libraries then lists. Also, if you use folders within a library, it limits the ability to use grouping and filtering.

- **Item Limit**: Specifies the number of items to show in the view and displays either in batches or limit overall.

- **Mobile**: Every list and library has mobile settings. The first setting allows you to limit the number of items returned and set a field that will allow you to edit the item.

With these settings, you can create straightforward views or complex views. A word of caution: be careful with the filter rules because a wrong filter condition can render zero items returned and becomes quite frustrating to find and resolve.

Permissions

The SharePoint Permissions model has always been a bit cumbersome because of the many places where permissions can be changed from sites, libraries, and items. With modern team sites, permissions management has been streamlined so adding users, whether they are a user of the organization or a guest, is now a lot easier.

On a modern team site, the members of the site are accessible via the member count in the upper right corner, as shown in Figure 2-27.

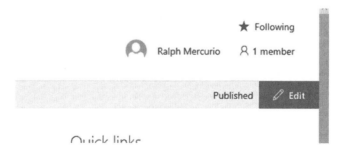

Figure 2-27. *Viewing members of a site*

Clicking "member" will open the Group membership dialog where new members can be added. In this interface, guests cannot be added to the site; they must be added through Outlook Web Access or Outlook 2016. For more information on adding guest users, please review Chapter 4.

To add organizational users (co-workers), by clicking on "member" as described above. In the dialog, click "Add members" and begin typing their name or email address. As you type the name or email address, the matches will begin to populate, and you can select the user from the list of suggestions. Click the Save button and the user will be saved and given the permission level of member. A member permission level allows the user to contribute to the site and ultimately to the Office 365 group. In this view, you can promote a member to an owner or remove the user from the group if needed.

In most cases, I would say to leave the permissions as is and not modify them because modifying them can indirectly cause users to lose access to the site or grant users too much permission. There are business cases where modifying the permissions are necessary, as in the case of employee reviews or a confidential site where permissions need to ensure that employees have the right level of access.

To modify the permissions in an advanced scenario, click "Site permissions" located in the Office 365 settings menu (cog or gear icon in the upper right corner). Clicking "Site permissions" will open the Site Permissions dialog. In this dialog, you can modify permissions of the SharePoint group such as modify the permissions of the group to be Read or Full Control. This is accomplished by selected the down arrow of the group and choosing the appropriate permission, as shown in Figure 2-28.

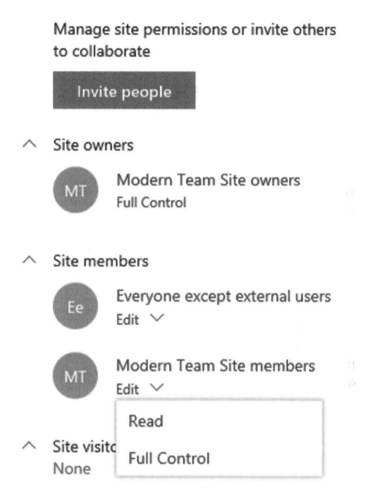

Figure 2-28. Site permissions dialog

This where most permission changes are done if needed. If the business requirements require that a different permissions scheme be created, that can be done by clicking the "Advanced permission settings" link shown in Figure 2-28.

For those users who are familiar with SharePoint 2010, 2013, or 2016 permissions management, the advanced permissions setting looks identical to Figure 2-29.

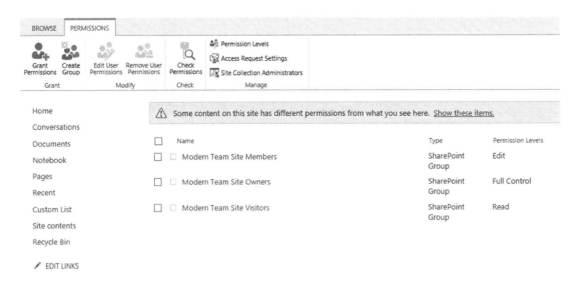

Figure 2-29. *Advanced permission settings*

Part of the purpose of this book is to provide a solid introduction to all of the Office 365 collaboration applications and not to focus solely on one application more than another. Because of this, I decided not to include advanced permissions in this book because that is a topic that is best reserved for an advanced SharePoint Online publication.

For classic experience sites, permissions are modified through a slightly different procedure. This procedure is exactly the same as it is in Microsoft's SharePoint 2010, 2013, and 2016 on-premises products. Again, advanced permissions are best reserved for a non-introductory book.

As a best practice, in most scenarios you manage the permissions through the Group membership dialog described at the beginning of this section. If advanced permission changes are needed, please consult with your Office 365 administrator prior to doing so.

Pages and Web Parts

Now let's explore pages. Pages hold all of the sites together and give the user an interface to connect to. SharePoint pages can be customized to include specific web parts, which can be used to show a user a different presentation of data or specific lists or libraries.

I will focus on editing a modern team site instead of a classic experience site. This is partly because modern team sites will always have a different set of web parts and modern team sites are part of Office 365 Groups.

Before you dive into editing a site, I want to highlight some of the available web parts and their uses because they have significantly matured throughout the years.

- **Text**: Adds text to the page. Allows for typical text formatting options.

- **Image**: Adds an image to the page

- **File viewer**: Embeds a file onto the page. It can be a .pdf, .docx, .xlsx, or another supported file type.

- **Link**: Adds a link to the page. Will show a preview of the website that the URL points to.

- **Embed**: Allows for embedded code to be added to the page. For example, you can embed a YouTube video. YouTube will generate the embed code automatically on the website.

- **Highlighted content**: Shows content based on a variety of metadata.

- **Bing maps**: Adds a Bing map to the page and shows a location.

- **Events**: Displays upcoming events or calendar entries.

- **Google Analytics**: Allows viewing of Google Analytical Summary site data. Google Analytics gathers metrics such as hits, user location, top pages, etc. At the moment, Google Analytics does not integrate natively with SharePoint Online.

- **Hero**: Adds the Hero web part to the page. The Hero web part allows content to be visually displayed and highlighted. This web part was introduced in the communication site.

- **Microsoft Forms**: Adds a survey to the site. Surveys are used to gather responses to a questionnaire. Microsoft Forms and surveys are discussed in Chapter 10.

- **Planner**: Integrates Microsoft Planner to show a plan and present the task associated with a plan in a visual representation. Microsoft Planner is discussed more in depth in Chapter 8.

- **Stream**: Embeds a video from a Microsoft Stream channel. Microsoft Stream is a video sharing platform that is integrated into the Office 365 suite.

Editing Pages

Editing pages in SharePoint Online is a simple task. The only trouble you will run into is figuring out which web parts to use or what page layout to use. To put the page into edit mode, select the Edit button in the upper right corner, as shown in Figure 2-30.

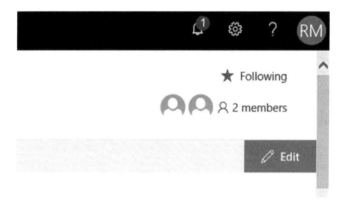

Figure 2-30. *Putting the page into Edit mode*

Clicking the Edit button puts the page into Edit mode. The interface will look like Figure 2-31. The layout contains some key components that I will highlight.

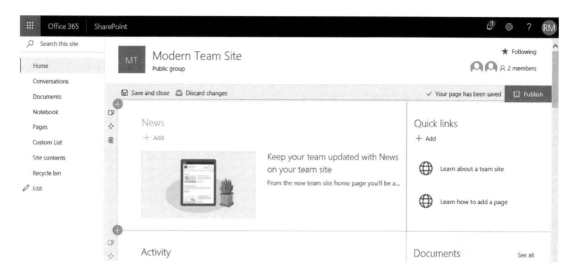

Figure 2-31. *The Edit interface*

On the top of the page layout beneath the Modern Team Site title, you will notice three buttons: "Save and close," "Discard changes," and "Publish." "Save and close" saves all the changes you made but does not publish the page to be visible. This is akin to draft mode and allows you to work on the page over the course of time without having to make all the changes at once. If you made a mistake and just want to start fresh, clicking "Discard changes" closes the page and allows you to reopen the page and start anew. It doesn't save any of your changes—even before you made a mistake in editing the page. The final button, "Publish," publishes the page and makes it visible to all users.

In this edit mode, you can edit either sections or web parts. In Figure 2-31, the News and Quick links are web parts while the section is the zone that contains both of the web parts. If you ever edited pages in other versions of SharePoint, the section is similar to the web part zone or the wiki zone on SharePoint Pages.

In the edit view, you can change the layout of a section, move the section, or delete the section completely from the page. The edit section icons are to the left of the section and are listed in a vertical format, as shown in Figure 2-32.

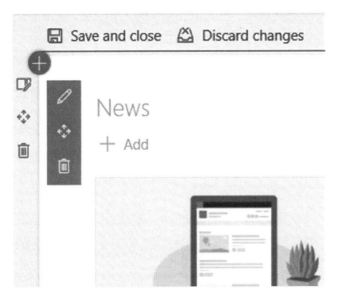

Figure 2-32. *Editing a section of a page*

The first icon allows you to change the layout of the section to one of five section layout choices. After you make your selection from the available choices below, click Save and the section will switch to the selected layout.

- **One column**: One single column. Web parts will stack vertically on each other.

- **Two column**: Two equal columns. Web parts will stack vertically on each other.

- **Three column**: Three equal columns. Web parts will stack vertically on each other.

- **One-third left column**: The section will be divided into two columns with the left column taking up 1/3 of the section.

- **One-third right column**: The section will be divided into two columns with the right column taking up 1/3 of the section.

The second icon is the Move Section icon. This icon allows the section to be reordered on the page. When moving a section, the entire section moves, including the web parts within the section. To move a section, click and hold the Move Section icon with your right mouse button. While the right mouse button is depressed, move the section anywhere on the page.

The third and final icon available when working with sections is the trash can icon. Clicking this icon removes the section and its included web parts from the page and deletes it all. Before the section is deleted, you will be asked for a confirmation. If you deleted the section in error, a previous page version can be restored. To restore a page to a previous version, follow these steps:

1. Click the cog (gear) icon in the upper right corner of the SharePoint site.

2. Select "Site contents" from the menu.

3. Open the Site Pages library.

4. Select the three vertical dots (ellipsis) and select "Version history."

   a. Select the version before the published version. Published versions always end in 0 while minor versions do not.

   b. Hover over the version you want to restore and from the drop-down menu choose "Restore."

Manipulating Web Parts

To add a web part to a section, make sure the page is in edit mode. If it is not, please follow the steps in the previous section to put the page into edit mode. Much like editing sections, adding web parts is a simple process. When hovering within a section, the "Add web part" dialog (as denoted by the red circle with a plus sign) will appear, allowing you to add any number of web parts; see Figure 2-33.

Figure 2-33. The "Add web part" interface

Clicking the "Add web part" will load the available web parts that can be added to a page. I discussed some of the most popular ones in a prior section, and the choices presented now are quite exhaustive. Because Office 365 integrates with a wide variety of third-party applications does not mean you have access to use them. They can be added to the page, but you must subscribe to use them explicitly within Office 365. There may be associated costs outside of Office 365 to make these third-party web parts work.

Let's add the Text web part to the section from the "Add web part" dialog. Adding the Text web part to the section will not only add the web part but also put the web part in edit mode, as shown in Figure 2-34.

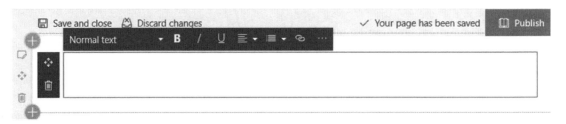

Figure 2-34. *Text web part in edit mode*

Because this is a Text web part, the familiar text styling tools appear. To add text, simply type your desired text and then style it with available tools. Every web part also can be moved to another section or within the section by clicking the move icon or can be deleted by clicking the trashcan icon.

The other web parts all work in a similar manner: add them to a section, edit as needed, and save your changes. Go ahead explore them all, see what works for your needs, and be sure to save your changes.

SharePoint Mobile App

Office 365 is designed to work across a variety of browsers and devices. This includes mobile devices on the Android, Apple, and Microsoft platforms. Microsoft released a SharePoint mobile app that allows you to connect to SharePoint Online sites, document libraries, and resources all with your phone.

To install the SharePoint mobile app, access the respective app store for your device. The below instructions are from the Android perspective, but the instructions and experience are similar regardless of the mobile platform. Access your respective store and search for "Microsoft SharePoint." Figure 2-35 depicts the app available in the Google Play Store.

Figure 2-35. *SharePoint mobile app in the Google Play Store*

Proceed to download and install the SharePoint mobile app. Once the app is installed, go ahead and open it. Upon opening the app, it will prompt you for your Office 365 email address and password. By entering your credentials, it connects the mobile app to Office 365 and will display the same information as the SharePoint portal site, which is accessible from the Office 365 app launcher in the browser.

The SharePoint mobile app will display the frequent sites and sites you are following, plus the News, Links, People, and Me icons, as shown in Figure 2-36.

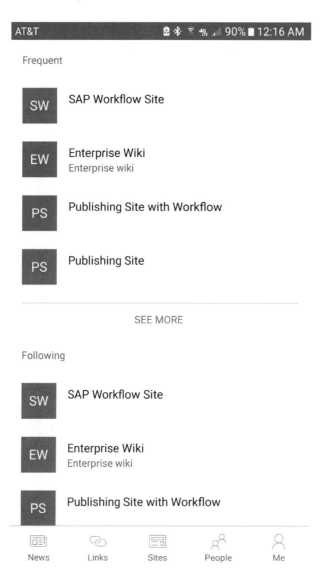

Figure 2-36. *SharePoint Mobile App interface*

Clicking a frequent site or a site you are following opens the respective site in the mobile app. Figure 2-37 depicts a modern team site in the mobile view; even though it is not identical to viewing a modern team site in a browser, the functionality is roughly the same.

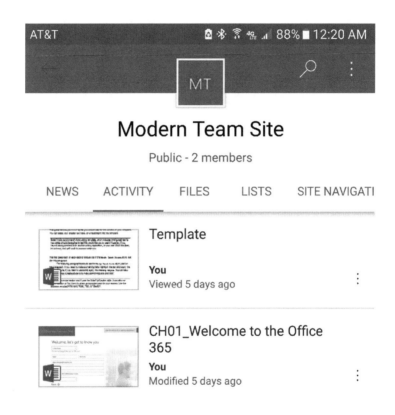

Figure 2-37. *Modern team site in the SharePoint mobile app*

The other aspects of the SharePoint mobile app pull information from Office 365. For instance, clicking the People icon in the app will allow you to search and find users within the organization. It will display their contact info as well as an activity stream of content that has been shared.

Clicking the News icon gathers all of the news articles that have been published within the modern team sites. I didn't cover creating and maintaining news articles in this book, but go ahead and give it a try. You can create news articles on modern team sites or within the SharePoint portal site.

Clicking the Links icon opens a list of links, which is managed by the Office 365 administrator. These links could be links to Human Resources portal, IT service catalog, or any other site.

The last two components of the SharePoint mobile app are the Me and search functions. The Me icon within the SharePoint mobile app allows you to modify your Office 365 profile as well as see an activity stream of your actions, files, and created content in Office 365. The search box, located in the upper right corner of the app, is not just a search into SharePoint Online sites; it also searches all of the Office 365 applications and content.

Summary

SharePoint Online is a workhorse application. It can help with document management, be the company's intranet, a place to search and find content, or a project management site with user tasks and documentation. SharePoint can be really whatever you need it to be and does so with elegance and ease.

Using lists and libraries to organize content with appropriate columns and views allows for data to be stored in a single location and provides business views into the data; by specifying metadata, you make the search experience even better. The metadata of an item gives the SharePoint Online search engine the ability to categorize an item and create a robust index, which ultimately gives you the best search experience possible.

Modern team sites and communication sites are modern templates that have been redesigned completely and allow for a mobile experience as well as new integrations with other products to bring information into a single site. This robust integration is only going to get stronger in the future.

OneDrive for Business, which is discussed in the next chapter, is built on the backbone of SharePoint Online document libraries, and you will notice that OneDrive functions in a similar manner and is centered around the document experience.

CHAPTER 3

OneDrive

In the last chapter, I discussed SharePoint Online and how it can help organize content around document libraries and sites at the organization level. In this chapter, I will discuss OneDrive, which allows content to be stored in Office 365 and always available. Microsoft OneDrive allows you to store up to 1 Terabyte (TB) of content, which is then accessible from any Internet-connected device. OneDrive is geared towards the individual user. There are two flavors currently offered by Microsoft: OneDrive and OneDrive for Business. I will focus on OneDrive for Business because it is included in your Office 365 subscription whereas OneDrive is targeted at consumers purchasing home subscriptions of Office 365. For our purposes and discussion, I will refer to OneDrive for Business as just OneDrive.

OneDrive is meant as a serious contender for file storage instead of using a local drive or a network location. As Internet-connected devices become more common and the Internet becomes available almost anywhere, it makes sense to store and access your files in the cloud. Microsoft also released a mobile version of OneDrive and introduced new features on the Windows 10 platform that greatly improve the storage, syncing, and accessing of your OneDrive files.

Where Is OneDrive Located?

Over time, OneDrive has been tightly integrated into Windows, Office, and mobile devices to allow ease of use and further adoption of the platform. The first and foremost way to access your OneDrive content is to use any modern web browser and access it directly from the app launcher (Figure 3-1) in Office 365.

© Ralph Mercurio 2018
R. Mercurio, *Beginning Office 365 Collaboration Apps*, https://doi.org/10.1007/978-1-4842-3849-3_3

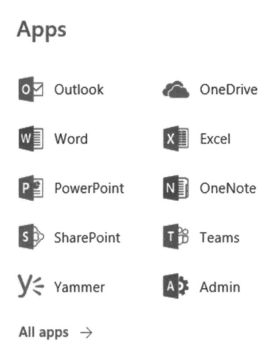

Figure 3-1. *OneDrive located in Office 365 app launcher*

Clicking the OneDrive icon opens OneDrive; I will discuss it further in the next section.

OneDrive also includes a sync client (Figure 3-2) that integrates into Windows Explorer and syncs content, additions, changes, or deletions with your OneDrive account.

Figure 3-2. *OneDrive sync client (blue cloud) installed on Windows 10*

OneDrive is also tightly integrated with the Microsoft Office suite and allows for opening and saving files directly from OneDrive. This integration is beneficial because you do not need to download files but can browse directly in OneDrive from the applications. Office Online, which offers the web versions of Word, Excel, PowerPoint, is also tightly integrated with OneDrive. I will discuss this further in Chapter 7.

Android and Apple mobile apps are available and allow you to browse and open files located in OneDrive. In conjunction with the mobile version of Office, you can also create and edit documents on your mobile devices, fortunately (or unfortunately) creating a modern workplace where you do not need to be in the office to work.

OneDrive via the Browser

As I demonstrated in the previous section, accessing OneDrive via the app launcher opens OneDrive. The OneDrive layout includes the content shown in Figure 3-3.

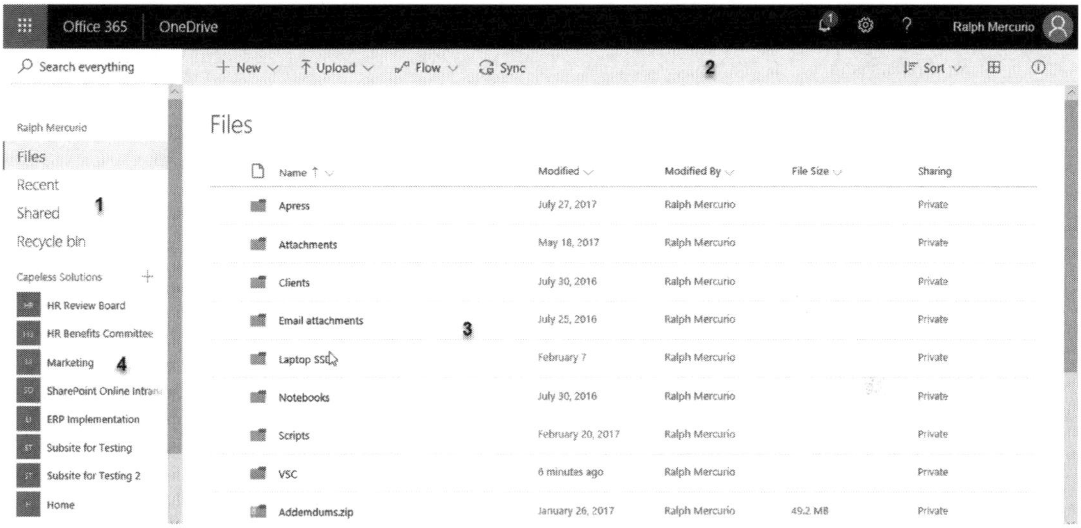

Figure 3-3. *OneDrive layout*

Each of the areas depicted by a number is explained below and elaborated on further in this chapter:

- Area 1 allows you to change the view to show files, recent additions, shared or private files, and the recycle bin.

- Area 2 depicts the OneDrive context menu, which shows/hides options based on your item selection.

- Area 3 is the main area of OneDrive where files and folders appear. It's similar to Windows Explorer.

- Area 4 shows the recent SharePoint or Office 365 Groups and allows you to quickly access the document portion of those sites or groups.

Views

Area 1, shown in Figure 3-3, allows you to show different views in OneDrive. This is useful because as your OneDrive grows and as you add more and more content, it can become cumbersome to view the content you're actively working on. Part of the goal of Office 365 is to always have the most recent content available. The OneDrive views attempt to help you; select the view you want by clicking one of the headings.

Files

The Files view is the bread and butter of OneDrive. This view contains all of the files and/ or folders that you upload or create in OneDrive. Taking a look around, you will notice that it is a mix of SharePoint functionality and Windows File Explorer. When you are in the Files view, the context menu shows the options shown in Figure 3-4 when no files are selected.

Figure 3-4. *OneDrive Files view*

The New command allows you to create a Word, Excel, PowerPoint, or OneNote Notebook using Office Web Apps (discussed in Chapter 7) and save the file directly in OneDrive. You can also create two other items: Forms for Excel and a Link. Forms for Excel allows you to create web-accessible forms and collect the responses from all participants. I discuss Forms in greater detail in Chapter 10. A OneDrive Link is a hyperlink to an existing item or webpage. The link then is stored in your OneDrive with an .url file extension.

The Upload command allows you to upload either file(s) or folders directly to OneDrive. The upload interface is similar to the SharePoint Upload interface and allows the selection of multiple files or folders. You can also drag a folder or file from your local device and upload into OneDrive. Simply right-click the item and drag it onto the browser window where OneDrive is open.

The third command, Flow, allows workflows to be contracted to perform a certain set of actions when an event (i.e., upload) occurs. I will discuss Microsoft Flow in Chapter 11 because it is a new product in Office 365 and I first need to lay the foundation so you can understand the impact and its use within Office 365.

The fourth command, Sync, syncs the contents locally to your PC utilizing the OneDrive Sync application. This application, which is discussed later in this chapter, allows for the contents of OneDrive (selective or all items) to be copied locally to your device. This device can be a laptop, desktop, tablet, or mobile device.

The final set of icons is located to the right of the context menu: Sort, Tiles preview, and Details. The Sort icon allows you to sort the contents of the OneDrive by the fields shown in Table 3-1.

Table 3-1. *Sorting Attributes*

Sort Attribute	What It Does
Type	Sorts based on file extension (.docx, .pdf, etc.)
Name	Sorts alphabetically
Modified	Sorts by time stamp
Modified By	Sorts by user who last modified the document
File Size	Sorts by file size
Ascending	Sorts by alphabetical or increasing number
Descending	Sorts by reverse alphabetical or decreasing number

Note   One thing to be aware of is that for the most part folders will always be first in any sort order, followed by files.

The Tiles preview (Figure 3-5) allows you to view the contents of the OneDrive graphically versus the standard details view that you see when the OneDrive loads. This is useful if you are looking for an icon or from a readability standpoint.

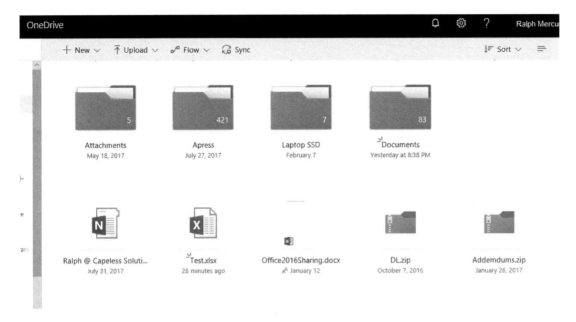

Figure 3-5. *Tiles preview for OneDrive*

The last icon is the Details icon, and it has two unique views. If no item is selected, clicking the Details icon displays the stream of recent changes that took place in your OneDrive. This recent stream is a history of what happened. However, you cannot revert any recent change from this window. If you select an item and then click the Details icon, it will show a preview of the contents of the file but not for every file type. For instance, .mp4 or .wav files will not render a preview but Office and PDF files will.

As part of the Details, you can see who has access and you can grant or revoke access. Below the Access Details are the recent changes, including the history of changes to the item. The last section is the Information Details, such as the type, modified, path (location), and size.

Recent

The Recent view displays a sorted list of files or folders starting with the most recently accessed item (Figure 3-6). It sorts descending (most recently accessed first) on the Last accessed column.

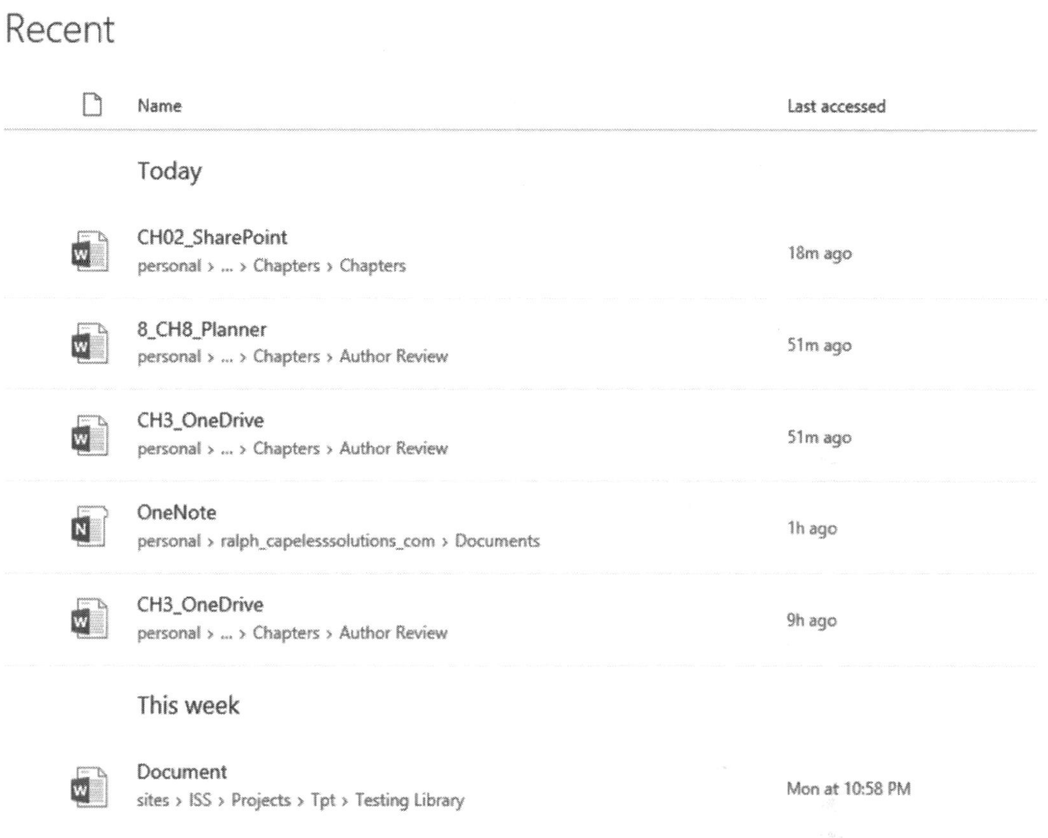

Recent

	Name	Last accessed
	Today	
	CH02_SharePoint personal › ... › Chapters › Chapters	18m ago
	8_CH8_Planner personal › ... › Chapters › Author Review	51m ago
	CH3_OneDrive personal › ... › Chapters › Author Review	51m ago
	OneNote personal › ralph_capelesssolutions_com › Documents	1h ago
	CH3_OneDrive personal › ... › Chapters › Author Review	9h ago
	This week	
	Document sites › ISS › Projects › Tpt › Testing Library	Mon at 10:58 PM

Figure 3-6. *OneDrive Recent view*

This view is beneficial because it allows you to quickly see the recent items first because those are the items that you are likely to share or continue to work on. In prior releases of OneDrive, this view was based on the `Modified` column but customer feedback most likely changed it.

Shared

The Shared view of OneDrive includes two child views. The first view is "Shared with me" and the second view is "Shared by me" (Figure 3-7).

Figure 3-7. *The "Shared with me" view*

The first view, "Shared with me," allows you to see any content that has been shared by other people and to which you have been given some level of access. This level of access can be read-only or edit. When an item is "Shared with me," the recipient will receive a link to the item and will be able to perform certain actions as designated by the owner of the item. The magic here is the file will and does reside on the owner's OneDrive, reducing the number of copies or email attachments.

The second view, "Shared by me," shows all the items that have been shared by the OneDrive owner. The power of this view is that you can quickly see what content is being shared and if you need to stop the sharing of the content and remove access for a user. In theory, this is great; it aims to cut down on information leakage or unauthorized access, but if the recipient saved a copy, this wouldn't protect the content.

Note   Protecting content once it leaves your Office 365 environment is the work of Azure Rights Management and is out of the scope of this book.

To view details about an item that is shared, the first step is to highlight the item by clicking the row. Once the row is highlighted, the context menu will change, as shown in Figure 3-8.

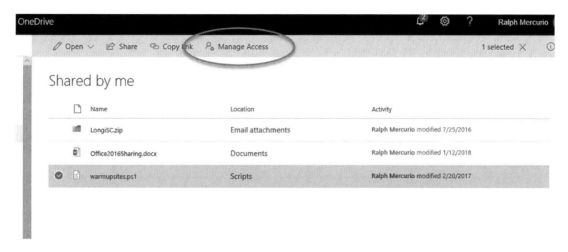

Figure 3-8. *Managing access to a file*

Clicking "Manage Access" opens a details pane. This details pane, shown in Figure 3-9, gives basic information about the sharing access. Currently, `warmupsites.ps1` is only shared with my organization and a single user has edit rights. You can quickly tell which user has edit rights by hovering over the user image; in a moment the user's name and email address will appear.

By clicking "Stop sharing" you can immediately remove all permissions from the item and only you (the OneDrive owner) will have rights to the file.

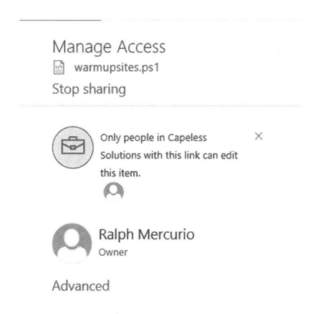

Figure 3-9. *The Manage Access details pane*

Clicking "Advanced" opens a SharePoint Online permissions management page (Figure 3-10) which shows not only the users who have access but also what level. The page should look familiar because it was discussed in the previous section and looks similar to a SharePoint Online permissions page.

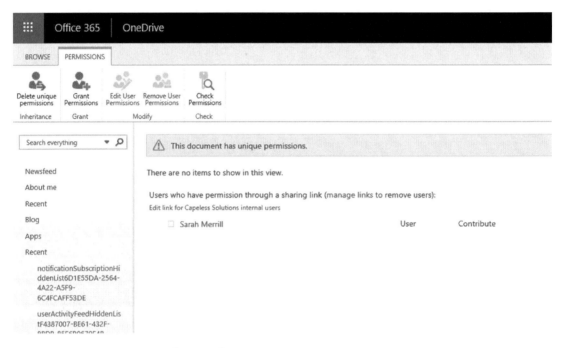

Figure 3-10. *Viewing advanced permissions on an item*

This looks familiar because OneDrive shares many of the same features as well as frameworks. This reduces development costs for Microsoft and allows the company to tailor and create products to serve different segments of the enterprise.

Recycle Bin

Any content deleted from OneDrive will appear in the OneDrive recycle bin. In OneDrive, the recycle bin has two stages. When you delete an item, it will appear in the recycle bin for 90 days, as shown in Figure 3-11. After 90 days, it will be moved automatically by OneDrive to the second-stage recycle bin where it will be available for another 90 days. After 180 days, it will be marked for permanent deletion.

The second-stage recycle bin is available by scrolling to the bottom of the recycle bin and selecting the second-stage recycle bin.

Recycle bin

	Name ⌄	Date deleted ↓ ⌄	Deleted by ⌄	Created by ⌄	Original location
📄	Document1.docx	2/22/2018 12:13 PM	Ralph Mercurio	Ralph Mercurio	personal/ralph_capel
📄	Book2.xlsx	1/12/2018 11:38 AM	Ralph Mercurio	Ralph Mercurio	personal/ralph_capel
📄	OneDrive - Capeless Solutions - Shortc...	12/12/2017 8:08 PM	Ralph Mercurio	Ralph Mercurio	personal/ralph_capel

Can't find what you're looking for? Check the Second-stage recycle bin

Figure 3-11. *The recycle bin and accessing the second-stage recycle bin*

Clicking the second-stage recycle bin changes the view, as shown in Figure 3-12, and displays the second-stage recycle bin.

Second stage recycle bin

	Name ⌄	Date deleted ↓ ⌄	Deleted by ⌄	Created by ⌄	Original location

Figure 3-12. *Second-stage recycle bin*

In my OneDrive, I don't have any files in the second-stage recycle bin, but I would be able to restore them if any were there.

Restoring a file from either the first or second-stage recycle bin is an easy process. To do so, simply click the item and choose "Restore" from the context menu, as shown in Figure 3-13.

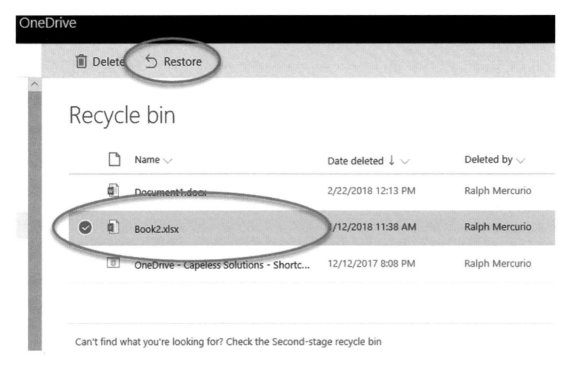

Figure 3-13. *Restoring an item from the recycle bin*

Note   If you manually delete a file from the recycle bin, you will not be able to restore or find it in the second-stage recycle bin.

Sites

Below the available OneDrive views, OneDrive catalogs and keeps tracks of the Office 365 Groups and SharePoint sites you can access. Clicking into a SharePoint Site or Office 365 Group opens the Documents library. Once the library opens, you can add items and have them available immediately.

Working with Items in OneDrive

OneDrive is very closely related to SharePoint Online document libraries and works similarly. OneDrive offers a myriad of actions depending on how and what you do within the OneDrive interface. By hovering over an item, two commands appear: a Share link and an ellipsis (Figure 3-14).

***Figure 3-14.** Share and ellipsis icons of a OneDrive document*

Clicking the Share icon allows you to share the item through the Office 365 sharing interface. This interface allows the item to be shared with the following:

- People within your organization

- People with existing access

- Specific people

You also have the ability to specify if the permission allows for editing or viewing only. You can also create a shareable link and send it directly to specific user(s).

Clicking the ellipsis (three vertical dots), as shown in Figure 3-14, renders a menu with a myriad of options. This context menu (Figure 3-15) shows the various options or actions per the selected item in your OneDrive, as shown in Table 3-2.

Figure 3-15. *OneDrive item context menu*

Table 3-2. *Context Menu Explanation*

Context Menu Option	Action
Open	Opens the item in the corresponding application, if available and known.
Preview	Renders a preview within the web browser. If it is an Office document, OneDrive will attempt to use Office Online.
Share	Allows the item to be shared with the following: People within your organization People with existing access Specific people

(continued)

Table 3-2. (*continued*)

Context Menu Option	Action
Copy Link	Creates a direct link to the item to share or access it.
Download	Downloads the item.
Delete	Deletes the item, sending it to the first-stage recycle bin.
Move To	Allows the file to be moved anywhere in the current OneDrive file/folder structure. The item will be moved, not copied, to the new location.
Copy To	Allows the file to be copied anywhere in the current OneDrive file/folder structure. The item will be copied, not moved, to the new location.
Rename	Renames the item to a new file name.
Flow	Starts a Microsoft Flow to perform a set of actions. Flows are discussed in detail in Chapter 12.
Version History	Shows previous versions and allows for a restore of a previous version if needed.
Details	Shows the details of the item, including properties and shared information.

Do not be overwhelmed by the available choices. In the previous chapter, I covered the context menu from the SharePoint perspective, and it is closely related to the available context menu in OneDrive.

OneDrive Sync Client

OneDrive also offers the ability to sync the contents of OneDrive with an OneDrive folder on your local device. A benefit of this architecture is that in the absence of an Internet connection you will still be able to access and consume your files. Any changes you make will automatically sync once an Internet connection is reestablished.

The OneDrive Sync client is available on Windows, Apple, tablets, and mobile devices through either the respective app store or a download from Microsoft. Now, I'll guide you through the process of an install and a basic configuration of the OneDrive client for reference. I suggest checking with your Information Technology department if there are any policies or special configuration needed within your enterprise.

Installing OneDrive on Windows 10

The OneDrive Sync client works on Windows 7 and higher versions, but Microsoft released an important update with the Windows 10 Creator's update that allows for selective syncing of items to your local workstation. This is important because OneDrive offers 1TB of online storage and you may not want to keep all of that content locally on your device. Also, if the hard drive isn't very big, you also run the risk of eventually running out of space and needing to upgrade to a larger hard drive.

The first step in the install process is to download the OneDrive Sync client. The download link is available via a hyperlink in the lower left corner of OneDrive titled "Get the OneDrive apps." Clicking the link opens a new web browser tab, and you can download the OneDrive Sync client. Once you give permission to install OneDrive after downloading, it will automatically install, as shown in Figure 3-16.

Figure 3-16. *Installing the OneDrive Sync client*

Once OneDrive finishes, a grey cloud will appear by the system time, and you will need to sign into Office 365 to activate the OneDrive Sync client. To sign in, left-click the grey cloud and sign in. Once you click "Sign in," OneDrive will begin the configuration process and ask you for your email account associated with Office 365. Figure 3-17 shows the first step in configuring the OneDrive Sync client.

Figure 3-17. *Signing into OneDrive via the OneDrive Sync client*

Once you enter your email address, choose the approriate platform to authenticate to OneDrive. In my case, it was Work. As discussed before, OneDrive comes in two flavors: personal or business. The OneDrive Sync client works the same in either version but OneDrive for Personal is not integrated into Office 365, and I have exclusively discussed OneDrive for Business in this chapter.

Once authenticated, the OneDrive client will create a default folder where it will sync the contents of your OneDrive account on your local device. Part of the simplicity of the OneDrive Sync tool is that any content that you want to sync must be in the default OneDrive folder. You cannot sync folders or content that is stored outside of this folder.

Accepting the defaults, the OneDrive Sync client will sync an exact copy of your OneDrive account to your device. In more advanced scenarios, you can selectively sync OneDrive folders instead of syncing your entire OneDrive account.

Now that OneDrive has been configured using the default configuration options, you will notice that the grey cloud has now turned blue and a OneDrive folder is now available within Windows File Explorer. You can save files directly into the OneDrive folder or drag files into it using Windows File Explorer.

Note   The following steps are specific to Windows 10 and having the Creator's Update installed only.

Now that you have completed the basic steps, let's explore some of the features of the OneDrive Sync client. The first feature I want to discuss is the ability to selectively sync content to the local device. By default, this feature is not enabled, and all content is synced between the two locations. To enable the selective sync, right-click the blue OneDrive cloud in the system tray (next to the system time) and select "Settings." Click the Settings tab, check the "Save space and download files as you use them" box shown in Figure 3-18, and click OK when complete.

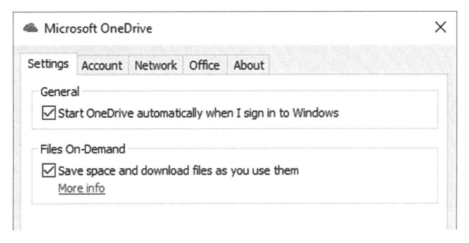

Figure 3-18. *Enabling files on demand*

Now that the feature is enabled, you can selectively enable Files On-Demand for the items you want. To do so, open the OneDrive default folder as designated by the blue cloud in Windows File Explorer.

With Files On-Demand enabled, three options become available to sync files. The three options are "online only," "locally available," or "always available." These settings are controlled by selecting the file or folder in Windows File Explorer and choosing the corresponding option.

To mark a file as "online only," open Windows File Explorer and navigate to the OneDrive folder. Right-click the item and choose "Free up space." This will change the status of the item from a green icon to a blue-outline cloud icon. See Figure 3-19.

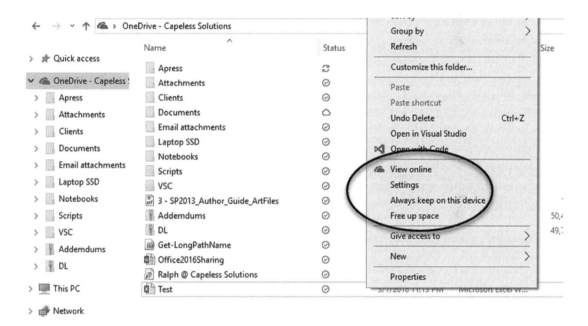

Figure 3-19. *Marking a file as "online only"*

The second option, "locally available," is when you open a file that was previously marked as "online only." This will cause OneDrive to download the file and also change from a blue-outline cloud icon to a green check mark. Once you are done working on the file and want to set it back "online only," follow the above steps.

The third option, "Always keep on this device," will ensure that the file is never marked as "online only" unless you reselect "Always keep on this device." This option ensures that a copy is stored on your device. This is denoted by a solid green circle with a white checkmark.

Note   Deleting an "online only" file from your local machine will delete it from your OneDrive in Office 365. The file will be available in the recycle bin if you need to restore it.

Experience Mobile OneDrive

Microsoft also released an app for both Android and iPhone platforms. The OneDrive client for these devices is available in the respective app stores. To access your OneDrive via your mobile device, open the download app and sign in with your Office 365 user id and password. Upon logging into the app, you will notice a familiar interface, as shown in Figure 3-20.

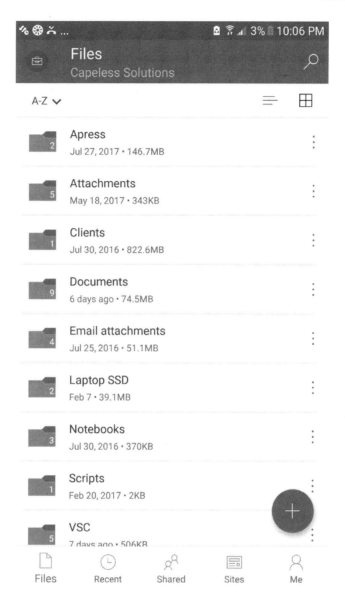

Figure 3-20. *OneDrive mobile interface*

The OneDrive for Mobile interface contains multiple views such as Files, Recent, Shared, Sites, and Me. These views are precisely the same as when viewing OneDrive through the browser. You can also select the appropriate options by clicking the ellipsis. Not every option is available, such as starting a Flow, which currently can only be done from the browser.

The Me view, which is not available when viewing OneDrive in the browser, contains some familiar settings I already discussed. For instance, the recycle bin is available and you can restore items much like the web version. To restore an item, navigate to the recycle bin and select the ellipsis to restore the item.

Another setting that is similar to Files On-Demand is that by default all items are available online only in the mobile version. This is by design because it limits the initial download of content and you have the ability to stream files as needed and sync the changes back to your OneDrive. If you want to download an item and have it available when an Internet connection may not be available, click the ellipsis and choose "Keep offline," as shown in Figure 3-21.

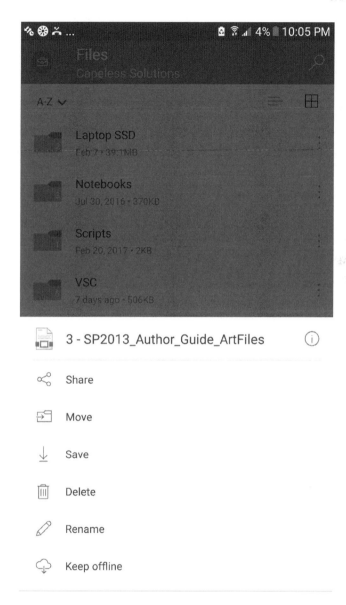

Figure 3-21. *Making a file available offline*

To view which files have been made available offline, select the Me view and choose "Files Available Offline."

Summary

Microsoft OneDrive offers you 1TB of storage that is secure and always available to you regardless of device or location as long as you have an Internet connection. By using OneDrive, you are almost guaranteed that you will not lose content via a hardware failure.

With OneDrive, not only is the content safe and secure but it becomes part of the Office 365 ecosystem and you can use the Office Online apps to view or edit your documents. This integration ensures that you have unfettered access to consume your content on your terms. Another important feature is the ability to selectively share content from your OneDrive with others, reducing email and ensuring that multiple versions do not get created.

In the next chapter, I will cover Office 365 Groups, which are a new feature of Office 365; they allow for a collaborative group experience built on Outlook and SharePoint.

CHAPTER 4

Office 365 Groups

In the previous chapter, I discussed OneDrive, which allows content to be stored in Office 365 and always available. In this chapter, I will discuss Office 365 Groups, which bring email, calendars, SharePoint sites, Planner, OneNote, and the ability to integrate other third-party sources into a single, concise application. Office 365 Groups are the ultimate tools for teams to collaborate and share information. This application mashup aims to bring together people from inside or outside the organization and collaborate using the familiar tools of Office 365.

Before I dive into Office 365 Groups, let's discuss what Office 365 Groups are not. They are not the same as SharePoint Groups; as I mentioned earlier, SharePoint Groups focus on permission-based access to your SharePoint sites. They also are not distribution groups like you use today to email a group of colleagues in Outlook.

Where Are They Located?

Office 365 Groups are accessible via the Outlook icon (Figure 4-1) from the Office 365 app launcher or within Outlook 2016 (Figure 4-2). You can access the Office 365 app launcher by logging into Office 365.com from any supported web browser. Any group of which you are a member will show in the Outlook left navigation and be accessible. Below the Groups heading are two more options: Discover and Create. These two options are used to find groups and to create your own groups for use.

© Ralph Mercurio 2018
R. Mercurio, *Beginning Office 365 Collaboration Apps*, https://doi.org/10.1007/978-1-4842-3849-3_4

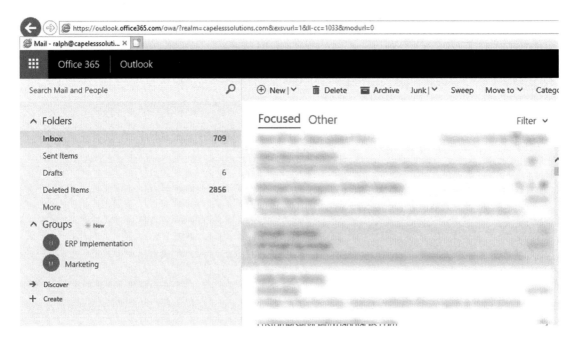

Figure 4-1. *Accessing Office 365 Groups from the Outlook icon in the Office 365 app launcher*

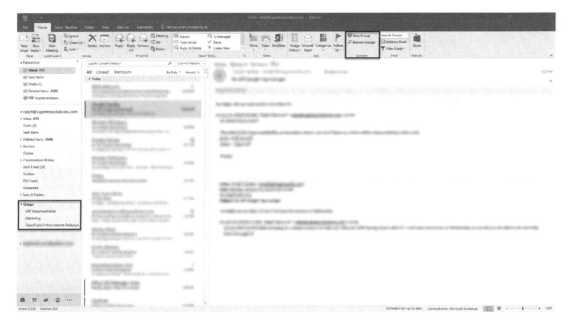

Figure 4-2. *Accessing Office 365 Groups from Outlook 2016*

Note   The interesting notion about Office 365 groups is that they do not rely on IT departments for creation. In Office 365, you can create a group and use it as you see fit to solve your particular challenges. With that, you should follow any governance or guidelines that your IT department has published around the creation and usability of Office 365 groups. There may be requirements or record retention laws around protecting and archiving any of the data in a group.

Discovering a Group

Depending on your particular organization, there might be some Office 365 groups already created and being used by the organization. To discover or find an Office 365 group, click the "Discover" link (Figure 4-1) located under the Groups heading in Outlook Web Access. Doing so will bring up an interface (Figure 4-3) where you can search for groups and view group suggestions that might fit your profile.

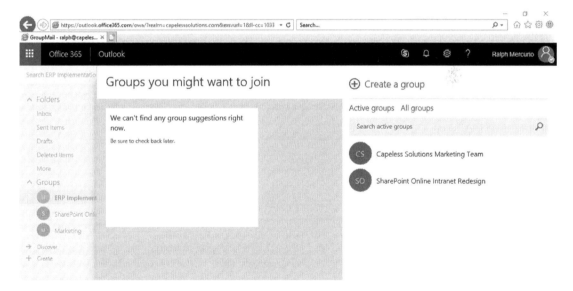

Figure 4-3.   *The Discover Office 365 Groups interface*

On the right side of the "Groups you may want to join" modal window you can also search for groups. The search contains two queries: Active groups and All groups. Active groups are noted by having a recent conversation event, although there may be other activity inside the group such as uploading a file or creating Planner (Chapter 8) tasks. The All groups query can search for all Office 365 groups. To find an Office 365 group, use the search bar. Depending on the total number of Office 365 groups, you may also be able to find one by viewing "Active groups" or "All groups" without entering search criteria.

Located in the middle of the page, Office 365 will suggest groups that fit your particular profile or share a common thread such a mutual colleague.

Creating an Office 365 Group

Creating an Office 365 group can be done multiple ways, some which I will not cover in this book. The first and easiest way to create an Office 365 group is by selecting the "Create" link (Figure 4-1) in Outlook Web Access. The link is located in the Discover section within the Groups section. You can also click the + sign to the right of the Groups heading.

Clicking the link displays the "Create a Group" interface to create your new Office 365 group (Figure 4-4).

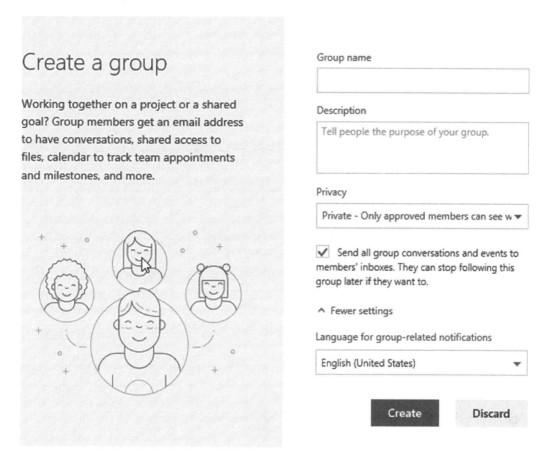

Figure 4-4. *Creating an Office 365 group through Outlook (web version)*

The form contains the following fields:

- **Group name**: This will be the display name for the Office 365 group.

- **Group email address**: You can add a friendly email address to be able to send mail directly to the group.

- **Description**: Describe the main use of the Office 365 group.

- **Privacy**: Choose public or private. I will discuss this in detail later.

- **"Send all group conversations" checkbox**: Any conversation will also be sent to the member's inbox. Members will not have to check the Office 365 group for communications because they will receive a copy in their own inbox.

- **Language for group-related notifications**: Choose the default language.

Once you are satisfied with the data you entered (Figure 4-5), click the Create button and your new Office 365 Group will be created.

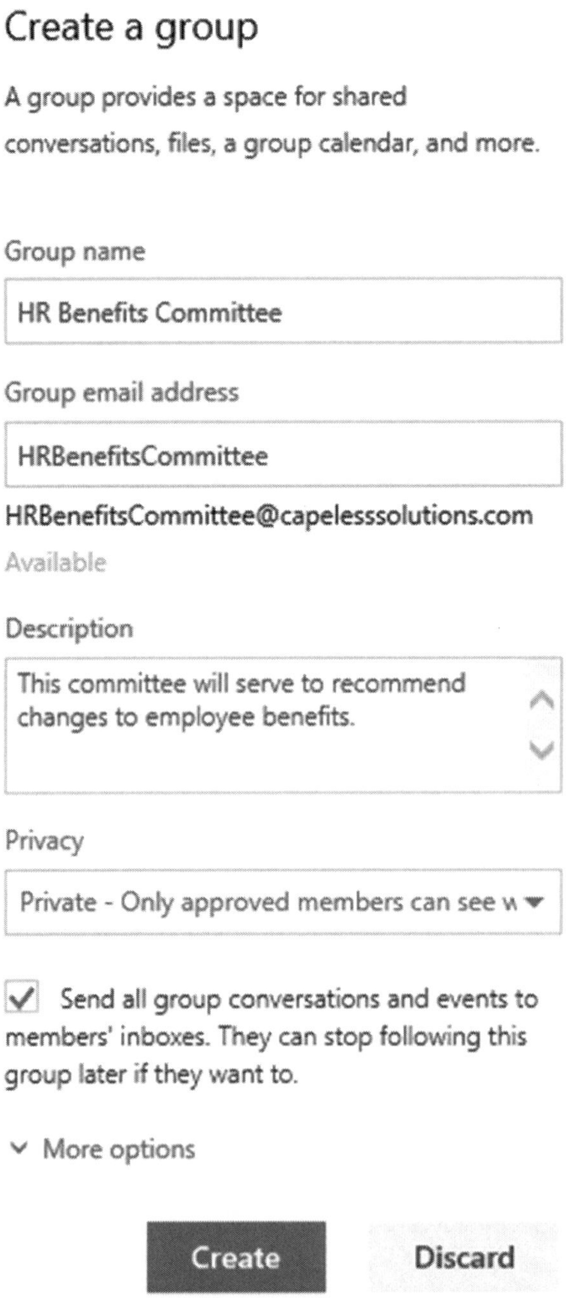

Create a group

A group provides a space for shared conversations, files, a group calendar, and more.

Group name

HR Benefits Committee

Group email address

HRBenefitsCommittee

HRBenefitsCommittee@capelesssolutions.com
Available

Description

This committee will serve to recommend changes to employee benefits.

Privacy

Private - Only approved members can see w ▼

☑ Send all group conversations and events to members' inboxes. They can stop following this group later if they want to.

∨ More options

Create   Discard

Figure 4-5. Creating your first Office 365 group

You also have the option to add members, or you can add them at a later date. I will discuss member management in detail in the next section.

But first, I want to spend some time discussing the privacy settings available in Office 365 Groups and what they mean within an organization. By default, all Office 365 groups are publicly accessible to your organization only and not available to outside guests. Thus a colleague might find an Office 365 group that they could contribute to, such as a software bug tracking. They could then submit or view the bugs and contribute in a collaborative way without formally being invited to the group.

On the other hand, you may want to set the privacy of the group to private and invite your colleagues to the Office 365 group. For example, if your HR team is examining the current benefits it provides to employees and is making changes or reviewing them, a private group would be ideal. This way, only invited members can review and make recommendations for changes without having confidential information available to all employees until the employee benefits are approved.

In either case, you can quickly change the privacy settings from public to private or vice-versa. In Outlook 2016, select the group from the left-hand navigation. Once the group is selected, click Edit Group via the Group Setting icon (Figure 4-6) in the Outlook ribbon.

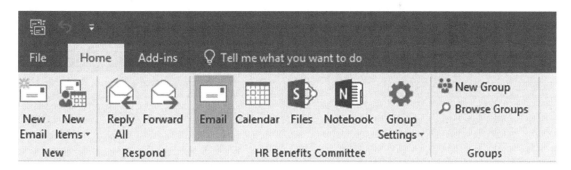

Figure 4-6. *Outlook 2016 ribbon, editing group permissions*

Once you click Edit Group, a new window will open, displaying the settings for the group (Figure 4-7). Choose either "Private" or "Public within organization" from the privacy drop-down menu. Press the OK button when complete.

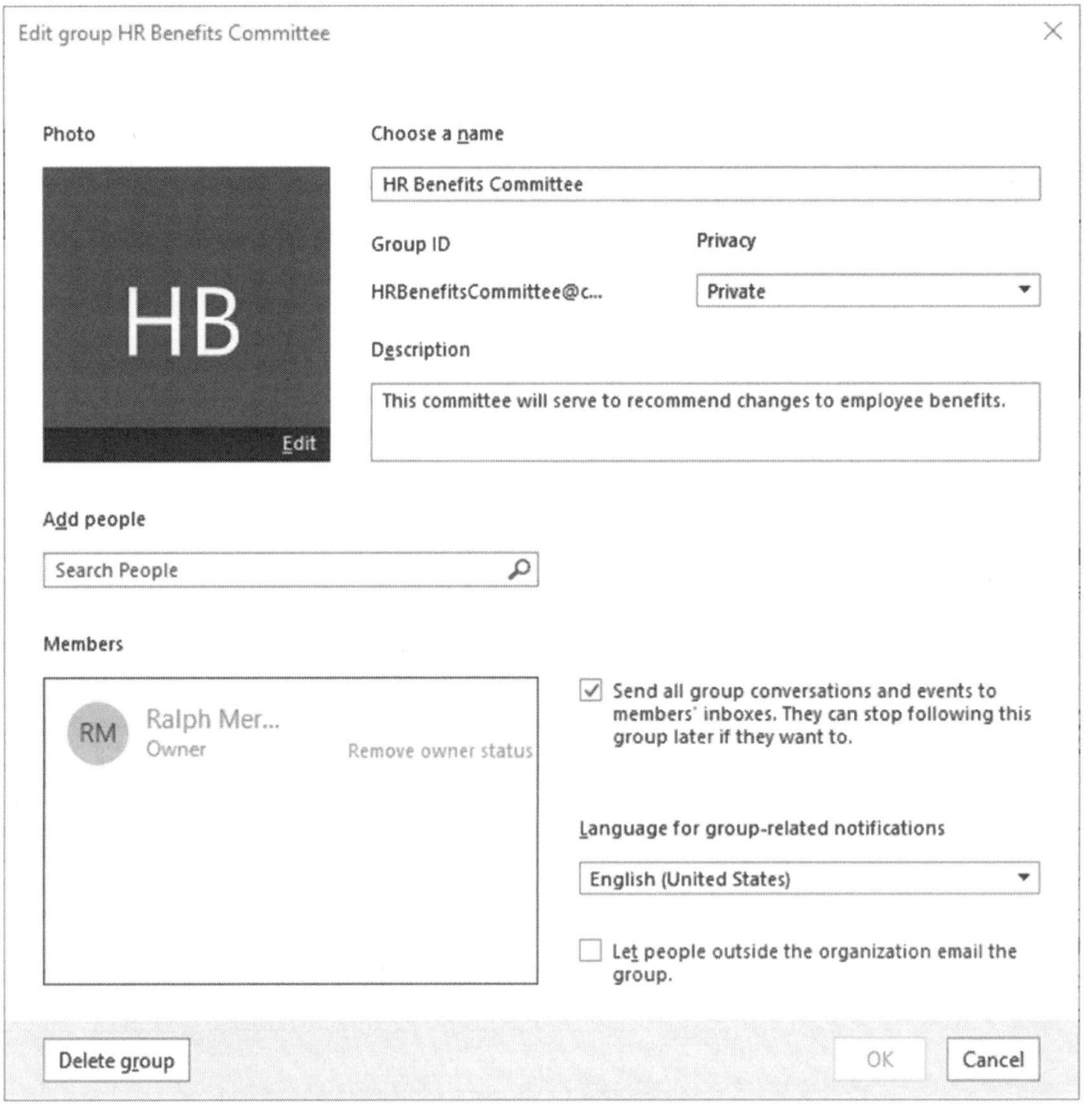

Edit group HR Benefits Committee   ✕

Photo

Choose a **name**

HR Benefits Committee

Group ID   Privacy

HRBenefitsCommittee@c...   Private   ▼

HB

Description

Edit   This committee will serve to recommend changes to employee benefits.

A**dd** people

Search People   🔍

Members

RM   Ralph Mer...
      Owner   Remove owner status

☑ Send all group conversations and events to
   members' inboxes. They can stop following this
   group later if they want to.

Language for group-related notifications

English (United States)   ▼

☐ Le**t** people outside the organization email the
   group.

Delete group   OK   Cancel

Figure 4-7. *Editing the settings of an Office 365 group*

The process is similar using Outlook Web Access through Office365.com. Select the group you want to edit in the Groups heading in the Outlook left-hand navigation. Once the group is selected, click the gear located in the upper right corner (Figure 4-8).

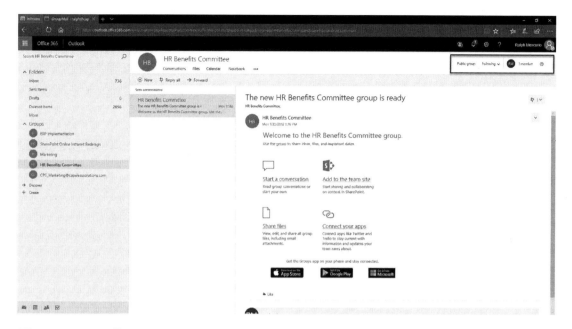

Figure 4-8. *Office 365 Groups settings through Outlook Web Access*

Clicking the gear icon reveals the Group settings dialog (Figure 4-9). Clicking "Edit group" opens a new menu (Figure 4-9), allowing you to change the privacy settings of the Office 365 group.

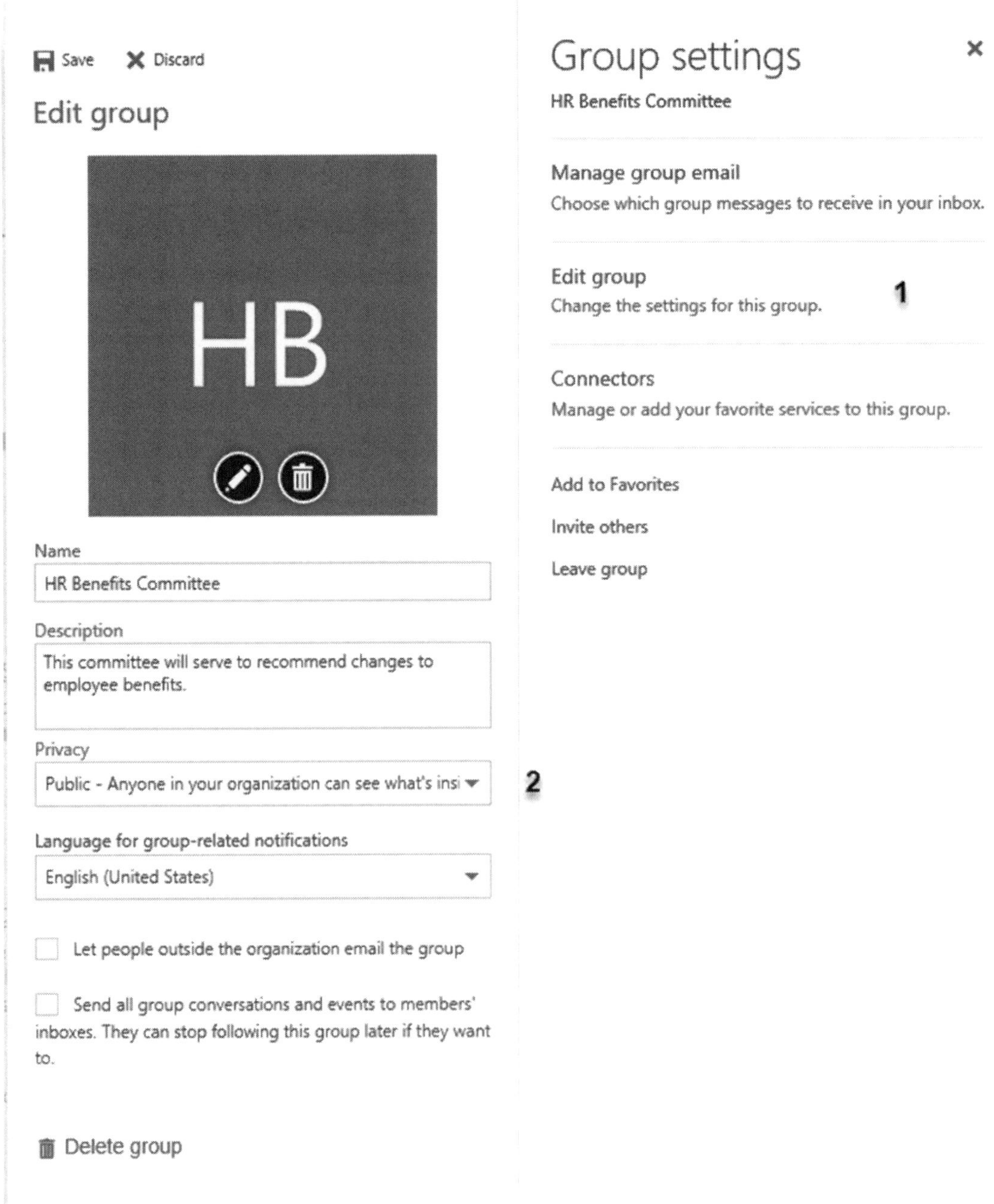

Figure 4-9. *Modifying an Office 365 Group Privacy setting in Outlook Web Access*

Within the Privacy drop-down, you can select either "Public – Anyone in your organization can see what's inside" or "Private – Only approved members can see what's inside."

Office 365 Groups Member Management

Office 365 groups need members to converse, upload files, and perform other collaborative activities to ensure that the groups are used to the fullest. Microsoft has recognized this and has made adding members very easy and efficient. To add members to a group, you don't need the intervention of IT because adding members is a primary Office 365 Group function.

Adding Internal Members

To add users to an Office 365 group within Outlook Web Access, select the group from the Groups heading. In the upper right corner next to the settings gear icon, you can see how many members (Figure 4-10) are in the group; clicking it allows you to add members to the group.

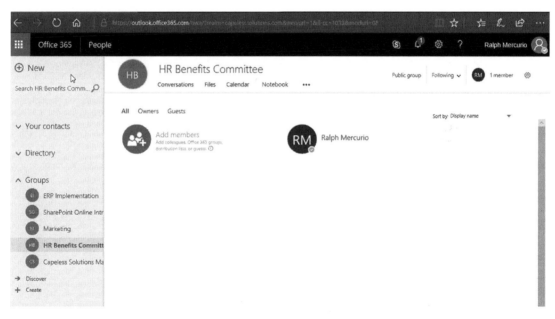

Figure 4-10. *Adding members to an Office 365 group*

To add a new user, click the "Add members" blue icon, shown in Figure 4-10 above. You can add four types of members to any Office 365 group: colleagues, Office 365 Groups, distribution lists, or guests. An easy way to distinguish between the different types of members accepted is the following:

- **Colleagues**: People you work with or within your organization. This includes members of any department.

- **Office 365 Groups**: You can add other groups to your group as members. This is useful if you decide to create groups around small teams that feed into a more substantial team. For example, you could have a group where all of HR has access and create smaller groups such as Retirement, Employee Relations, Benefits, HR Administration, and Training. In this model, you would just add all the smaller groups to the larger HR group.

- **Distribution lists**: Contains the email addresses of contacts available through the Global Address Book of Outlook. You cannot use a personal distribution list.

- **Guests**: Any user who is not part of the organization. This includes vendors, partners, and external users.

Once you click the "Add members" icon, a new dialog box will open, as shown in Figure 4-11. Simply begin to type the name of a user (colleague), an Office 365 group name, a distribution list, or the email address of an external user.

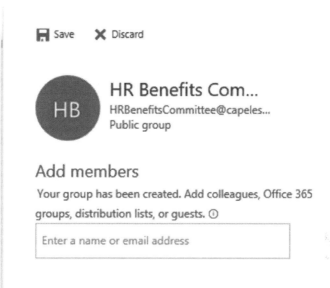

Figure 4-11. Adding members to an Office 365 group

Type the name of the user or distribution list, and it will appear in the window. Select the user and press the Save button in the upper left corner of the window.

Guest Users

Guest users are considered users who are not part of your organization. These guest users can be vendors, partners, consultants, etc. Please make every effort to be aware of the guest users and create a process to validate guest users to ensure that they are still needed and valid.

Adding External (Guests) Members

Adding internal colleagues, distribution lists, or Office 365 groups will provide a seamless experience and login for users already on the Office 365 platform. The process and experience for guest users is a little different. To demonstrate it, let's invite RobertSMercurio@gmail.com, who is an external user of the organization, and add him the HR Benefits Committee Office 365 group.

1. Within the HR Benefits Committee group, click "Members" in the upper right corner and then "Add members."

2. Enter RobertSMercurio@gmail.com as the external guest whom you will invite. This email account is only for the purpose of demonstrating guest access and is unmontiored.

3. Once he is added to the group, he will receive an email similar to Figure 4-12 in his Gmail inbox.

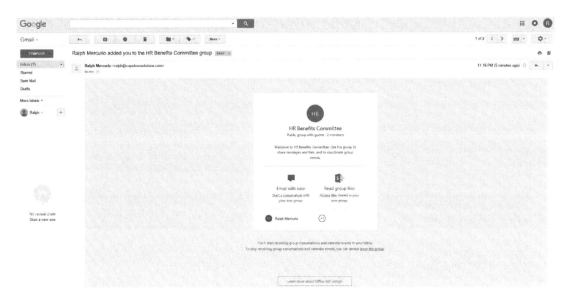

Figure 4-12. *Guest user invite after being adding to an Office 365 group*

At this point, Robert (guest user) has the ability to start a conversation and even contribute or create a conversation within the group through the email client. He does not get access to the actual Office 365 group via Outlook or Outlook Web Access.

Guest Experience within Office 365 Groups

Being an external user vs. an internal user is a slightly different experience. Internal users have access to all the features of an Office 365 group in Outlook or Outlook Web Access.

The second link in the introduction email contains a link to access the files shared within the group. Clicking the link will ask the user to create an account in Office 365, as shown in Figure 4-13.

Office 365

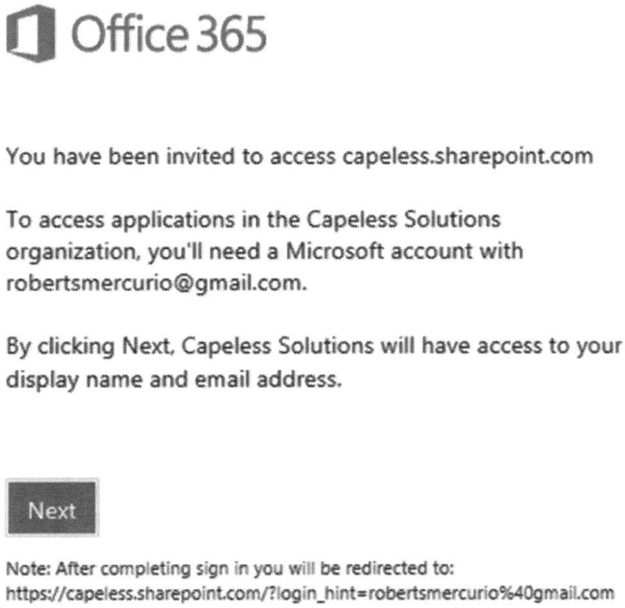

You have been invited to access capeless.sharepoint.com

To access applications in the Capeless Solutions
organization, you'll need a Microsoft account with
robertsmercurio@gmail.com.

By clicking Next, Capeless Solutions will have access to your
display name and email address.

Next

Note: After completing sign in you will be redirected to:
https://capeless.sharepoint.com/?login_hint=robertsmercurio%40gmail.com

Figure 4-13. *Creating a Microsoft account to access applications in the Capeless Solutions tenant*

Office 365 will create an account for robertsmercurio@gmail.com and allow the user to create a password to access it, as depicted in Figure 4-14.

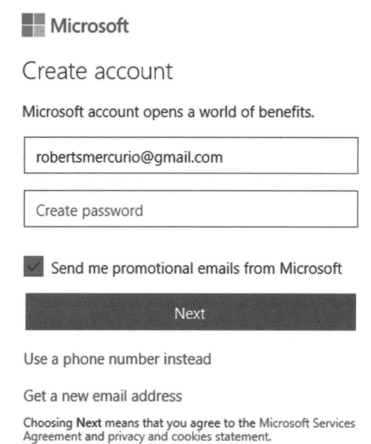

Figure 4-14. Creating a password to access the applications

Once the user creates a password, the Office 365 service will validate the user by emailing the user (in this case `robertsmercurio@gmail.com`) a validation code. The user will enter the validation code that was sent by Microsoft; if the correct code is entered, the account is validated.

After the validation process, the user is granted access to the Office 365 group through the web browser. The guest user will have access to the OneNote notebook, OneDrive, and SharePoint site (Figure 4-15) associated with the group. The guest user will not have access to the conversation stream of the Office 365 group.

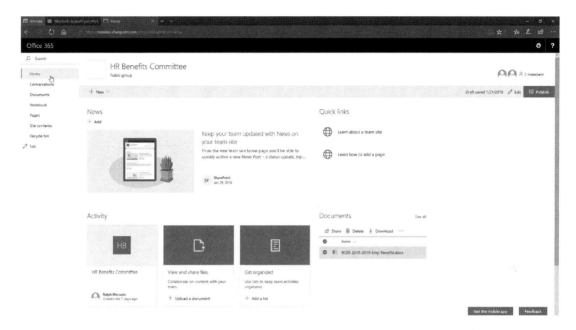

Figure 4-15. *Office 365 Group SharePoint site logged in as a guest user*

Components of an Office 365 Group

As mentioned, an Office 365 Group is a combination of a few familiar applications that bring people together to collaborate. In this next section, I will discuss each component and what it can do for the Office 365 Group.

Conversations (Outlook Inbox)

Conversations are essentially emails that can be viewed by all members of the Office 365 group. These conversations remain in the group forever until they are deleted by someone. The foremost benefit of the conversations is that these conversations are available from the day the Office 365 group was originally created and any members who join after can see all the conversations. This reduces the task of forwarding important emails or copying all the pertinent emails and giving them to the new group member.

Conversations retain many of the same features of emails (Figure 4-16); a member can create a new conversation, reply to all, or forward the conversation.

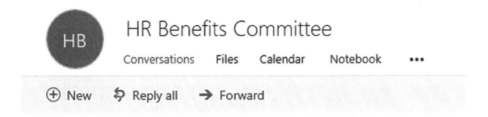

Figure 4-16. *Available actions for a converstion*

Currently, all members can send, forward, and view messages while external members cannot delete conversations.

Calendar

Every Office 365 group contains a calendar where members can post events and have a single calendar to hold all the group appointments. The calendar also functions like the one in Outlook and can even be overlaid with other calendars to create a seamless calendar viewing experience.

To access the group calendar, click the Calendar link shown in Figure 4-16. My personal calendar is on the left while the HR Benefits Committee group calendar is on the right and is shaded light blue, as shown in Figure 4-17.

Figure 4-17. *Viewing a calendar in a group*

To overlay the calendars and create a single view of multiple calendars, click Merge in the upper right corner of the window; see Figure 4-18.

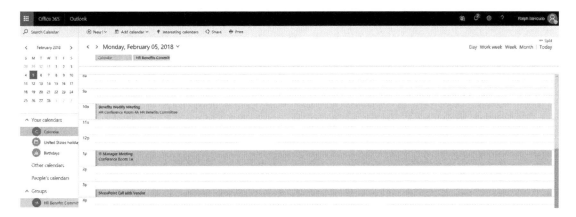

Figure 4-18. *Merging two Outlook calendars*

Merging two or more calendars does not create or move any appointments between the calendars selected; it simply overlays each calendar in a different color to create a seamless view. To unmerge the calendars, click Split in the upper right corner.

Site (SharePoint)

I discussed SharePoint Online in Chapter 2 and the same principles discussed also hold true in Office 365 groups. As content is generated or there is a need to collaborate on a document, SharePoint makes an appearance. Behind every Office 365 group is a SharePoint site, which is accessible via the ellipsis (three dots) and selecting Site (Figure 4-16). The interface presented at the time of publishing (Figure 4-19) contains an area to post news articles, an activity stream, a document library, and a comments section (not visible in Figure 4-19) as well as the ability to edit the pages.

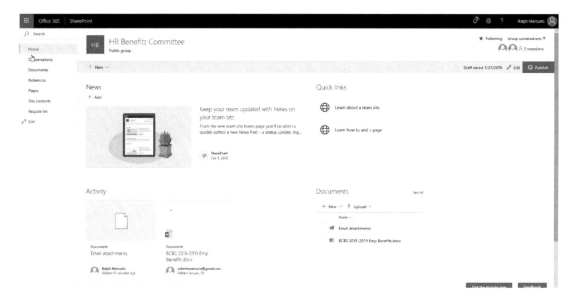

Figure 4-19. *SharePoint site associated with a group*

Files

Members have the ability to upload content for the Office 365 group to consume. Click the Files link located between the Conversations and Files links, shown in Figure 4-16.

Now there is a bit of trickery going on because "Files" is actually the SharePoint site document library presented in a different view. This view presents content with minimal options; for example, you cannot create views or add new columns. In this document library, you can click the following options (Figure 4-20):

- **New**: Create an Excel, PowerPoint, or Word document by creating documents in Office Online. I discuss the Office Online applications in Chapter 7.

- **Upload**: Upload content from your local workstation using the familiar Windows Explorer interface.

- **Tiles**: Shows the document in the tile format.

- **Browse library**: Opens the document library on the SharePoint site.

Figure 4-20.   *The Files view*

When you click an item in the document library, the item becomes highlighted and three options become available (Figure 4-21):

- **View**: Opens the file in Office Online.

- **Email**: Opens Outlook Web Access, allowing you to email the document as an attachment.

- **Download**: Downloads a copy of the document.

Figure 4-21.   *Document options*

As mentioned, "Browse library" will open the same document library in the SharePoint site associated with the Office 365 group. Once the library is open in SharePoint, you can then manipulate the library through the common SharePoint Online features discussed in Chapter 2. This includes creating different views and adding different column types.

Planner

Microsoft Planner is discussed in greater detail in Chapter 8, where I will detail the ins and outs of Planner and how to use it to manage any tasks. To open Planner in an Office 365 group, click the ellipsis (three dots) and select Planner (Figure 4-16).

In this example, Planner can be used to keep track of which members are reviewing benefit proposals and when they are due. As you will see in Chapter 8, Planner offers a simple way to manage tasks and a basic reporting dashboard to view statuses quickly.

Notebook

An Office 365 group also contains a OneNote notebook where all members can share their notes as they collaborate, and which can serve as a repository for non-document-centric or conversation content; access it by selecting Notebook, as shown in Figure 4-16. OneNote Online is discussed in Chapter 7.

Third-Party Connectors

Lately Microsoft has been allowing third-party services to be able to connect to Office 365 in various ways. Within Office 365 Groups, Microsoft has allowed several vendors the ability to connect its Office 365 service. Some of these vendors are Twitter, Google Analytics, and MailChimp. I am not going to dive into connecting to third-party services here but I will discuss connecting and consuming third-party sources in Chapter 11, which details Microsoft Flow.

Deleting a Group

To delete an Office 365 group from Outlook 2016, select the group from the left navigation of Outlook 2016, and in the Office Ribbon select "Group Settings" and then "Edit Group." In the Edit Group modal window, click "Delete group" in the lower left corner.

Because Office 365 believes in second chances, it will offer a confirmation window informing of the deletion and what happens to the data. When deleting an Office 365 group, the entire conversation stream, SharePoint files, the shared OneNote notebook, and the associated Planner tasks are deleted. If you still wish to delete the group, check the checkbox confirming your understanding that the data will be deleted and press the Delete button.

The experience is similar if you are deleting the Office 365 group from Outlook Web Access. From within Outlook Web Access, select the Office 365 group you would like to delete from the Groups heading. Once the group displays, select the cog or gear icon in the upper right corner below the initials or image of the user logged in. Clicking the cog/gear icon opens the Group Settings menu; choose "Edit group" and then "Delete group" and confirm the deletion.

Note   If you accidentally delete an Office 365 group, there is about a 30-day window where it can be restored. This is an IT administrator activity only and is done with the administrator sections of Office 365.

Office 365 Groups Mobile App

Office 365 provides the ability for users on an iPhone or Android device to utilize a mobile application to access Office 365 Groups. Currently, the Outlook application available on the mobile platforms doesn't integrate with Office 365 Groups; however, that ability is forthcoming and will be released soon.

To install the Office 365 Groups app, download the appropriate version from the Apple or Google Apps store (Figure 4-22).

Figure 4-22. *Outlook(Office 365) Groups mobile application via the Google Playstore*

Once the application is downloaded and installed on your device, open the application. It will prompt you for your credentials and password. Once your credentials are validated, the Office 365 groups you currently are a member of will appear in the app (Figure 4-23).

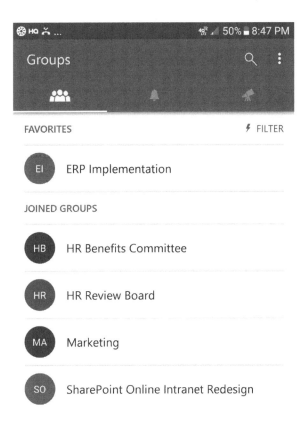

Figure 4-23. *Office 365 Groups mobile app introductory screen*

As with many mobile apps, there isn't one-to-one functionality in accessing groups through the web browser or in Outlook 2016. In the mobile version, there is no SharePoint Site or Planner navigation. You do have access to the conversation stream, calendar, and OneNote notebook.

Accessing the HR Benefits Committee group in the mobile app opens the mobile interface, shown in Figure 4-24.

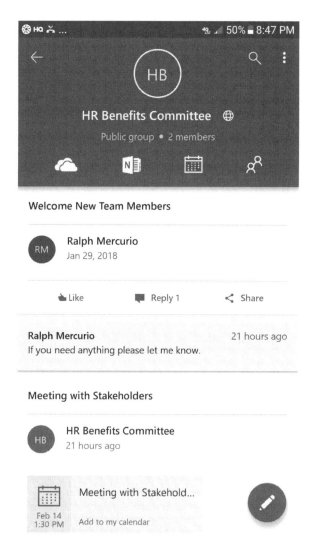

Figure 4-24. *HR Benefits Committee group viewed on the mobile platform*

In this view, you have access to files, calendar, and OneNote notebook plus the
ability to view the members of the group. When you first open an Office 365 group,
you will be presented with a time-based view of the most recent calendar events and
conversations.

In this view (Figure 4-25) you can add new conversations by clicking the Pencil icon
in the lower right corner of the application. The new conversation interface not only
allows you to take a photo with your camera but you can also attach a saved image or
document and add a location or a gif.

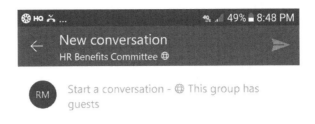

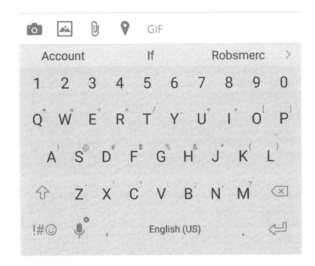

Figure 4-25. *Adding a new conversation in the Office 365 Groups mobile application*

You can like, reply, or share a conversation. When liking or replying to a conversation, everything will happen in line with the conversation and the updates will be available immediately.

To access the files of an Office 365 group in the mobile application, simply click the OneDrive Cloud icon. Within this view, you can open any supported file type in the appropriate mobile Office version of PowerPoint, Excel, OneNote, and Word. To upload a file or create a new folder, click the + sign located in the lower right of the Files view.

To view the OneNote notebook associated with the Office 365 Group, click the OneNote icon located to the right of OneDrive Cloud icon. This opens the notebook in OneNote mobile. You can view, edit, and add new content and it will become available to all members in either the mobile app, the group from a web browser, or within Outlook 2016.

The calendar of the Office 365 Group with the mobile application works similarly to the Outlook Calendar you know since the early versions of Outlook. To add a new calendar event, click the + sign located in the lower right corner of the Calendar view. It will ask for basic information such as event subject name, if it is an all-day event, start and end time if it is a repeating event, location, and any notes associated with the invite. The mobile application introduces a new interface for specifying the start and end time of a calendar appointment (see Figure 4-26). Once you are satisfied with the appointment, click CREATE in the upper right corner.

Figure 4-26. *Setting the time of the calendar appointment*

The final available icon with an Office 365 group is the members icon. When you click it, you will see all members, the owner of the group, and if there are any guest members. Click each of the headings to see the members and their respective assignments.

You also can add members into the group by clicking the "Add Members" icon in the lower right corner. You can add external users by typing their email address. You can also type the names of colleagues you would like to add; because it's integrated with your organization's Active Directory, Office 365 will be able to resolve the typed names.

Retention Policies for Office 365 Groups

A big gap in Office 365 has been around preservation of content and recovery. Think about it for a moment: when systems were located within a company's data center, the company had the tools needed to back up data to ensure easy recovery and preservation. With the shift as IT to a service, the need has become less and less.

Recovery of email is no longer needed because it is the responsibility of the vendor (Microsoft) to ensure that it is available, and the same is true for the other systems. Did you ever lose the contents of your personal email account with Google or Yahoo?

Back to the task at hand, rentention policies allow the IT administrators to set policies to ensure that data can be placed on legal hold or for eDiscovery cases. Office 365 now includes preservation policies around Office 365 Groups, where the data inside the group is preserved.

Microsoft has the ability and capability to offer retention policies around the majority of the content in Office 365. These policies can only be created and activated by an IT administrator with appropriate access in Office 365. The content of an Office 365 group can be retained for a number of years and can be custom tailored to the specific needs of the organization.

Summary

Office 365 Groups combine a SharePoint site, a OneDrive location, and a conversation stream (Outlook) into a convenient package. There is less focus on a document-centric approach but it does include the ability to incorporate documents. In this example, an HR Benefits Committee can leverage the various components of a group. There are conversations between internal HR members, and the conversation log is viewable by everyone without the need to forward messages. There is a need to have the proposals be viewed or consumed by members of the group, which the SharePoint site allows. There is integration with Planner, allowing the team to assign and track tasks to meet their deadlines, which can also be added to the shared calendar.

In the next chapter, you will explore Microsoft Teams, which is another collaborative mashup for teams to use. Microsoft Teams differs from Office 365 Groups because Teams is based on the concept of chat, not email.

CHAPTER 5

Teams

Office 365 presents different ways of working, each with a different set of capabilities. For example, SharePoint is best suited for document and item management and as a place to share information. Office 365 Groups combine the familiar inbox with a SharePoint site. Teams works in a completely different way: it employs the concepts of chatting and collaboration.

This is a new way to work and collaborate with users throughout the enterprise. It moves the team away from an email-centric approach to a fluid, chat-based approach where ideas can flourish and interactions can occur. This is especially important for users who are geographically dispersed and not located in the same office as their colleagues. Imagine for a moment that you are a user who works from home and thus you do not have the daily interaction that your colleagues do in the central office. Teams gives you the feeling of being connected to your colleagues and contributing to the work effort.

As this is a Microsoft flagship application within Office 365, there are a lot of pieces and integrations. In this chapter, I want to take the approach from a high level and provide an overview of the critical features; I hope to disseminate enough information to make you feel comfortable with Microsoft Teams by the time you finish this chapter.

Using Microsoft Teams

In the Office 365 tenant, click the app launcher in the upper right corner and select Microsoft Teams, as shown in Figure 5-1.

Figure 5-1. *Microsoft Teams application*

© Ralph Mercurio 2018
R. Mercurio, *Beginning Office 365 Collaboration Apps*, https://doi.org/10.1007/978-1-4842-3849-3_5

Once you click the application, you will be presented with the Microsoft Teams interface. The interface contains a few critical areas, as shown in Figure 5-2.

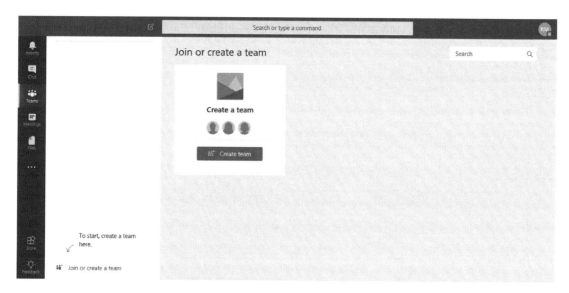

Figure 5-2. *Teams interface*

There are six available menu options located on the left that allow you to do a variety of different functions. Let's review each of them before you explore Teams further.

- **Activity**: As the name suggests, the Activity dashboard displays recent unread chats, if you are mentioned, replies to chats, what items you are following, any likes of content, missed calls, and any voicemails. The latter two options are dependent on your organization's Office 365 plan.

- **Chat**: The chat dashboard shows chats you are a part of and allows you to either place a voice call or video call to a particular user.

- **Teams**: Clicking the Teams icon opens the Teams dashboard and allows you to create or join a team.

- **Meetings**: The power of Office 365 is that there is substantial integration between all of the applications. You can see your Outlook Calendar in the Meetings view and any meetings that are scheduled.

- **Files**: Clicking the Files icon condenses files you recently viewed, files in your OneDrive, and files shared among teams of which you are a member.

Now let's explore each area more to gain a broader sense of understanding. Teams is very different than any other Microsoft product you may have used in the past but with a little guidance you can make sense of it all.

Walking Through Teams

Teams is based on the fundamental concept of a team: a group of people working towards the same goal. These teams provide the building blocks that allow channels to be created and utilize Microsoft Teams to the fullest.

Creating Your First Team

To create your first team, click the Teams icon located on the left in the Microsoft Teams application. You'll see the Teams dashboard open, as shown in Figure 5-3.

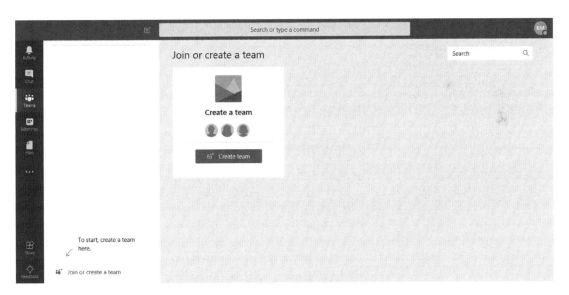

Figure 5-3. *Creating your first team within Microsoft Teams*

Click "Create Team" from the center of the dashboard; this initiates the creation of a team, as depicted in Figure 5-4.

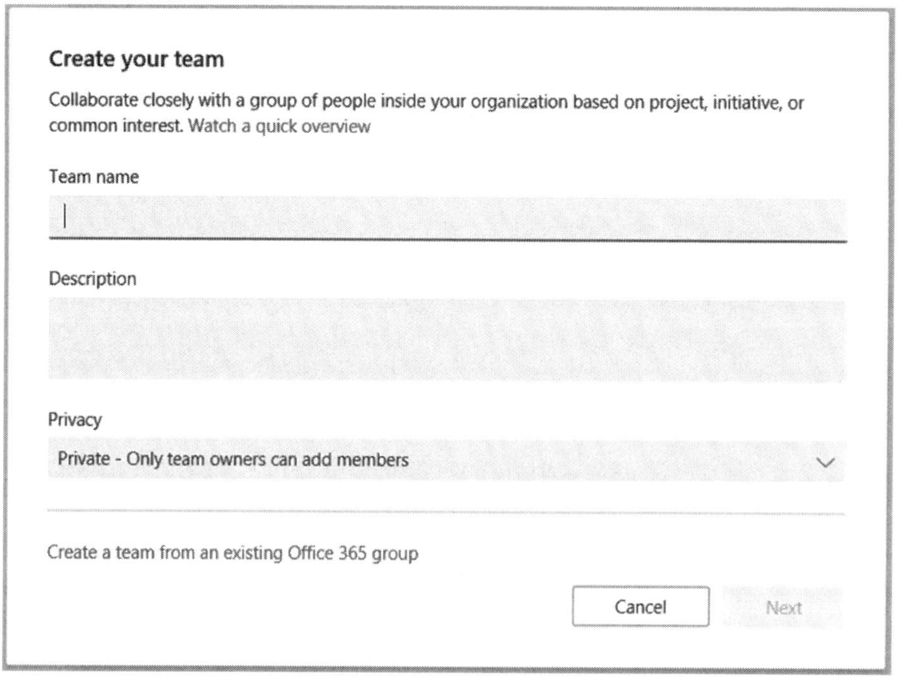

Figure 5-4. *Team settings*

Populate the fields as needed. This includes a team name, a description, and a privacy setting. The privacy choice can be set to private, which means only team owners can add members, or public, which means that the team is open for anyone to join. This is very similar to the process to create Office 365 groups. Once you are satisfied with your selections, click the Next button in the lower right of the form.

After clicking Next, you'll see a permissions screen, as shown in Figure 5-5.

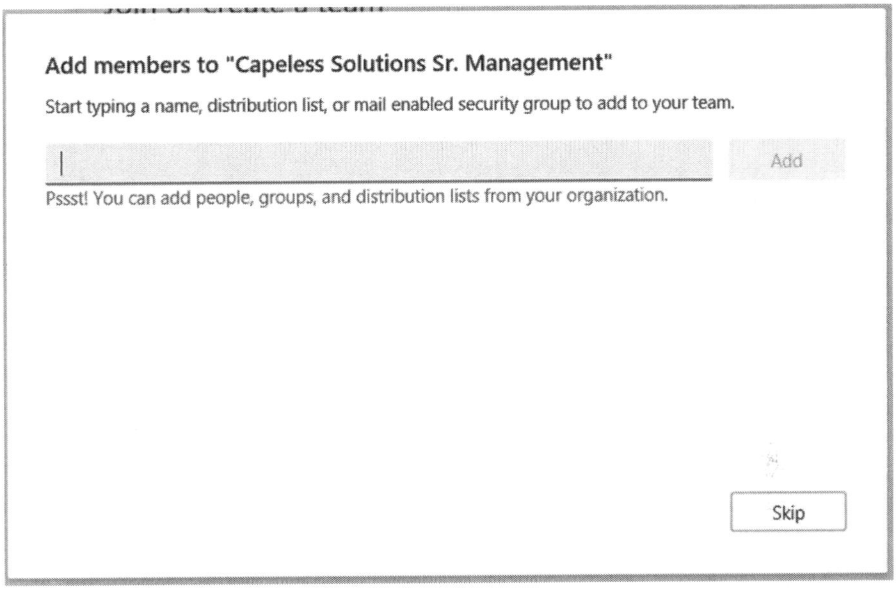

Figure 5-5. *Adding members to a team*

This screen allows you to add members to the team by populating the text box with their name or email address. You can use a distribution list or mail-enabled security group to add users in large batches. Contact your IT department for more information to see if you can benefit from a distribution list or mail-enabled security group.

There is an interesting integration between Microsoft Teams and Office 365 Groups. Teams allows the creation of a team from an existing Office 365 group. The option to do so is called "Create a team from an existing Office 365 group," as shown in Figure 5-4. Clicking the link allows a team to be created from a group without losing data or changing the existing group in Outlook or SharePoint. Select the Office 365 group for which you want to add Teams functionality and click "Choose team."

Note   At the time of this publication, there does not appear to be more integration between Teams and Office 365 Groups; the two apps do not share information or membership besides the standard fields of Name, Description, and Privacy settings.

Managing a Team

In the above example, you created a team for the senior management of Capeless Solutions. Now that the team is created, let's explore the available options. Similar to SharePoint or OneDrive, click the ellipsis (…) next to the Microsoft team. Doing so will open a context menu with different options, as shown in Figure 5-6.

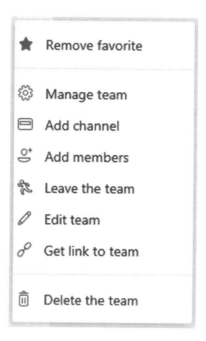

Figure 5-6. *Available menu options for managing a team*

The first available option within the context menu is "Remove favorite." Clicking the link removes the team from the favorites menu. Don't worry; it does not delete the team. To add the team back, click "More." Find the team you recently removed as a favorite and click the ellipsis. You will have the option to restore it as a favorite.

The second available context menu item is "Manage team" and is depicted in Figure 5-7.

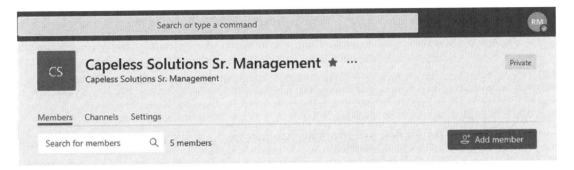

Figure 5-7. *Managing members, channels, and settings*

Clicking "Manage team" allows you to manage memberships, modify settings, and channel information. The Members tab allows you to search for members, view members and their associated permission, and offers the ability to remove or add a member. To remove a member from the team, click the X all the way to the right of the row you want to remove. To add a member to the team, click "Add member." Adding a member opens the same interface as shown in Figure 5-5. Begin to type the user's name or email address or, as mentioned, you can also add a distribution list or mail-enabled security group. Once the user or group is added, assign it an appropriate permission level through the interface.

Note   You cannot remove any members who have the "Owner" right assigned. You must change their permission before removing them.

The Channels tab allows you to create a channel, which is a way to organize a project, discussion, or content and is a logical container. An example is to create a channel for senior managers to collaborate on a pending acquisition or to create a collaborative environment to discuss confidential matters. Let's create a channel by clicking "Add channel" within the Channels dashboard. This will open the interface for channel creation, as shown in Figure 5-8.

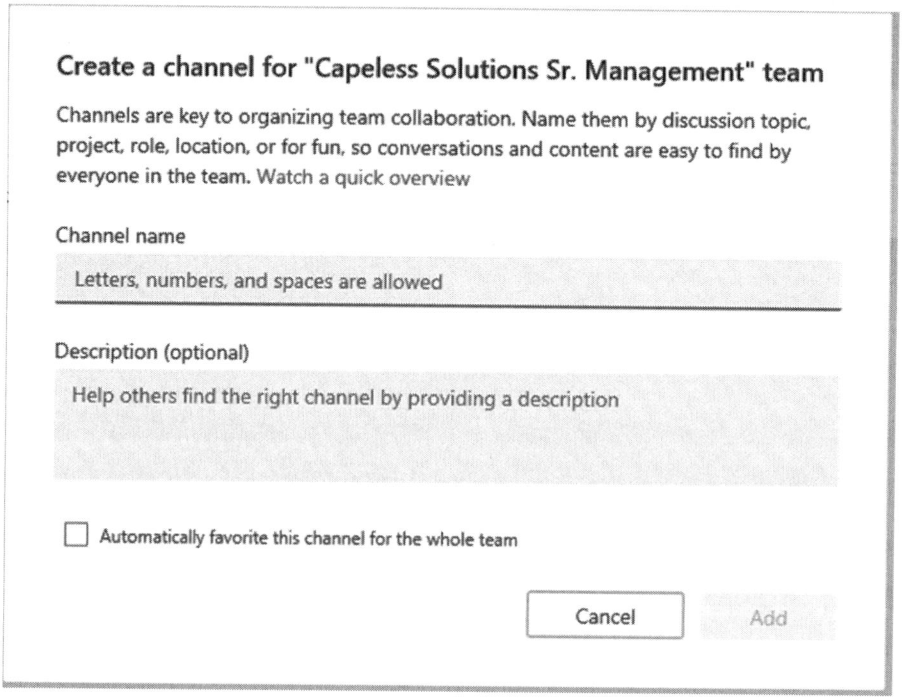

Create a channel for "Capeless Solutions Sr. Management" team

Channels are key to organizing team collaboration. Name them by discussion topic, project, role, location, or for fun, so conversations and content are easy to find by everyone in the team. Watch a quick overview

Channel name

Letters, numbers, and spaces are allowed

Description (optional)

Help others find the right channel by providing a description

☐ Automatically favorite this channel for the whole team

Cancel   Add

Figure 5-8. *Creating your first channel within Microsoft Teams*

The first step is to name the channel appropriately and give it a description (if desired but not required). You also have the ability to make the channel a favorite for all members of the team. Press the Add button when complete. You will explore channels in their entirety in the next section.

The third and fourth options from the context menu are "Add members" and "Leave the team." Clicking "Add members" opens the same interface as in Figure 5-5 and the steps are the same. Clicking "Leave the team" allows a member to leave the team and stop receiving updates or being included. Prior to removal, the user will receive a warning confirming the selection.

The last three options from the context menu are "Edit team," "Get link to team," and "Delete the team." Clicking "Edit team" allows you to modify the team name and description. At the moment, it does not seem possible to change the privacy of a team or to toggle between private and public. The "Get link to team" option generates a URL that can be copied into an email or shared via another method such as chat. The party will still need access if it is a private team. The final option, "Delete the team" allows the owner to delete the team and the data behind it. The owner needs to confirm the request for deletion.

Exploring Channels

You created your first channel in the previous section, and now you will take an in-depth look at the components of a channel within a team. In the Teams dashboard, you will see the team and channel you created earlier. The first thing you will notice is that there are two channels: General and Acquisition of SharePoint Consulting firm, as shown in Figure 5-9.

Figure 5-9. *Teams and channels*

The General channel is created by Office 365 as the default channel. This default channel contains and catalogs all the activity in a team and displays it on the homepage of the channel. The default General channel and any channel you create will share the following options via the ellipsis to the right of the channel: "Connectors," "Get email address," "Get a link to the channel," and "Follow this channel."

The Connectors option allows you to connect the channel to a variety of sources. Connectors exist to connect Microsoft Forms, Bing News, Dynamics 365, or other sources with the team. As Teams is adopted by more and more companies, the list of connectors will grow and the intergration will grow as well.

The "Get email address" allows mail to be sent to the channel. Clicking the "Get email address" option within the context menu reveals an email address. Any mail sent to the address will show in the Conversations tab of the channel. You also have the option to download the original email if desired.

The last two options, "Get a link to channel" and "Follow this channel," allow you to generate a URL to share with colleagues and mark the channel to be followed so you will receive updates concerning the channel.

The non-General channels also have a set of exclusive options. These options are "Edit this channel" and "Delete this channel." Clicking "Edit this channel" allows the channel name and description as well as automatically favoring the channel to be modified. Clicking "Delete this channel" deletes the channel and any associated chats, but the files remain in a SharePoint document library.

Now that you know the basics of creating and maintaining teams and channels, let's take a ride through the components of a channel and how they work together to provide a seamless experience.

Clicking any channel opens the channel within Microsoft Teams. For this example, let's use the channel you created earlier in this chapter titled "Acquisition of SharePoint Consulting firm." When the channel opens, you'll see four options along the top: Conversations, Files, Wiki, and (+) sign.

The Conversations section contains the chat stream for the team. A conversation can be started by typing into the conversation text box located at the bottom of the channel, as shown in Figure 5-10.

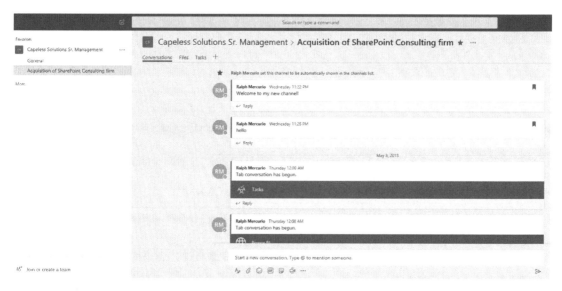

Figure 5-10. *A conversation stream within a channel*

A chat or post can be edited by using the following options by clicking on the corresponding icon underneath the textbox: formatting text, attaching an item, emojis, gifs, stickers, and the option to meet now. Once a post is posted, it is viewable by all members of the team in the conversation stream, and members can reply back to your post.

First and foremost, if you posted a post and decided it shouldn't have been posted, the post can be deleted from the conversation stream by choosing the Delete option from the ellipsis when you hover over your post. When deleting a post, it does not delete the replies to the post and will display a "This message has been deleted" message in the conversation stream. You also have the ability to undo the deletion by clicking "Undo" within the deleted post.

Your posts can also be edited by selecting Edit from the context menu. Clicking "Edit" allows you to edit the post with the same tools when you originally posted the post with the exception of the "Meet now" option. Editing any post will mark the post with an "Edited" message, indicating it is not the original post.

The final two options via the context menu of a post are "Mark as unread" and "Copy link." Marking a post as unread will not separate the post but will separate all the posts that were created after the post you are marking as unread. The "Copy link" option generates a link back to the channel and copies the post so it can be posted in an email or document.

Every post also has the ability be saved as well as liked; both of these options are available in the upper right corner of any chat. Saving a post saves it and allows it to be accessed at a later date in a single convenient location regardless of the channel you are on. To like a post, just click the thumbs icon in the message and you liked the message.

To view your saved messages and modify a subset of settings for Teams, click in the upper right corner of the application. The icon will be your initials or some combination, as shown in Figure 5-11.

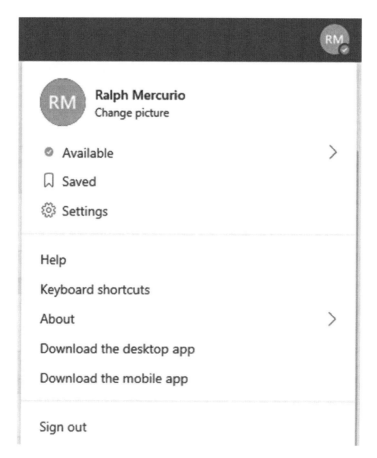

Figure 5-11. *Accessing a subset of settings*

The first option is Available, and it relates to what is known as presence, which can be Available, Busy, Do not disturb, and Away. Each presence status relates to a particular color, and this indicator is used throughout the Office 365 applications. Next is the Saved option, clicking it loads all of the posts you have saved.

The Settings menu allows you to change the color scheme of Teams from the default interface to Dark and High contrast. You can also modify the notifications from Mentions, Messages, and Other categories. To begin, I would leave these as is until you feel comfortable with Teams and know what information you want to see in the Activity stream, Banner, and email notifications.

Within the channel, there is also the Files link. The Files link allows members to upload files into a SharePoint document library, as discussed in Chapter 2. A surprising option that Microsoft has released is the ability to add cloud storage that is not part of Office 365, specifically OneDrive. You have the ability to add Dropbox, Box, ShareFile, and Google Drive. You will need a subscription (paid or free) to use these cloud storage providers, but it shows that Microsoft is open to integrating with the tools people use and to bring those technologies into a central application like Teams.

The Wiki link allows a wiki to be created and have members of the team add content. I have never liked wikis and always viewed them to be challenging to create and manage. However, you should explore the wiki. If you don't want that functionality, remove the Wiki link by selecting "Remove" from the drop-down arrow.

The last link in a channel is the + link, which allows you to add a tab from a variety of sources, as shown in Figure 5-12.

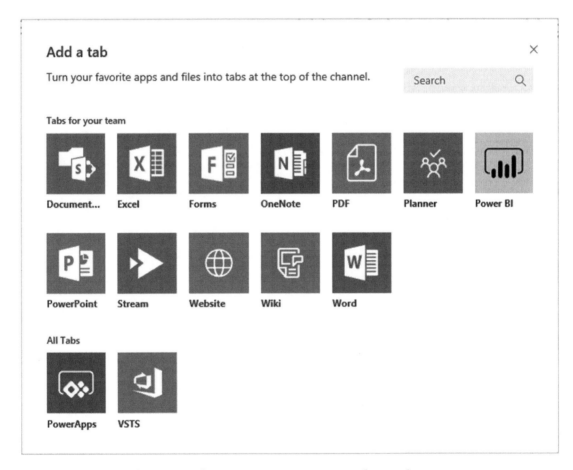

Figure 5-12. *Adding one of many integrations to a channel*

For example, I discuss Planner in detail in Chapter 8, but the primary purpose of Planner is task management. You can create a plan from the channel and have the ability to add tasks, assign them to members, and view it all in a dashboard that shows the tasks and their status. Not only will you have a conversation stream and any supporting files, but also the tasks that need to be completed. This allows for a 360-degree experience without ever leaving the Office 365 applications or purchasing additional applications or signing in multiple times.

Activity

The activity feed catalogs the activity on the channels you follow and offers an audit trail of what you have been doing in Teams, as shown in Figure 5-13.

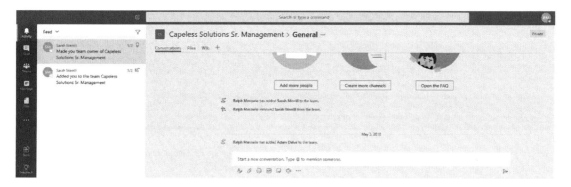

Figure 5-13. *Activity dashboard*

Clicking the Activity icon on the left-hand side of the application opens the Activity dashboard. You can toggle from Feed to My Activity. You also can filter the Activity feed to show only specific items as noted:

- **Unread**: Displays unread messages (chats).

- **Mentions**: Displays when you are mentioned in a post. Mentions are formatted as @username.

- **Replies**: Display all replies to your posts.

- **Following**: Displays users that are following your posts.

- **Likes**: Displays posts that you have liked.

- **Missed call**: Displays all missed calls.

- **Voicemail**: Displays all voicemails (pending licensing and setup).

- **Apps**: Displays updates from integrated apps.

However, you can't filter the My Activity feed and instead will see all of the activities you have made in Microsoft Teams.

Chat

As described earlier, Teams is based on the concept of chatting not emailing, so it only makes sense that chat is integrated into the Teams platform without the need to open another application. Figure 5-14 shows the Chat dashboard.

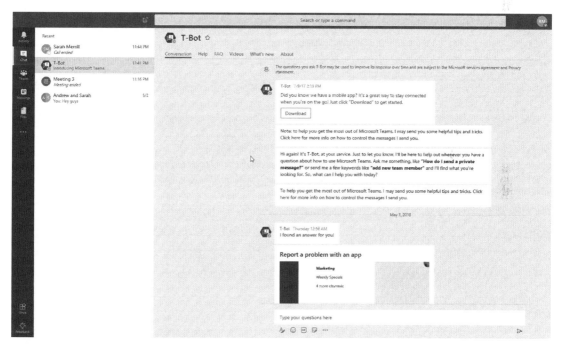

Figure 5-14. *Chat dashboard*

Access the Chat dashboard via the Chat icon located below Activity on the left-hand side of Teams. Once the screen refreshes, you will be able to chat with your colleagues and the T-bot. The T-bot (Teams-bot) is an AI chatbot that is there to guide you and answer any questions you may have about Teams. Just type your question in the question box of the Conversations section of the T-bot chat. The T-bot will attempt to find the best answer based on your question. If the T-bot is unable to answer your question correctly,

Microsoft has also made available Help, FAQ, and Video sections with appropriate resources.

To start a chat, click the new chat icon to the left of the "Search or type a command" text box in the center of the page. Clicking this icon allows you type the name of your colleague and send a message via the same interface you explored in the Conversation section of channels, as shown in Figure 5-15.

Figure 5-15. *Chat interface with a colleague*

Not only are you able to chat with a colleague but seven other options exist. These options are Files, Organization, Activity, and the + symbol as links. The other three options are Video, Phone, and Add members. The last three icons are located to the right of the chat window.

Focusing on Files, Organization, Activity, and the + sign, let's explore each option to gain better an understanding of what can be done. The first option, Files, is a location for files to be uploaded and shared among the chat members. Adding files is a simple process and involves dragging the file to be added to the files screen. The uploaded file will also be added to the chat or conversation screen.

Note   At this time you cannot delete the file once it has been uploaded via the Files tab. The only way to delete the file is to delete the specific chat post in which the file was uploaded.

The next option, Organization, displays the organizational hierarchy, as seen in Figure 5-16, if the appropriate fields are populated within Active Directory.

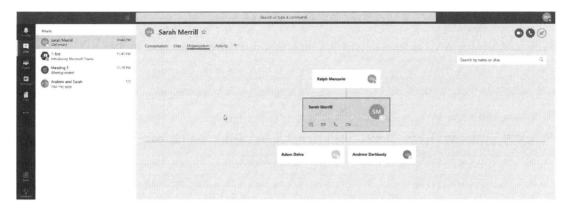

Figure 5-16. *Viewing the employee organizational hierarchy*

Active Directory is a system that contains all the users and their properties in a central location. These properties include name, phone number, manager, and a variety of other fields to identify and catalog users. The organization hierarchy depends on the Manager field being populated. Hovering over a contact will also allow you to chat, email, call, or video call with them. This is not available if you are chatting with more than one person.

The Activity Link is slightly different than the Activity dashboard I described earlier. This Activity link displays updates based on the teams that are common between you and a singular chat participant. This is not available if you are chatting with more than one person.

The + sign link to the left of Activity allows you to add a tab to the chat window. This is very similar to how it works within channels, as described earlier. Unfortunately, you can only add a Power BI or Website tab. This is not available if you are chatting with more than one person.

Meetings

The Meetings icon, located under the Teams icon on the left-hand side of the application, allows meetings to be scheduled in a variety of ways to have the most significant impact on communicating. Depending on the situation, a scheduled meeting might be the best route or maybe you want ad hoc meetings, keeping the team more fluid and adapting to day-to-day operations.

Meetings can be scheduled within a channel or with a particular colleague. Figure 5-17 depicts the "New meeting" interface, which is available when clicking "Schedule a meeting" within the Meetings dashboard.

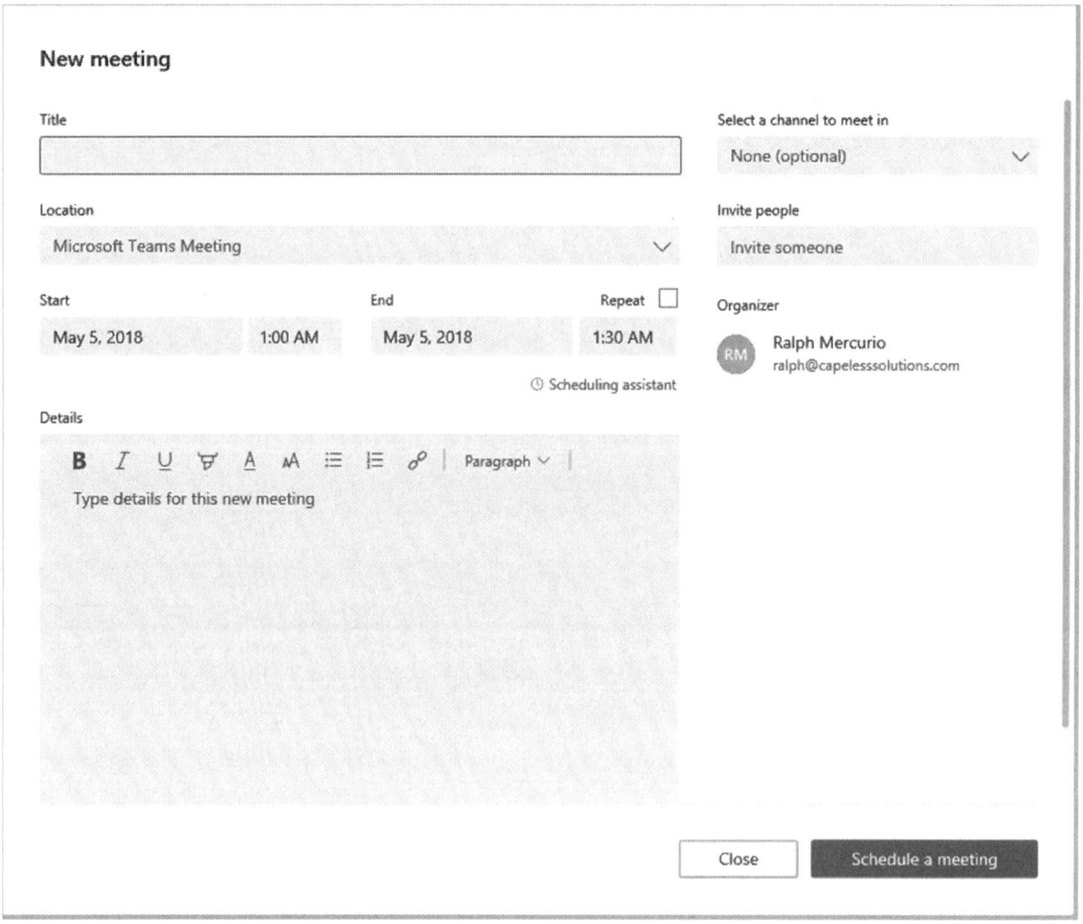

Figure 5-17. The "New meeting" interface

To schedule a meeting, the fields must be filled in to ensure the accuracy of the invite. Picking the "Select a channel to meet in" option and choosing the appropriate team allows the meeting to take place and be open to anyone who has access to that specific channel. You can also "Select a channel to meet in" and invite a small subset of users. This creates an openness of communication and transparency with the team. Members of the team will also be able to join if needed.

Video and phone meetings can also be started from within a chat conversation by selecting the Video or Phone icons from the chat area. These meetings are referred to as ad hoc because they are generally not scheduled and also are private.

Files

The last area to discuss with Microsoft Teams is the Files icon located on the left-hand side of the application. The Files icon, when clicked, opens the Files dashboard and allows you to see recent files, Microsoft Teams, and OneDrive files. Also, if any cloud storage was added previously, it will be accessible through the Files dashboard. Figure 5-18 shows the Files dashboard of Teams.

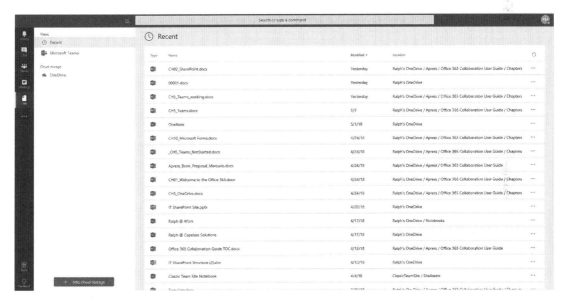

Figure 5-18. *Storing files within teams*

The files, if supported by Office 365, can be edited by clicking the ellipsis menu in the rightmost column. Editing files is a similar experience in almost every Office 365 application; for reference, I discuss Office and Office Online in Chapter 7.

Microsoft Teams Mobile App

Microsoft released a mobile version of Microsoft Teams, as it did for almost every one of its core products (SharePoint, Planner, OneDrive, etc.) The mobile application is supported on both Android and Apple platforms and is available from the respective app stores.

To install your specific version, download the mobile app from the correct app store. Once the app is downloaded and installed on your mobile device, open it and specify your Office 365 credentials. Once Office 365 authenticates you, you will be presented with a very similar interface to the web version. Figure 5-19 shows the mobile view and the associated icons available.

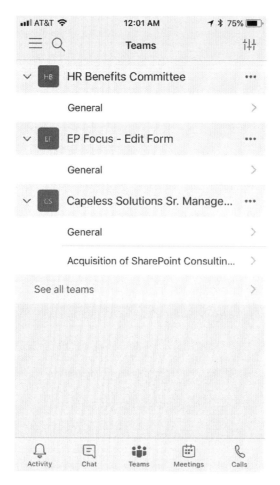

Figure 5-19. *Microsoft Teams on an Apple iPhone*

Summary

Microsoft Teams is situated to become the next significant collaborative tool for teams. It couples the power of SharePoint and OneDrive plus the ability to make video/phone calls without the need to use multiple applications.

By shedding email, the collaborative experience can now take place in teams and channels. These areas allow for a fluid, collaborative effort centered around documents, conversations, and integrations with the Office 365 stack of applications for now. In the future, the integration will grow, and Microsoft Teams will be able to interface with a whole new bunch of third-party applications.

The next chapter will focus on Yammer, which enables enterprises to create a social site to share information.

CHAPTER 6

Yammer

In the last chapter on Microsoft Teams, I introduced a new Office 365 application that allows collaboration in an email-less environment. In this chapter, you will explore Yammer, which is similar but different to Teams.

Microsoft Yammer is very similar to an enterprise social network application that allows colleagues to find relevant information or people, find and use content, and collaborate and join the conversation. This is where the differences become apparent, in my opinion. Yammer is designed for the entire enterprise while Teams is designed for smaller groups of users who collaborate on specific projects or work efforts, as you explored in the previous chapter.

The story behind Yammer is that it was acquired in the late 2000s and has been around since then in a variety of versions. What is different this time is that it is an integrated, featured application within Office 365, which allows Microsoft to provide value to it, whereas before it was always considered a sort of bolt-on application within SharePoint and didn't really fit into the SharePoint platform.

Using Microsoft Yammer

In Office 365, click the app launcher in the upper right corner and select Microsoft Yammer, as shown in Figure 6-1.

Figure 6-1. *Microsoft Yammer*

© Ralph Mercurio 2018
R. Mercurio, *Beginning Office 365 Collaboration Apps*, https://doi.org/10.1007/978-1-4842-3849-3_6

Once you click the application, you will be presented with the Microsoft Yammer interface. The interface contains a few critical areas, shown in Figure 6-2.

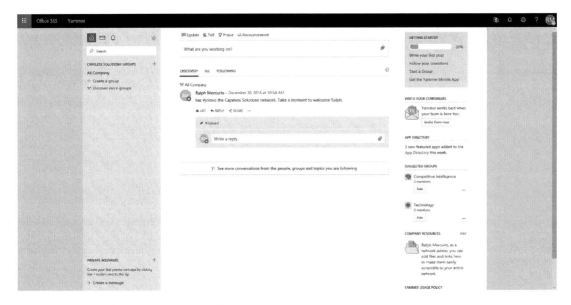

Figure 6-2.   *The Yammer interface*

The leftmost area of the application contains the bulk of the actions such as creating and finding groups, sending messages, viewing messages, viewing notifications, and searching across Yammer.

The right side of the application is primarily used for displaying group information, posting to groups, viewing memberships, and a few other actions that you will explore later in this chapter.

Walking Through Yammer

Yammer looks intimating upon logging in but once you're familiar with its interface, it is quite simple. The first area I will discuss is around groups. Groups in Yammer are not the same as Office 365 Groups. Yammer groups do not contain an inbox or a SharePoint site or some of the other Office 365 Groups functions you explored in Chapter 4. Yammer groups are like a team in Microsoft Teams but, as discussed, Yammer groups are meant for the enterprise where Teams is more suited towards smaller groups of people.

Creating a Yammer Group

Under the search box to the left of the Yammer application, you will see the current groups in Yammer as well as the ability to create or discover groups. Your first objective is to create a group. To begin the process, click "+ Create a group", which opens a modal window titled "Create a New Group." See Figure 6-3.

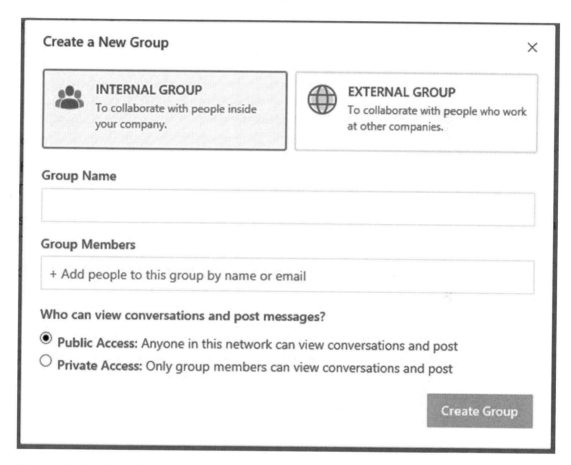

Figure 6-3. *Creating a new Yammer internal or external group*

The first thing you will notice is that you have the ability to create two types of groups: an internal group or an external group. Internal groups allow your colleagues to communicate and belong to a group; an external group allows external members to join.

Both groups share a few common fields. The first is "Group Name" and it is used to identify and title the Yammer group. The second field is "Group Members" and this field gives you the ability to add group members to the group. The third option is where the biggest difference is between an internal group and an external group.

If you select internal group, your choices for "Who can view conversations and post messages" are the following:

- **Public Access**: Anyone in this network can view conversations and post. This setting allows anyone to join the Yammer group and participate in it. With Yammer, once you have access to the group, you can perform a majority of the actions.

- **Private Access**: Only group members can view conversations and post. With this setting, you must be sure to add members to the group. You also have the option to allow the group to be visible to all colleagues even though they cannot join the group unless specified.

If "external group" is selected, you have two different choices to view conversations and post messages. The two options are

- **Approved members from other networks and anyone in this network**: This setting allows anyone in your organization to join the group as well as specified users from other networks. This is similar to the public access permission when creating internal groups.

- **Only group members:** This is very similar to the private access permission of internal groups. You also have the option to have the group be visible in search.

Once you have populated the required fields, click "Create a new group." Yammer will create the group behind the scenes; after a few moments, you will be presented with your group, as shown in Figure 6-4.

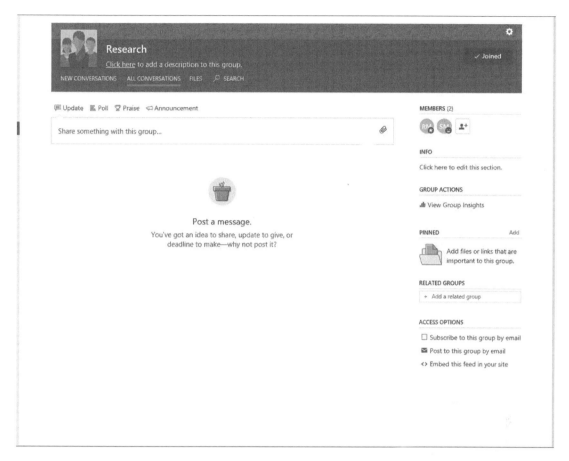

Figure 6-4. *Viewing a Yammer group*

Basics of a Yammer Group

A Yammer group allows you to view "New Conversations, "All Conversations," and "Files." You also have the ability to search within the Yammer group. These options are located below the description of the group, as shown in Figure 6-5. Each one of these choices is self-explanatory so I won't define them.

Figure 6-5. *Yammer group options*

Also, within a Yammer group, you can see the members of the group and invite new members. There's also an Info section, plus Group Actions, Pinned, Related Groups, and Access options. These options are located on the right side of a group, as shown in Figure 6-4 above. I'll define the above options because they are Yammer-specific:

- **Members**: This section shows the current members of the site. It also provides the ability to invite others to the group, depending on the privacy settings of the group. Clicking a user icon will not only show you the conversations, posts, and files of that user referred to in the Yammer profile but also allow you to send a message, make a call with Skype, and choose to follow the user. See Figure 6-6.

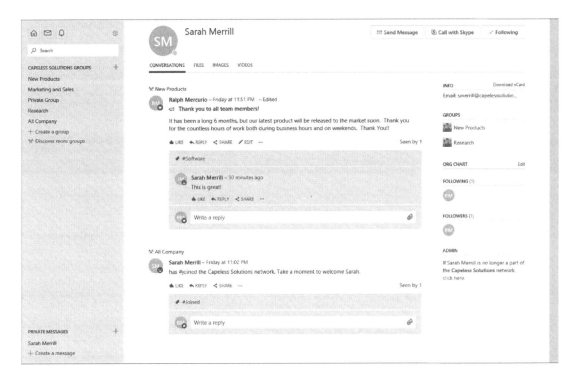

Figure 6-6. *Member options in a Yammer group*

- **Info**: Gives the group owner the ability to add more information about the group. The owner can add rules on postings or files. To add info about a Yammer group, click the link and then the Edit link to provide information. Be sure to save your changes after.

- **Group Actions**: The only available link is for Group Insights, which is a visual dashboard of the activity of the group. Yammer collects information such as members, active people, number of posted messages, read messages, and a few other metrics over 7 days, 28 days, and 12 months. You currently can't alter the time period. The report can be downloaded for further analysis in CSV format.

- **Pinned**: You can "pin" files or links that are relevant to the group in an easily accessible location. Files can be selected from SharePoint or within Yammer by selecting the appropriate link. Links can also be posted through the same interface. See Figure 6-7 for more details.

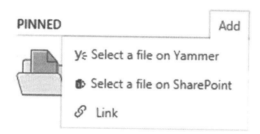

Figure 6-7. *Adding a file or link to the Pinned section of a Yammer group*

- **Related Groups**: Related groups are groups that the current Yammer group might find useful and worthwhile to join. Simply search for the group and you can select the group(s) to add.

- **Access Options**: Located on the bottom of the right hand of the Yammer group are the access options. These options are "Subscribe to this group by email," "Post to this group by email," or "Embed this feed in your site."

  - **Subscribe to this group by email**: Yammer notifications will be sent to your inbox.

  - **Post to this group by email**: Offers the ability to send mail directly to the Yammer group via an email address. Click "Post to this group by email" for the generated link.

- **Embed this feed in your site**: Clicking this link generates an HTML code snippet that can be posted on any HTML web page including SharePoint Online sites. I discussed SharePoint and editing pages in Chapter 2.

To change any of the settings of a Yammer group, select the cog (gear icon) in the upper right corner of the group. You can edit the group name, description, group image and color, group pattern, membership, and the privacy settings.

Adding users is a critical component of Yammer, and without them, Yammer wouldn't exist. Unfortunately, adding users is not as easy as it is SharePoint or Teams because at the time writing this chapter Yammer is not fully connected to Active Directory. This means that the interface to add members to a group is limited, unlike some of the other Office 365 applications. There are a few different methods to add users to Yammer; I will explain the most straightforward method to the most complex method.

The first method of user management in Yammer is to add a user to a Yammer group. This is done by clicking the Add Members icon under the Members section when viewing a group. For reference to the location of the Members group, see Figure 6-4.

Clicking the Add Members icon opens a model window where you can specify the email address of the user. As you type the email address of the user and begin to type the domain after the @ symbol, the email address of the user will appear in the "Suggested People for This Group" area. Click the appropriate email address of the user and click "Add To Group." This will add the user to the group; however, they will need to confirm their invitation in their inbox.

This method isn't feasible if you need to invite a large number of users. Yammer will accept a CSV (comma-separated values) document, which needs to be in a specific format. This action is only available to Yammer Administrators but is the easiest way to add users in bulk. This is especially important if you create a group for all users such as Company News or another enterprise-wide group.

Posting to a Yammer Group

The second area that I will discuss is the ability to post an update, poll, praise, or announcement, as shown in Figure 6-8, in a Yammer group.

Figure 6-8. *Posting to a Yammer group*

There are four types of posts that can be made in a Yammer group. Each of these posts has a unique purpose, and you will explore them below in further detail.

- **Update**: An update to a Yammer group is the simplest of all posts. Type your message in the text box and if you want you can also add a gif, a file from Yammer, SharePoint, or upload directly from your computer. You also have the ability to notify people of the update by specifying their name in the "Add people to notify" textbox. See Figure 6-9 for more details.

Figure 6-9. *Posting an update to a Yammer group*

- **Poll**: A poll is akin to a single question survey (Figure 6-10). For now, you can only post a single question. No other data types are available. It's similar to an update post because you can also attach a file or notify a person.

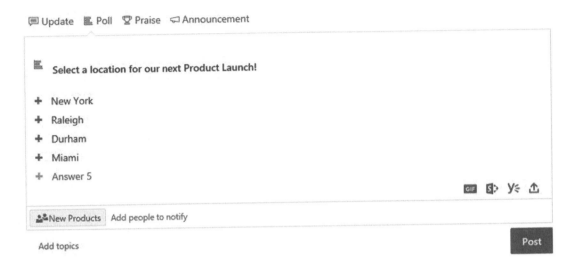

Figure 6-10. *Creating a poll for a Yammer group*

The poll isn't as robust as Microsoft Forms, which is discussed in Chapter 10. In this scenario, a Microsoft Form can be created and the link to the form can be pasted into an update post.

- **Praise**: Built upon the update post, but gives you the ability to give your post a little more detail, as shown in Figure 6-11.

Figure 6-11. *Creating a praise post in Yammer*

A praise post contains two parts: "Who do you want to praise?" and "Share what they've done." You also have the same ability as the previous post types to notify people or add files.

- **Announcement**: The final post type is an announcement, as shown in Figure 6-12.

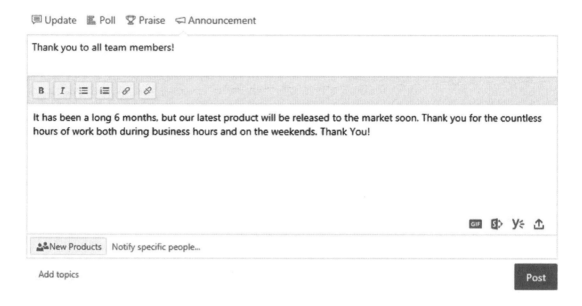

Figure 6-12. *Creating an announcement post in Yammer*

An announcement post is most similar to an update, but an announcement post contains two sections. The two sections are "What do you want to announce?" and the second section is the body of the announcement. You also have the ability to notify people and upload files.

Interacting with Yammer Posts

Similar to Microsoft Teams, which was discussed in Chapter 5, Yammer is also a chat-based collaboration tool. Every post (update, poll, praise, and announcement) can be liked, replied to, shared, or more options can be selected via the post context menu (…), as shown in Figure 6-13.

Figure 6-13. *Options for interacting with posts*

To like a post, select the Like icon located under the post. Clicking the post will change the icon from Like to Unlike. If you choose to unlike a post at a later date, click the Unlike icon. Replying to a post is a similar action to liking a post. Click the Reply link and a text box will appear underneath the original post. Type your message and choose to notify others, add a file, or post text.

The Share icon allows you to share a post with another group or within a private message, as shown in Figure 6-14 when clicking "Share."

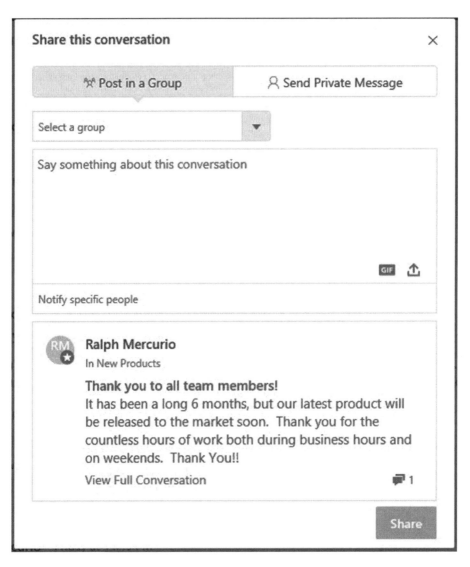

Figure 6-14. *Sharing a conversation*

Within the "Share this conversation" modal window, select a group from the drop-down to share to a Yammer group. The list will populate with groups you have access to. You can add context to sharing a post by adding your comments, uploading a file, and notifying specific people. In order to share the conversation directly in a private message, select the "Send Private Message" option. This option requires you to add specific participants because you are sending a private message. You also have the ability to add a gif or upload a file. When you are satisfied with your selections, click "Share" in the lower right corner to post to a group or send a private message.

If you are the creator of the post, you will also see the Edit link. Clicking this link allows you to edit your post, correct context, or spelling. All edited posts are labeled as edited. You can't edit a poll post.

The final menu option is the post context menu as depicted with an ellipsis (...). The context menu includes the following options:

- **Stop Following**: Unfollowing a conversation will stop the updates from appearing in your Yammer inbox. You can always follow a conversation by selecting it in the context menu.

- **Bookmark**: Bookmarks the conversation to your Yammer profile page. Your profile page can be viewed by selecting your member icon, as shown in Figure 6-15.

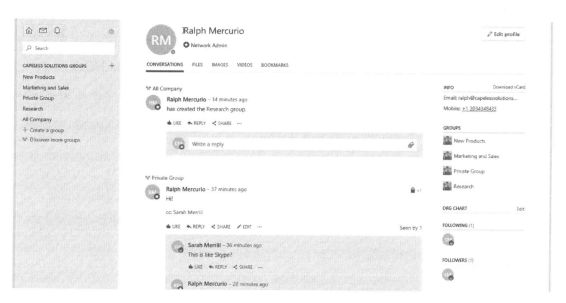

Figure 6-15. *Accessing your Yammer profile page*

- **Move Conversation**: Allows a conversation to be moved to another group, as shown in Figure 6-16. You need to populate the fields as requested in the form.

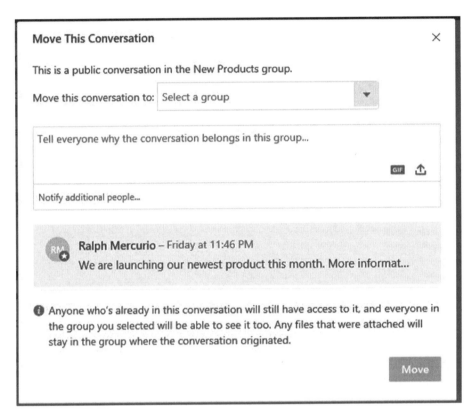

Figure 6-16. *Moving this conversation to another group*

- **Copy link to Clipboard**: Copies a link to the conversation, which can be pasted in an email, Microsoft Teams, Skype conversation, etc. The user needs the correct permissions to access the conversation.

- **View Conversation**: Opens the conversation stream in the same window.

- **Add Topics**: Allows you to search and add topics to the conversation. A topic name will be preceded with the # symbol. Adding topics will increase the search relevancy and allow all conversations tagged with the same topic to be viewable on a single page.

- **Hide Conversation**: Hides the conversation from your view unless others reply to it. It does not hide the conversation from others.

- **Delete the Message**: Deletes the conversation.

Messages

Messages are very similar to posts, and messages can be posted in a group or sent to any colleague using the Yammer platform. To send a message, select "Create a message" in the lower left corner, as shown in Figure 6-2.

A "Create a Message" modal window will open, as shown in Figure 6-17. You will be able to post an update to a group or send a message. When sending a message to a group, note that only public groups are listed in the "Select a group" drop-down. The remainder of the fields are similar to posting an update within a group.

Figure 6-17. *Creating a message to send to either a group or as a private message*

Sending a message to another colleague(s) is similar to posting an update; the difference is you need to select the colleagues to send the message to. Once you select the colleague(s), type your message, attach any items if needed, and press "Send Message." All conversations outside of a group will be listed in the lower right corner. Clicking the colleague's name opens the chat interface and allows you to chat.

An interesting feature with private messaging on the Yammer platform is that a conversation can be moved to a private or public group if deemed appropriate. To move a conversation to a group, select "Move to Group" from the available options within a chat, as depicted in Figure 6-18.

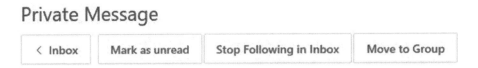

Figure 6-18. *Moving a private message to a group*

Clicking the link will ask you which group to move the message to. Once the message is moved, it can not be undone. Also be aware if your message contained sensitive or confidential information, it will be visible to all members of the group.

Yammer Mobile App

Microsoft released a mobile version of Microsoft Yammer, as it did for almost every one of its core products (SharePoint, Planner, OneDrive, Teams, etc.) The mobile application is supported on both Android and Apple platforms and is available from the respective app stores.

To install your specific version, download the mobile app from the correct app store. Once the app is downloaded and installed on your mobile device, open it, and specify your Office 365 credentials. Once Office 365 authenticates you, you will be presented with a very similar interface to the web version. Figure 6-19 shows the mobile view and the associated icons available.

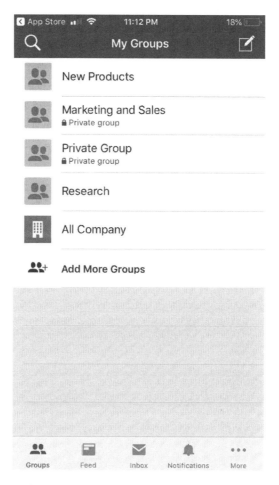

Figure 6-19. *Accessing the Yammer mobile application*

On the Yammer mobile app, you will see a list of your groups; you also have the ability to add and discover more groups. Along the bottom of the application, you can navigate to the Yammer feed, Inbox, Notifications; you can also access the Yammer People Directory and invite people via the ellipsis menu (…).

The functionality of the Yammer mobile application is well thought out and compliments the web version of Yammer. As depicted in Figure 6-20, viewing a group allows a colleague to view the feed of updates and be able to post an update, announcement, or praise.

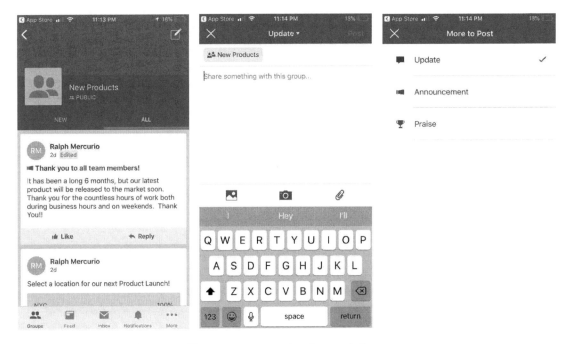

Figure 6-20. Posting to a Yammer group in the mobile app

To post to a Yammer group, click the "Create Post" icon in the upper right corner when viewing a group. Similar to the web version of Yammer, you can add a photo, take a photo, or upload a file via the interface. To change to a different posting type, select the drop-down arrow shown in the second image of Figure 6-20. You can choose to create an update, announcement, or praise post.

Business Retrospective

I want to touch base on a past experience concerning Yammer and a business problem that the executives wanted to solve. The company was dinged by their employees on the yearly employee survey for not being transparent with information, so the company wanted to create a culture of employee empowerment. After a discussion with them, they agreed to greenlight Yammer as a PoC (Proof of Concept). Part of winning them over was to show that Yammer had the features needed to solve the issues and increase employee engagement.

Part of the success of the project was to ensure that the executives would be responsible and willing to post updates and engage with employees. I would love to tell you that once we configured Yammer in the enterprise, created a public group, and had the executives begin posting short updates about what the company was going through, that user adoption shot through the roof and employees felt they were informed.

That didn't happen, and it would appear on the surface that we failed. However, we noticed something odd: we engaged at the wrong level in the organization. Having executive buy-in was needed, but employees felt they couldn't relate or shouldn't respond to upper management.

Because of this, we started to engage other managers, and Yammer became a more widely used platform. A year later, the yearly employee satisfaction survey showed that they were moving towards their goals of dissemanting information and engaging employees.

Summary

A common thread throughout this book is that Microsoft has shifted from providing a single application to solve the many collaboration challenges we face to building applications that allow us to choose the best ones for our needs.

Yammer is similar in many ways to Microsoft Teams but is geared towards connecting colleagues at the enterprise level and not on the project or team level. The key to Yammer is to create groups, public or private, and to ensure that all users have access to the Yammer network. For this to happen, users need to be added in bulk by your IT administrator.

The key to working with Yammer is to ensure that posts are made, whether they are updates, polls, praises, or announcements, and that those posts are replied to. This is important because without any content or current updates, users won't see the value in contributing to or using Yammer.

In this chapter, I covered the basics of Yammer including groups, users, and interacting with posts, and the Yammer mobile application. In the next chapter, I will discuss another cornerstone of Office 365, the Office 2016 suite including Outlook, Word, Excel, OneNote, and PowerPoint.

CHAPTER 7

Office

In the last chapter, you explored Microsoft Yammer and its ability to deliver communication for the entire enterprise. In this chapter, you will explore Office 2016, Microsoft's flagship productivity end-user application, which is available with most subscriptions to Office 365. It includes Outlook, PowerPoint, Word, Excel, OneNote, Publisher, OneDrive for Business, Skype for Business, Access, and Sway (web version only). I will highlight the key applications in the suite and provide a quick overview and some functionality of each.

There is no separate cost or buying the Office DVD from your favorite retailer because it is included in your SaaS (Software-as-a-Service) monthly cost. Your user license to Office 365 allows for five installations of the product on a variety of devices: PCs, Macs, and tablets (iPad and Android). The software is also supported on mobile device platforms.

The difference between purchasing the DVD from a retailer vs. using it as part of the Office 365 subscription is that you are allowed five installs across any devices that support it. There is product key that will not allow you to install more than five times, and each install is cataloged by Office 365 during product activation. Companies that use Office 365 may choose not to use Office 2016 from the Office 365 portal but rather the more traditional Office 2016 license available depending on their license agreement.

Not only do you get access to download and use the Microsoft Office 2016 client applications but you can also use the Office Online versions of Outlook, PowerPoint, Word, Excel, and OneNote in any modern supported browser. These Office Online versions of the popular client applications allow for most tasks to be completed in the browser version. However, certain tasks aren't possible with the Office Online versions.

© Ralph Mercurio 2018
R. Mercurio, *Beginning Office 365 Collaboration Apps*, https://doi.org/10.1007/978-1-4842-3849-3_7

Installing Office 2016 from Office 365

Log into Office365.com with your credentials. On the main page, you will notice an "Install Office apps" link; see Figure 7-1.

Figure 7-1. *The Install link in Office 365*

Click the link and two options (Figure 7-2) will be presented to you. One option is to download and install Office 2016 while the other option is "Other install options."

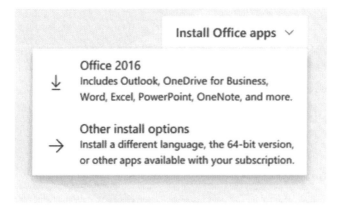

Figure 7-2. *Office 2016 install options*

Office 2016

There are two variants of Office; 32-bit and 64-bit. There are some differences between the two variants; one notable difference is that Excel 64-bit offers support for many more rows then Excel 32-bit. You can't install the Office 32-bit version in conjunction with Office 64-bit products; all Office applications must be the same version. Most users choose to install the 32-bit version, which is what Office 365 defaults to.

If you currently have Office installed on your device, it is considered a good practice to uninstall that version and install the latest version. However, please check with your IT department because there may be business reasons to use a version of Office specified by a company's IT department.

To install the 32-bit version of Office 2016, click "Office 2016" from the context menu (Figure 7-2). This will launch the click-to-run version, which is automatically updated from Microsoft (Figure 7-3).

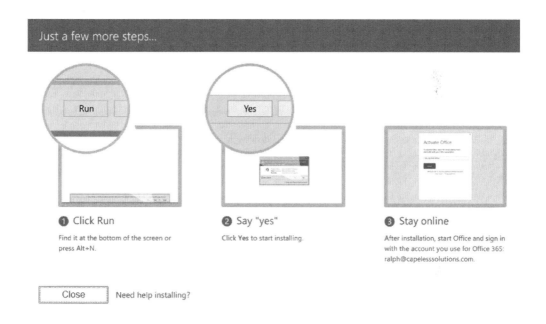

Figure 7-3. *Office 2016 32-bit click-to-run installer*

In Internet Explorer, a dark grey download prompt appears at the bottom of the window (Figure 7-3). It will offer the following download options: Run, Save | Save as, or Cancel. Choose Run and allow the installer to begin the install process. It may prompt for permission to make changes, but that is dependent on your specific security settings. Once the installer proceeds, follow the on-screen prompts to finish the install.

Office 2016 Application Overview

My intention with the next sections is not to provide an in-depth guide to each application but rather to give a brief overview of each application in the Office 2016 suite and some of the improvements that will make your life a little easier.

Outlook

Outlook is the most well-known mail client in the world and is used by most people at some time in their working career or even privately. Outlook contains five mini-applications that together provide a seamless experience.

- **Mail**: This application is your inbox for email communication. You can send/receive emails to anyone just as you do now.

- **People**: This is your standard Outlook address book.

- **Calendar**: Just like the Outlook Calendar you may have been using for years. Use it to schedule meetings with other people, days you might not be in the office, etc.

- **Tasks**: This application contains all the tasks from Outlook that you may have created or the application has created on your behalf.

- **Notes**: A virtual sticky note-like application where you can keep notes about anything, just the like the ones that currently clutter your desk and the bottom of your monitor.

Mail

Launch the Outlook 2016 client from your device by going to Start and opening Outlook 2016 if you're on a version of Windows. If Outlook 2016 is already configured, you will be presented with the Outlook interface (Figure 7-4).

Don't worry; your eyes are working fine. I intentionally blurred the image below because it contains sensitive information I do not wish to disclose.

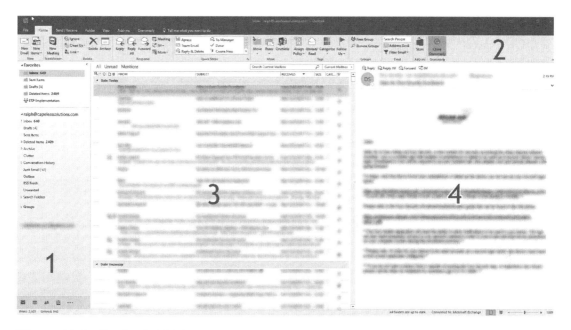

Figure 7-4. *Outlook 2016*

The application contains four main areas:

- **Area 1**: The leftmost area is known as the Folder pane and contains the Outlook Email account (Inbox). This is where you will find not only the Inbox but also sent and deleted items.

- **Area 2**: The Outlook ribbon contains actions such as "Create a New Email," "Replying to All," or "Forwarding." You can also access the Outlook address book or install Office add-ins from the Microsoft Office store.

- **Area 3**: The main window of the Mail application, it contains the mail items dependent on the folder chosen in the Folder pane.

- **Area 4**: The rightmost area is known as the Reading pane. Its main function is to display the contents of the item selected in the mail window such as the Inbox. It can be a position to the right, bottom, or completely off.

Microsoft listened to customer feedback and introduced some new features in Outlook 2016. One of the most notable enhancements, and one that was at the top of my list, is the ability to add recently accessed documents to emails. There is no need to search for the file you just saved to an unknown location on your device. To add a recent file, select "Attach File" from the Include section of the Office Outlook ribbon in a new email, as shown in Figure 7-5.

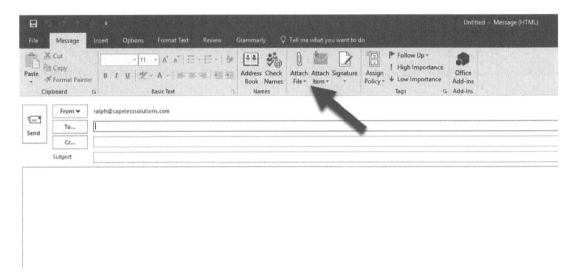

Figure 7-5. *Attaching a recent file to an email*

Clicking the Attach File icon not only allows you to add recently accessed documents (Figure 7-6) but also documents from other locations such as OneDrive or an Office 365 Group.

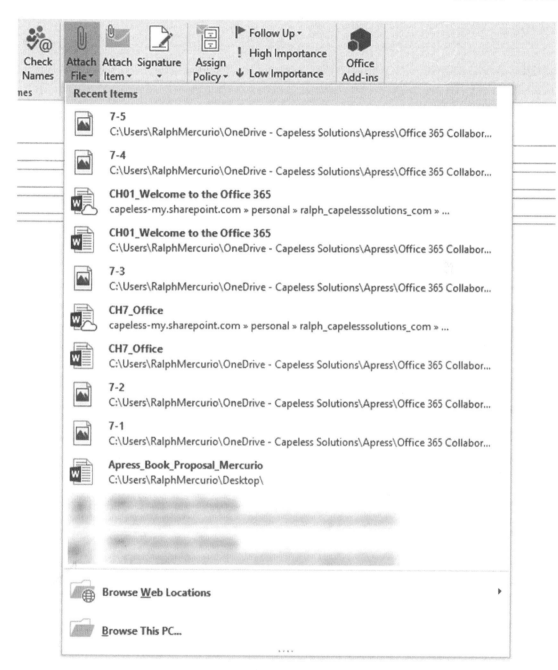

Figure 7-6. *Attach File options in Outlook 2016*

Of course, you can still access your documents locally by clicking "Browse This PC." You will see the familiar Windows Explorer interface to find and attach your files. Microsoft also included a way to attach files from Microsoft OneDrive and Microsoft Groups. This creates seamless integration between Outlook and where you store your files in the other applications.

Attaching a File from OneDrive

Attaching a file from OneDrive is straightforward and simple. To attach a file, follow these steps:

1. In a new mail message in Outlook, select "Attach File" (Figure 7-6) from the Outlook ribbon.

2. Select "Browse Web Locations" from the menu and choose "One Drive" (Figure 7-7).

   It will be named slightly differently in your Outlook.

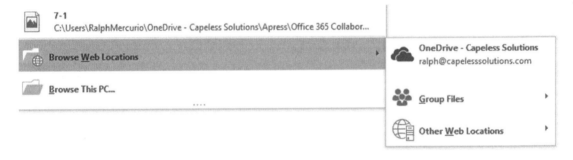

Figure 7-7. *File attachment options*

3. Selecting the OneDrive link opens Microsoft OneDrive via File Explorer. It may seem like it is the local copy of OneDrive, but it is the Office 365 storage location.

4. Select your file. You will be presented with two options. The first option, "Share as OneDrive Link," shares the file directly from your OneDrive. This adds the user as a reader and allows them to see

174

and access the file. The other option, "Attach as copy," sends the recipient a copy of the file. The second method is the traditional method of sending files as attachments.

5. Compose the remainder of the message and send the email to the recipient.

Attaching a File from Office 365 Groups

The process is similar to attaching files from OneDrive. Follow the below steps to attach a file from Office 365 Groups.

1. In a new mail message in Outlook, select "Attach File (Figure 7-6)" from the Outlook ribbon.

2. Select "Browse Web Locations" from the menu and choose "Group Files" (Figure 7-8).

    It will be named slightly differently in your Outlook.

Figure 7-8. *Selecting the Group Files link lists all the Office 365 groups of which you are a member*

3. Select the Office 365 group and select the file you want to attach. You will be presented with two options. The first option, "Share Link," shares the file directly from your Office 365 Group. It adds the user as a reader and allows them to see and access the file. The other option, "Attach as copy," sends the recipient a copy of the file.

4. Compose the remainder of the mail message and send the email to the recipient.

People

Connecting with others is the cornerstone of Microsoft Outlook. The Outlook address book allows you to connect and remember the people you are connected to.

The Outlook address book (Figure 7-9) keeps track of contacts and their associated details. These details include multiple email addresses, phone numbers, or any other details you deem important.

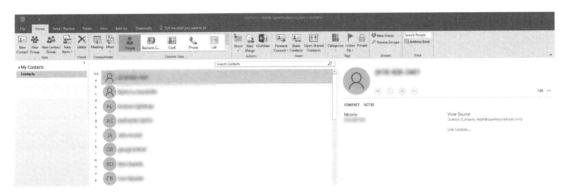

Figure 7-9. *Outlook address book (People)*

In my opinion, Outlook's address book hasn't evolved through the Office product lifecycle. It will be interesting to see how Microsoft plans to integrate it into the Office 365 stack with some of their recent acquisitions, specifically LinkedIn.

Calendar

The infamous Outlook Calendar: keeping track of our meetings, events, doctor's appointments, and when we are not in the office. Outlook has introduced incremental changes over the years to include calendar overlays (superimposing calendars on top of each of other) but the calendar has remained roughly the same throughout the Office iterations. The current interface of the Outlook Calendar is shown in Figure 7-10.

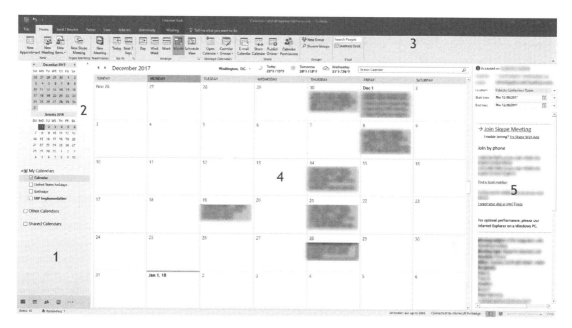

Figure 7-10. *Monthly view of Outlook Calendar*

The Calendar application contains five main areas:

- **Area 1**: This area displays your Outlook Calendar as well as any Exchange Group Calendars and any other calendars that may have been shared with you.

- **Area 2**: This area will always show the current month as well as the next month. It quickly lets you pinpoint a date and will update Area 4.

- **Area 3**: The Outlook ribbon contains actions such as "Create a New Appointment" and various views of the calendars such as Day, Work Week, and Month.

- **Area 4**: This view reflects the view chosen from the Outlook ribbon.

- **Area 5**: This area shows the meeting details of a selected appointment from the calendar.

Tasks

Outlook also can manage tasks either from flagged emails, create new tasks directly from emails, or create new tasks. Tasks created from flagged emails are known as To-Do items and tasks created emails are tasks. These tasks are different than tasks created in Planner or SharePoint and are not integrated with those products. I will discuss Planner tasks in Chapter 8; SharePoint tasks were described in Chapter 2. I will explain Outlook To-Do items and Tasks and their slight nuances next.

To-Do Items

To-Do items are generated when an email is marked for follow-up. An email can be marked for follow-up by right-clicking the email and choosing "Follow Up." This will not only mark the email with a colored flag but will also create a To-Do item in Outlook Tasks. Be aware that when a To-Do item is deleted, the email is deleted as well.

Tasks

Creating a task can be done in two ways: either through the Outlook ribbon (Figure 7-11) or within Outlook Tasks.

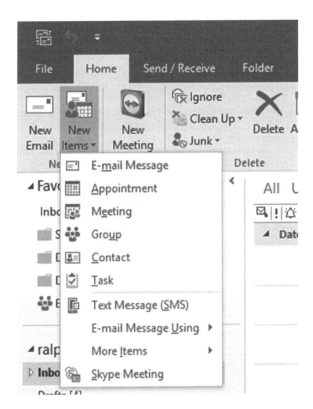

Figure 7-11. *Create a task from the Outlook ribbon*

When creating a new task, you need to specify the values such as subject, start date, end date, status, etc. Tasks can be assigned to others in the organization by selecting "Assign Task" in the Outlook ribbon (Figure 7-12).

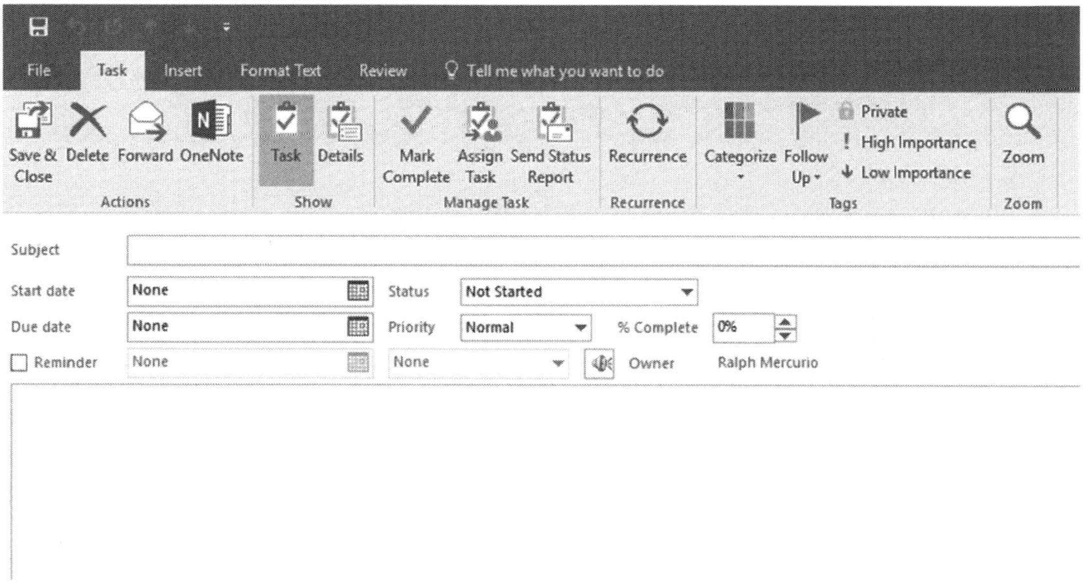

Figure 7-12. *Task settings*

Tasks from Emails

The third way tasks are generated is by dragging an email directly onto the Tasks icon in Outlook Quick Launch in the lower left corner of Outlook. Dragging the email to the Tasks icon opens a new Task window with the subject and the contents of the email added to the task (Figure 7-13). You can then set the other details of the task and save it to Outlook.

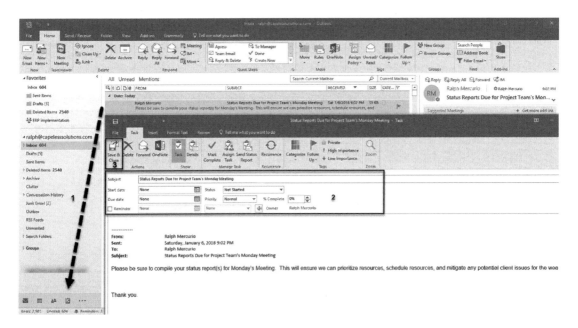

Figure 7-13. *Creating a task from an email*

Notes

Notes in Outlook was introduced in the early 2000s and hasn't received a major redesign since. The purpose of Notes is to give users a place to take and store notes about a project, meeting, or even passwords. Outlook Notes and Microsoft OneNote are not the same product, but OneNote is far superior to Notes and is my preferred editor for notes in the Microsoft stack. I am not going to explore Notes in too much detail but I will give a basic introduction.

To access Notes, click the ellipsis located in the lower left corner of Outlook (Figure 7-14) and select the Notes application from the pop-up menu.

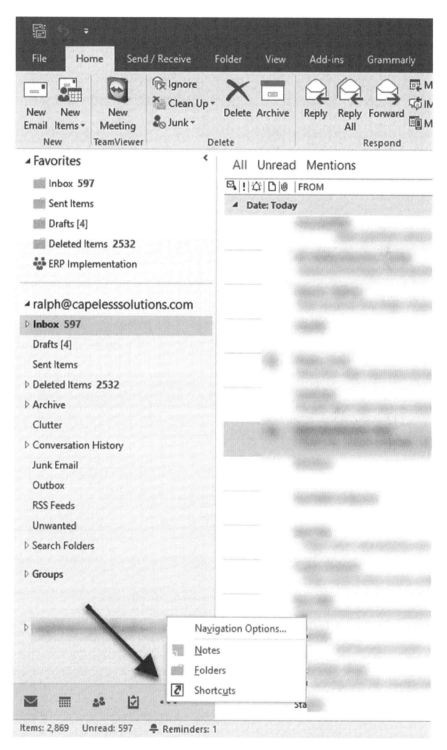

Figure 7-14. *Accessing the Notes application from the Outlook bar*

Accessing the application opens the Notes interface (Figure 7-15). You will notice the interface is like the other applications: E-Mail, People, Calendar, and Tasks.

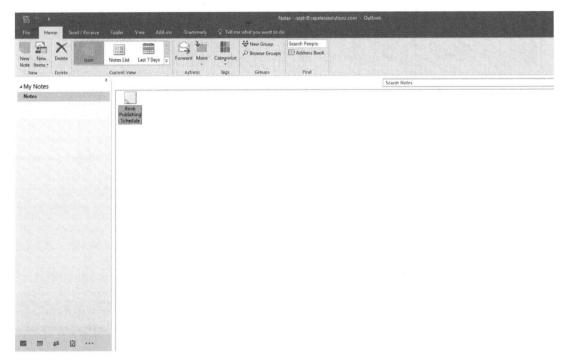

Figure 7-15. *The Notes application within Outlook*

The interface contains the Outlook ribbon with the appropriate actions just for Notes, the Notes window, and a My Notes navigation control.

Creating a Note

From the Outlook ribbon or by right-clicking the main Notes window, select "New Note." A yellow sticky note will appear and you can add text to it. You can only add text to the note. The note is timestamped, and once you click out of the Note, it is automatically saved.

Viewing and Sorting Notes

Notes can be sorted and viewed in three distinct views to quickly access and find them. The views include Icon, Notes List, and Last 7 Days. Currently, you cannot customize the views further.

Icon

The Icon view displays the notes as sticky notes. These notes can then be arranged and grouped in any manner you see fit. The Icon view is the default view and can be seen in Figure 7-16.

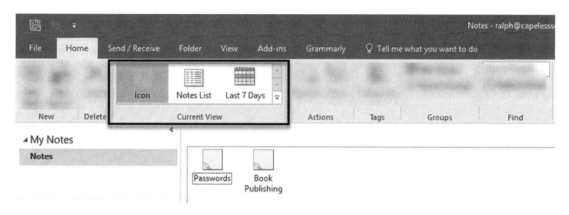

Figure 7-16. *Available views*

Notes List

The Notes List view simply lists the notes in a list (Figure 7-17). You can sort by either the subject or created columns.

Figure 7-17. *Notes List view*

Last 7 Days

This view shows the notes that have been created in the last seven days. In this view, you can also sort through a variety of fields.

Deleting a Note

To delete a note, simply highlight the note and choose Delete from the Outlook Ribbon or right-click the Note and choose "Delete Note" from the menu.

PowerPoint

Microsoft PowerPoint is arguably the most-used software to craft presentations for business, education, or personal presentations. PowerPoint allows the user to create presentations with numerous slides. The trick to creating an amazing and well-thought presentation is to keep the content of each slide concise and to ensure that the prestation stays on track and delivers a clear message.

The PowerPoint layout contains three main areas: the Office Ribbon, the current slide being edited, and a list of slides (Slide Sorter) in the presentation (Figure 7-18). When editing a slide, the Office ribbon changes, allowing only the appropriate commands.

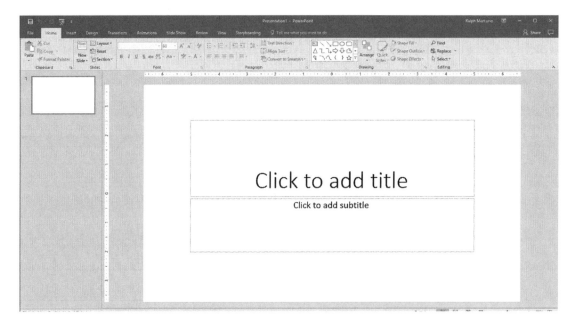

Figure 7-18. *PowerPoint layout*

Edit the slide as needed, adding text or images. When complete, click "New Slide" from the Insert tab of the Office ribbon or right-click in the Slide Sorter (leftmost) and choose "New Slide."

To view your presentation as if you were presenting to an audience, press F5 on your keyboard; to end your presentation, press the Escape key. Continue to customize it as needed by adding slides and content.

Word

Microsoft Word is used throughout to world to write and edit essays, resumes, business documents, and a whole host of other types of documents. Word is simple to use but at times can be frustrating when trying to line up text with the correct margins or when trying to make a document to look perfect. The Microsoft Word layout shares some commonalities with the PowerPoint layout; the Word layout is shown in Figure 7-19. The Word layout contains the Office ribbon and the document area.

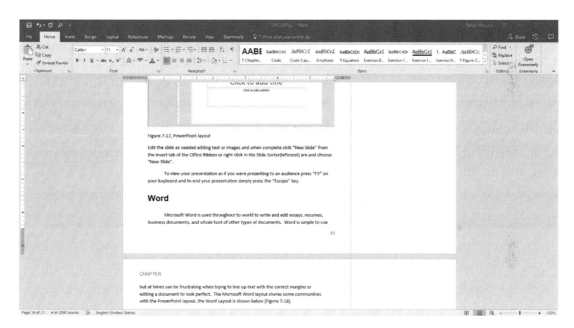

Figure 7-19. *Word layout*

Excel

Microsoft Excel is a spreadsheet program that contains calculations and formulas, graphing capabilities, and even the ability to track a household budget. The Excel layout contains the Office ribbon (a common theme in both client and web apps) and the spreadsheet (Figure 7-20).

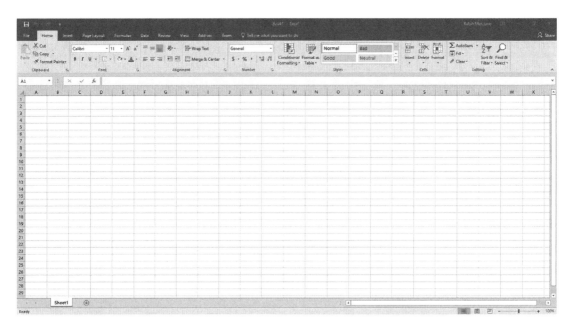

Figure 7-20. *Microsoft Excel 2016 layout*

To create a basic line chart and to explore some of the new features of Excel 2016, create two column headings as depicted in Figure 7-21.

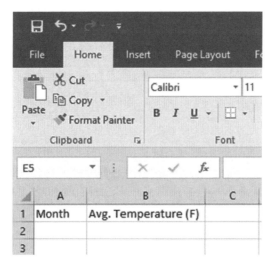

Figure 7-21. *Column headings*

In cell A2, type **January** into the cell and drag the lower right corner to row 13. To drag the corner, hover your mouse over the lower right corner of the cell A2 until a black cross appears. Once the cross appears, hold the left mouse button and drag the cell down. If done correctly, Excel recognizes the month (January) and fills in the remaining months. In the second column, add the average temperatures for each month. Once done, it should look like Figure 7-22.

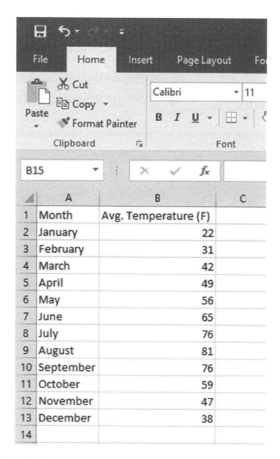

Figure 7-22. *Completed dataset*

Now that you have a complete dataset, you can quickly generate a chart to show the data graphically. This is useful to embed into a PowerPoint or Word document or send via email to a group of recipients. To generate the graph, select the dataset and select "Recommended Charts" from the Insert tab of Office ribbon, as shown in Figure 7-23.

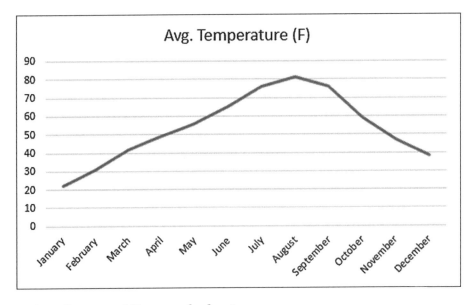

Figure 7-23. *Using Excel's Recommended Chart option*

Excel will analyze the dataset and present the most appropriate charts based on the data. Select the recommended Line Chart and Excel will generate the chart in Figure 7-24.

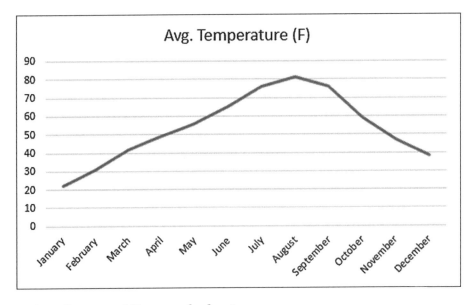

Figure 7-24. *Generated line graph chart*

The chart can be tailored by adding a legend, series labels, or other cosmetic additions.

OneNote

Microsoft OneNote is like Outlook Note's foreign cousin. In OneNote, you can keep "sticky notes," mark up your notes in color, insert images and other content, and easily share them across multiple devices or with other users. The OneNote interface (Figure 7-25) is intuitive if you're familiar with the Office layouts of Outlook, PowerPoint, Excel, and Word.

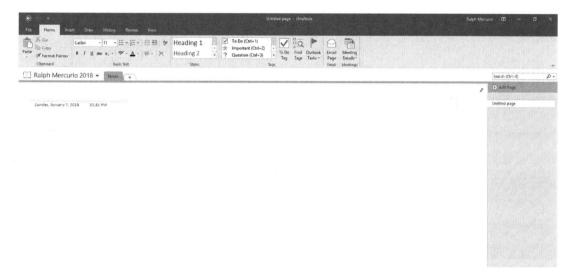

Figure 7-25. *OneNote interface*

The OneNote interface includes not only the Office ribbon but also the Note area. To add a note, simply add the text or content directly onto the note. To continue from the previous section, I copied the Excel chart that was generated from the dataset and pasted it directly into OneNote; see Figure 7-26.

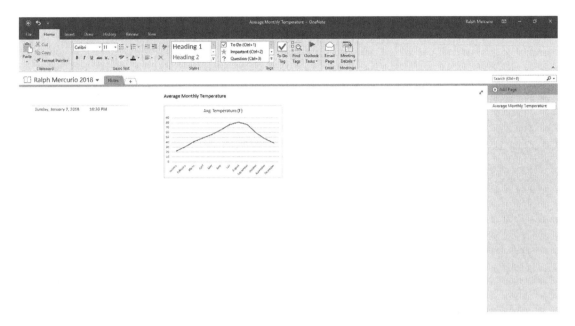

Figure 7-26. *Creating a note with an Excel-generated graph*

With OneNote, you can mark up your notes with color or markings, which is truly different from Outlook Notes. This flexibility of marking up your notes translates really well to the tablet and touchable screen laptops. To access the markup features of OneNote, simply select "Draw" on the Office ribbon.

Publisher

Microsoft Publisher is an Office product for creating and publishing books, newsletters, and other publication materials. It has been an Office staple since 1991 and is only available on the PC platform; it is not available on the Apple or tablet platforms at this moment.

Launching Publisher opens the interface (Figure 7-27), which is similar to other layout and publication software such as products from Adobe or Quark.

Figure 7-27. *Microsoft Publisher layout*

I hope these quick blurbs about the key Office products did provide enough of a background to get you started and to understand the purpose of each application. Learning Microsoft Office isn't easy, and it doesn't come overnight, but there is a wealth of resources in books, videos, and training to help you succeed.

Office Online Overview

With Office 365, Microsoft made Microsoft Word, Outlook, Excel, PowerPoint, and Sway available within any modern supported browser. This also allows tight integration with the other SaaS applications within the Office 365 suite.

The Office Online applications are not a one-to-one relationship with the client applications discussed in the previous sections. Part of the reason for this is that developing an application to be installed and run from within a browser is extremely complex, and there are limitations and security concerns that Microsoft can't change and must comply with.

Outlook

To open Outlook from Office 365, navigate to `Office365.com` and log in. Once you are logged in, click the app launcher (upper left corner) and click the Outlook icon. This opens a new tab and in turn opens Outlook (Figure 7-28).

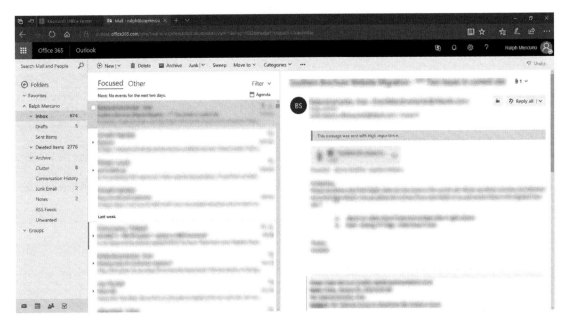

Figure 7-28. *Outlook interface viewed in a web browser*

Viewing Outlook in the web browser is quite similar to the installed Outlook 2016 version; each contains Mail, Calendar, People, and Tasks icons but the web version of Outlook has Notes removed.

When viewing the Inbox, you will notice that Microsoft has introduced two views: Focused and Other. These views attempt to streamline the grind of inbox management and try to separate mail that is relevant vs. mail from nonrelevant sources such as advertisements, sales proposal, blind emails, etc.

Note   The focused inbox is slated to be rolled out to Office 2016 sometime in calendar year 2018 during an update cycle. It should appear after the applications update themselves or the updates are pushed out via the IT department.

Word Online

To launch Word Online, launch the Word application from the Office 365 app launcher. Opening Word Online presents an interface (Figure 7-29) where you can open a recent document, create a new, blank document, or choose from a variety of templates to create resumes, cover letters, and other document types.

Figure 7-29. *Word Online start-up layout*

Let's create a new, blank document by selecting the document type from the list of available templates. Word Online prepares and creates the document and presents an interface similar to Word 2016. The interface contains the Office ribbon, the document, and the ability to edit in Word if the Word Online version becomes unwieldy or you need to perform an advanced function not available in Word Online.

An interesting function of Word Online is that there is no Save button. Word Online continuously saves the document back to your OneDrive as you work on it. You can see the status in the header of Word Online; see Figure 7-30.

Figure 7-30. *Word Online's saving feature*

Since OneDrive is the default location to save Word Online files within Office 365, you can view the versions within the OneDrive application. Word Online saves major versions of the document you are working on but not every single change. Because of this, you will not have access to all versions of the document you were working on but you will have access to all major versions. To access the versions, navigate to OneDrive and select the "Version history" link within the context menu.

At first glance, it appears that the Office ribbon and Office Online ribbon are the same, but as you examine the available commands, you will quickly see they aren't. For example, the Review tab (Figure 7-31) of Word Online and the Review tab (Figure 7-32) of Word 2016 are not the same. You will notice that the infamous Track Changes functionality is missing. In these cases, Track Changes can only be done in Word 2016.

Figure 7-31. *Word Online Review tab*

Figure 7-32. *Word 2016 Review tab*

For most users and most purposes, Word Online will suffice. Not only do you get the benefit of using any web browser from any PC or Mac but the ability to view and edit documents is key to being productive in situations where Office may not be installed, such as kiosk machines, remote employees who can't get an Office license assigned to them, or underpowered devices where the client software can't be installed.

PowerPoint Online

PowerPoint Online is similar to Word Online, and they share a common layout, much the same way the Office 2016 products feel. With PowerPoint Online (Figure 7-33) you can create presentations and work on them completely in the browser.

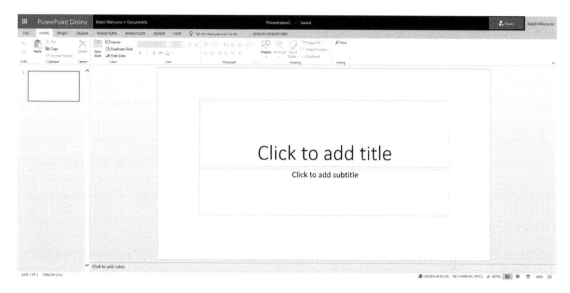

Figure 7-33. *PowerPoint Online interface*

PowerPoint Online contains the same Office Online ribbon, the ability to open PowerPoint Online documents in PowerPoint 2016, auto-saving, and most of the functionality of its older brother, PowerPoint 2016. There are gaps, however, much like Word Online vs. Word 2016. I believe those gaps are quite minimal for most presentation creators.

Using PowerPoint Online does have advantages over PowerPoint 2016, and the traveling workers come to mind. Years ago I would have argued that PowerPoint Online, if existed, wouldn't be very good, simply because of the reliance on having an Internet connection. However, as time has passed, Internet connections are abundant either through cell devices, public access hotspots, or your home Internet provider.

Think of a traveling salesman whose PowerPoint 2016 continues to crash and won't start. Having access to PowerPoint Online alleviates that frustration and still allows for the presentation to be consumed or collaborated on. There have been situations where I have gone to a client's location only to be told that that Office isn't installed on the conference room PC or I forgot my converters to connect to their system. With Office 365 and PowerPoint Online, I can present directly from the browser.

Excel Online

Excel Online (Figure 7-34), like the other online versions of Office, offers the same layout and feel as Excel. For most users, Excel Online will suffice to create and view content.

Figure 7-34. *Excel Online layout*

Once you require features such as macros, PowerPivot, power query, data tools ("Text to Columns," "Remove Duplicates," and the other features), you will need to use the Excel 2016 version.

OneNote Online

OneNote Online is a great companion to Office Online. It shares a similar look and feel to OneNote 2016 and for the most part will suffice as an excellent application to create and store notes.

Like the other Office Online products, there are some limitations and features that have been removed to make it work within the confines of a web browser. However, I feel that those limitations should not hinder the ability to create and markup notes.

Sway

Microsoft Sway, available from the app launcher in Office 365, is aimed at storytelling and is not necessarily a presentation slide deck like PowerPoint. PowerPoint will always have its place in the business world because it is an excellent way to communicate an idea or slide deck to an audience.

Sway tries to shift the consumption from an audience to a single user. It does this by introducing "Sways" and forces the end user creating a Sway to focus on the message rather the focus on generating content for a slide deck.

Sway is available through Office 365 as part of Office Online, a downloadable application from the Windows Store, and a variety of mobile devices. Microsoft has not integrated Sway 2016 as part of Office 2016.

Co-Authoring

Office Online allows one of the most powerful collaborative features ever released in Office 365. True co-authoring allows multiple people to edit and view a document and see the changes in real time as they are made, regardless of location.

In order to allow for co-authoring, the following two conditions must be met: the document must be saved in either OneDrive or SharePoint Online. This is required to ensure that the 365 services can maintain the document and stream of changes. The final condition is that users must be invited to collaborate on the document.

Note   Office 2016 recently introduced real-time co-authoring but it is dependent on having the appropriate Office 2016 updates installed. The process is similar to co-authoring in Office Online but to ensure real-time the user must agree to automatic sharing. I will focus on co-authoring in Office Online because the platform is already configured for real-time co-authoring.

Co-Authoring in Office Online

Each Office Online application (Word, PowerPoint, and Excel) does have certain co-authoring rules that dictate what and how things can be edited. For instance, only one user can edit a cell at the same time in Excel Online, while the other two Office Online applications are more lenient. Without these rules, the stream of changes would simply override the others and co-authoring would fall flat.

Excel Online

From your specific OneDrive, select "New" and choose "Excel workbook." This will create a new Excel Online document and will serve as the example to show co-authoring in Excel Online.

From the Office Online ribbon, choose File ➤ Share ➤ Share with people (Figure 7-35). Opening the "Share with people" dialog allows you to invite users from either inside your organization, specific people, people with existing permissions, or anyone. For the Anyone permission level to be enabled, your IT administrators must enable certain settings with Office 365 to make it work.

Choose "Users from inside your organization." Your screen will be different from what you see in Figure 7-35 because these images are based on my organizational name and settings.

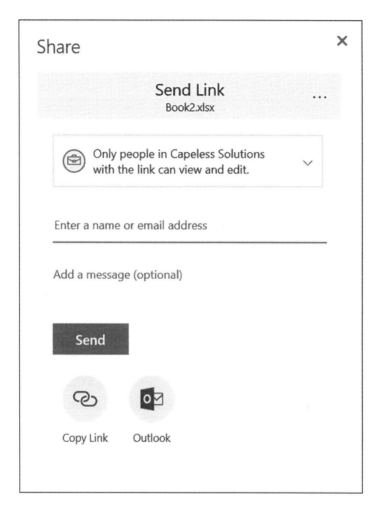

Figure 7-35. *Excel Online sharing a document*

In the Share dialog box, enter a name or email address of a user within your organization. I am going to share the Excel Online document with Sarah Merrill, a user in my organization. Simply type the user's name in the "Enter a name or email address" textbox. Once the user is entered and recognized by Office 365, you can share the link either by creating a shareable link or sending it via Outlook.

Sarah will receive an email with a link to the document to edit it. When she clicks the link specified in the email, it will open the Excel Online workbook in read-only mode. At this point, the document is just being viewed; once she selects to edit the workbook with Excel Online, the workbook will go into co-authoring mode (Figure 7-36).

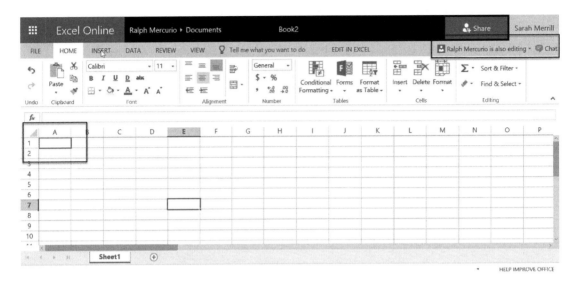

Figure 7-36. *Co-authoring an Excel Online workbook*

When the workbook is in co-authoring mode, you will notice two things: a red box around a cell (in this case A1), and who is editing the document. User Ralph Mercurio was assigned a red editing color by Office 365 and he is currently editing cell A1. If you hover over "Ralph Mercurio is also editing," you will notice that it shows exactly what cell he is editing.

From my perspective (Figure 7-37), I can see that Sarah Merrill is editing cell F6 and was assigned a blue color.

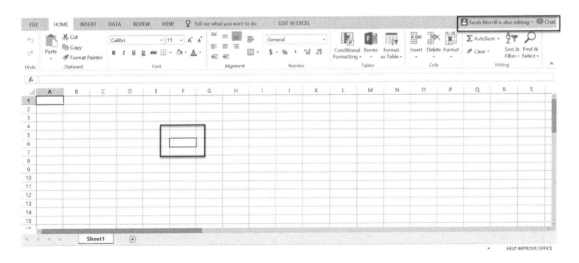

Figure 7-37. *Excel Online co-authoring with a user*

As I add content to the workbook, it will display in the workbook and Sarah will be able to see the edits I make without delay. Figure 7-38 shows a side-to-side comparison of what I see as I edit the workbook and what Sarah sees as she views the workbook.

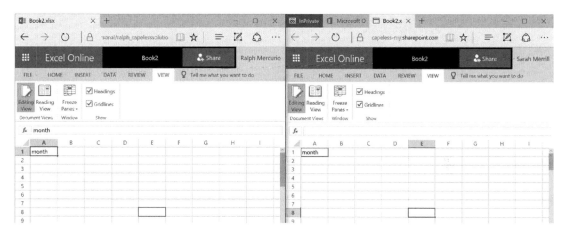

Figure 7-38. *Side-by-side view of the Excel Online co-authoring experience*

At this point, Sarah will not be able to edit the cell A1 until I move onto another cell. The two users may continue to edit the workbook, and once the editing is complete, the document will be saved back to my OneDrive.

With co-authoring in Excel Online, you can also have a web chat with the user(s) editing the workbook. This is innovative in two ways: it's integrated completely with the Excel Online workbook and doesn't use any other outside application to facilitate the web conversation. To begin a chat from within Excel Online, select "Chat" (Figure 7-39). This opens the chat window and asks you who you want to chat with. You may only chat with users who are currently editing the document. This feature is enabled in all Office Online applications, not just Excel Online.

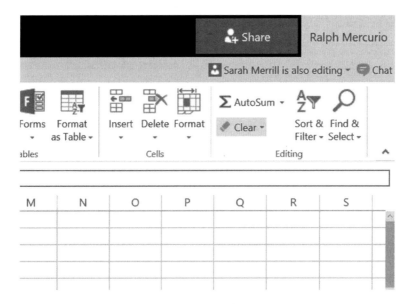

Figure 7-39. *Starting a chat during a co-authoring session*

Go ahead and try to edit an Excel Online document with a colleague; see Figure 7-40. You will notice that it is an efficient and innovative way to collaborate on documents.

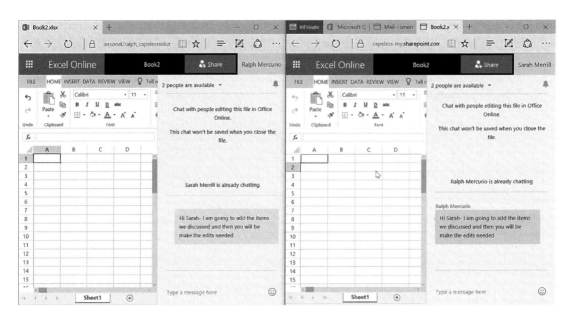

Figure 7-40. *A chat between two users, a side-by-side view*

Word Online

Like co-authoring in Excel Online, the experience is similar in Word Online. You still need to ensure the document is located in OneDrive or SharePoint Online and the user you want to share with also has a valid Office 365 license. In most cases, this won't be an issue because an entire organization will be on Office 365, but if Office 365 is being rolled out to an organization in a slow manner, it's possible that not all users will have the appropriate license.

To co-author a Word Online document, the process is similar to co-authoring in Excel Online. Once the document is saved in OneDrive or SharePoint Online, go ahead and share the document via File ➤ Share in the Office Online ribbon.

In Word Online, the co-authoring restrictions are relaxed compared to Excel Online. In Word Online, you can edit the same cursor location; Excel Online will not allow you to edit the same cell. Figure 7-41 shows the experience in Word Online between users.

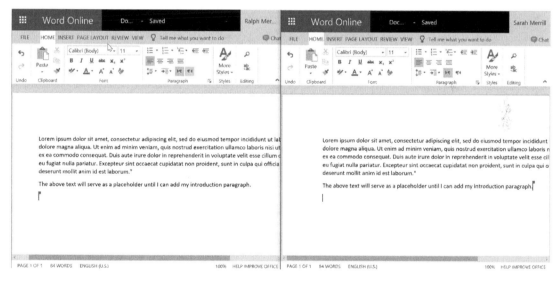

Figure 7-41. *Word Online co-authoring*

PowerPoint Online Co-Authoring

Like Excel and Word Online, PowerPoint Online co-authoring shares the same common functionality and experience. This is to ensure that the experience from an end-user perspective is as unified as possible in Office Online and provides a seamless experience.

To share a presentation for co-authoring, follow the same steps as Excel and Word Online to invite a user to the PowerPoint document. Another way to share a document (PowerPoint, Word, Excel) is to click the Share button in the upper right corner of the PowerPoint document. It will direct you to the same sharing interface as the previous method.

In Figure 7-42, Sarah and I are both editing the same PowerPoint document. I am working on Slide 2 while Sarah is currently editing Slide 1 of the presentation.

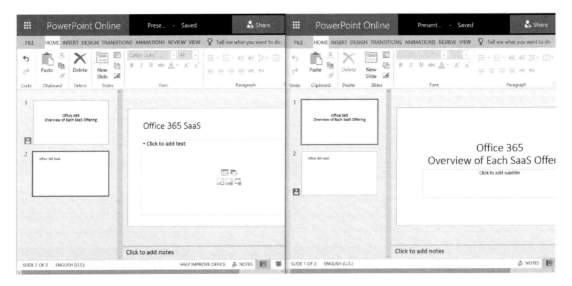

Figure 7-42. *PowerPoint co-authoring*

In my opinion, co-authoring in PowerPoint Online is the most collaborative of the three Office Online applications. Being able to edit the same presentation while working on a different slide within the presentation offers a powerful collaborative experience and means that teams can build out a PowerPoint document quickly.

Summary

Office Online and Office 2016 offer the best tools for collaborating, creating, and editing content, and creating effective documents to convey the appropriate message. For most users, Office Online will be sufficient enough, but some power users will need to use the Office 2016 applications for the advanced features.

However, the ability to create content with Office Online is very powerful because you do not need the Office client installed locally on the device you are using. For Office Online, you only need a working Internet connection, an Office 365 license, and a supported web browser. This makes it possible to work from most locations and have access to your documents in OneDrive or SharePoint Online.

When you need to do advanced data exploration in Excel or track changes within a Word document, you must use Office 2016. As an Office 365 subscriber, you have the ability to download and install Office 2016 up to five times on a variety of devices. For users who have relied on InfoPath 2013, you will notice that InfoPath 2016 is not available. In this case, you can use InfoPath 2013 but should plan on transitioning to PowerApps eventually.

Co-authoring is a powerful toolset in the Office 2016 and Office Online ecosystems. Co-authoring is a great tool to foster collaboration with users who are geographically dispersed and may not want to send documents continually back and forth via email.

In the next chapter, I will Microsoft Planner, which offers task management far superior to that of Outlook, SharePoint, or any other Microsoft task amanagement program. Planner is aimed at project task assignment and reporting for which Project 2016 or Project Online is overkill.

CHAPTER 8

Planner

In the previous chapter, I discussed the familiar Office applications and some of their benefits. In this chapter, I will review Microsoft Planner, which is an Office 365 product that allows you and your team to create tasks and plans to manage tasks and projects. With Planner, you can assign tasks to users, monitor their statuses, and report on them. By utilizing this Office 365 application, you can finally get rid of all the Post-It notes littering your desk, the countless Microsoft Excel spreadsheets, and not have to utilize Microsoft Project to manage simple or ad hoc projects which might not be available in your workplace.

I am not discounting the need for project managers or project management software, but Planner does offer the ability to manage tasks and resources. Microsoft Project has its place, and it's a great tool to manage enterprise projects but it does require licensing outside of the traditional Office suite licensing, and there is a bit of a learning curve to using it. Microsoft Planner is more focused on task management for projects and does not encroach on the features of Microsoft Project but does share some commonality with task management.

As I dive deeper into Microsoft Planner, I am going to touch upon some key areas that I think you will find useful. Regarding task management, you will explore not only creating tasks but also the ability to track and group them with buckets. You will also dive into reporting on tasks and their statuses. In Chapter 11, you will explore connecting Microsoft Planner with Microsoft Flow to create a truly remarkable integration between the two services.

But before we get too far ahead of ourselves, let's look at how to access Planner and get familiar with the interface and where you can find certain actions within Planner.

© Ralph Mercurio 2018
R. Mercurio, *Beginning Office 365 Collaboration Apps*, https://doi.org/10.1007/978-1-4842-3849-3_8

Overview of Planner Interface

Within Office 365, click the app launcher in the upper right corner and select Microsoft Planner, as shown in Figure 8-1.

Figure 8-1. *Launching the Microsoft Planner application*

Once you click the application, you will be presented with the Planner Hub (see Figure 8-2). This Planner Hub displays all the Planner plans you create. I will discuss plans shortly.

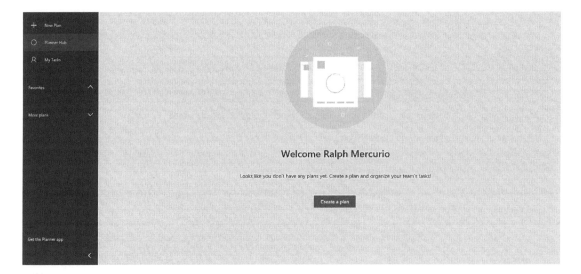

Figure 8-2. *Microsoft Planner Hub dashboard*

The Planner Hub also contains options to the left of the main section of the dashboard; see Figure 8-3. The options include to creating a new plan (+ New Plan), a shortcut link to the Planner Hub, My tasks, Favorites, Recent Plans, getting the Planner app, and an icon (<) to minimize the left menu.

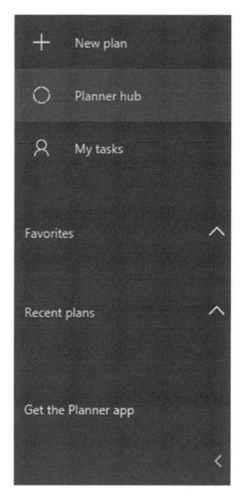

Figure 8-3. *Planner Hub left menu options*

Now that you know the layout and where actions are located within the application, let's move on to discussing plans, which provide the foundation for Planner.

Plans

Plans are a foundational element of Planner. Each plan provides the foundation for task buckets, charts, and schedules. It also provides an integration point for Office 365 Groups and Teams. Office 365 Groups was discussed in Chapter 4 and Teams was explored in Chapter 5.

Creating a New Plan

To create a new plan, click "+ New Plan" in the left-hand menu. A modal window appears with the title "New Plan," as shown in Figure 8-4.

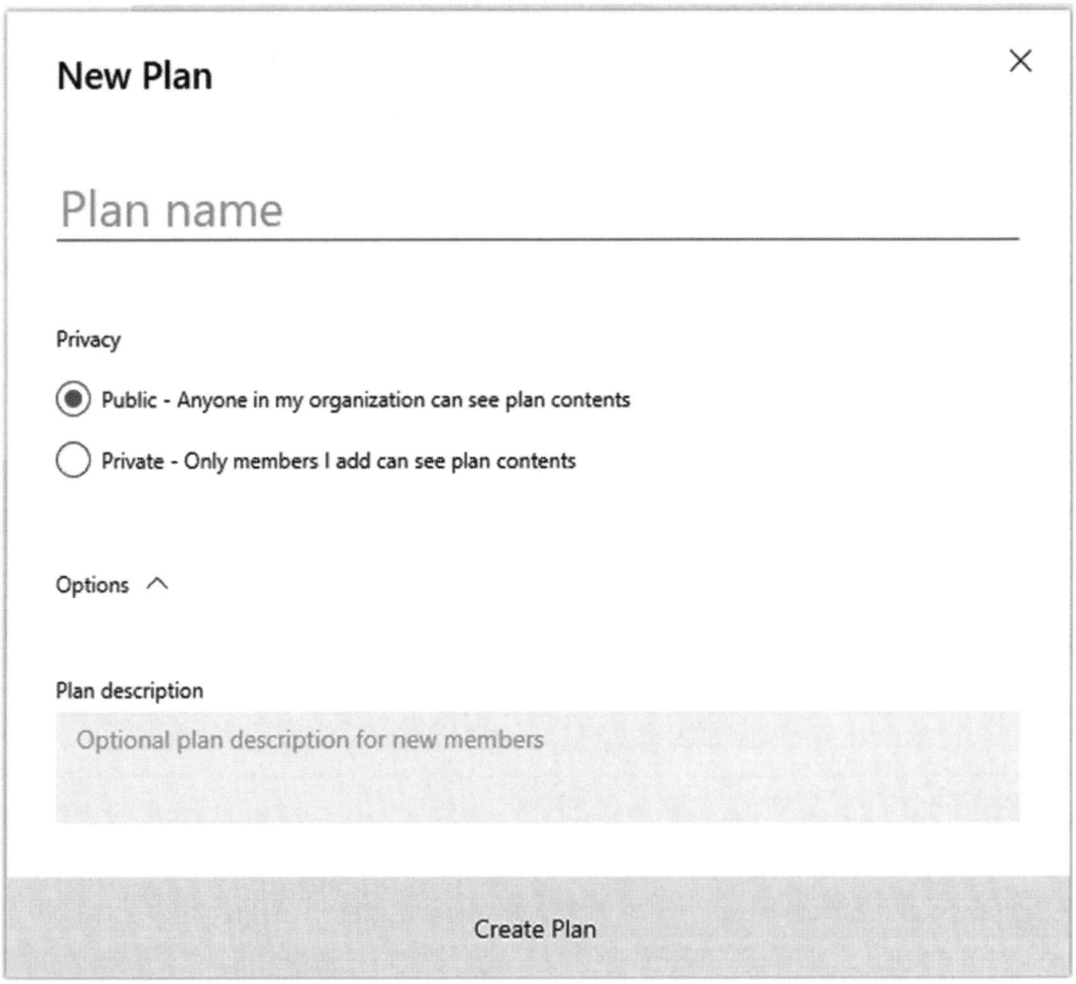

New Plan   ✕

Plan name

Privacy

◉ Public - Anyone in my organization can see plan contents

○ Private - Only members I add can see plan contents

Options ∧

Plan description

Optional plan description for new members

Create Plan

Figure 8-4. *New Plan window*

Creating a new plan is as simple as specifying a title for the plan, entering a plan description if desired, and selecting the privacy settings. There are two privacy settings: public and private. If public is selected, any user within the organization can view the plan; if private is selected, the onus is on you to give access to the correct users. The easy way is to make all the plans public, but there may be reasons why this is not desired.

For example, if the project deals with sensitive information about an acquisition or other business activity, that could be sufficient reason to make it private.

Let's create a new plan with the following settings:

- **Title**: ERP Implementation

- **Privacy**: Private – Only members I add can see plan contents

- **Plan description**: Plan to select an ERP system

Once the plan details are entered, press the Create Plan button. See Figure 8-5.

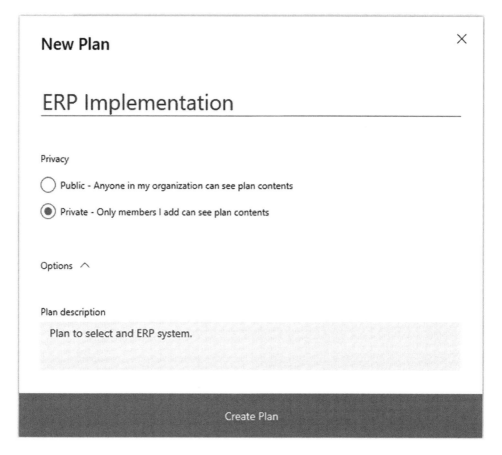

Figure 8-5. *New Plan settings*

Now that you have created a plan, let's get familiar with the plan's dashboard. Each plan also contains more settings available by an ellipsis (…) next to the Schedule link. This context menu contains some interesting connections as well as Planner-specific settings. Opening the menu, you will see icons for Conversation, Members, Files,

Notebook, and Sites. These five options are connected to other Office 365 services, and you will explore some of these options later in the chapter. The remaining four options are "Add to favorites," "Copy link to plan," "Add plan to Outlook calendar," and "Plan settings." The Plan dashboard contains settings to create tasks, add new buckets to contain tasks and group by, invite members, three different views to view data (Boards, Charts, and Schedule), and a settings menu. See Figure 8-6.

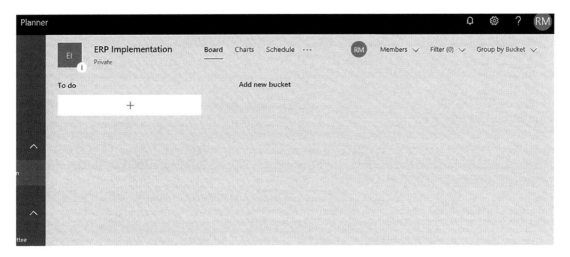

Figure 8-6. *Planner plan dashboard*

As you add tasks, I will explain the available options and settings. Buckets contain tasks that are assigned to resources. Buckets also contain a few settings that can be manipulated; they can be renamed, moved left or right on the Plan dashboard, and deleted. The Settings menu can be accessed by hovering over the bucket title and clicking the ellipsis (...). This will bring up the context menu for buckets.

There are times when you may want to group tasks by a common theme. Out of the gate, Planner creates a To-Do bucket, but you can create as many buckets as you need. Creating buckets is as simple as clicking "Add new bucket" and typing a name. For this exercise, let's create a bucket called "Internal Tasks." Now that you have a bucket to hold your tasks, let's invite users so you can assign tasks.

To invite users to a plan, click "Members" in the upper right corner. Simply type the name of a user you want to add and Office 365 will automatically show the users that match your query. I am going to invite Tony Smith, Sarah Merrill, and Andrew Darkbody to the plan; the users you add will be different because these users are specific to my

Office 365 tenant. If you created a trial tenant, you will also need to create users; this can be accomplished by going to the Admin settings, creating the users, and assigning them an appropriate license.

Note   If you made a mistake adding a user, click "Members" and hover over the name you want to remove. By hovering over the name you want to remove, an ellipsis will appear and you can select the "Remove" option from the menu.

As Planner takes off in your organization and more and more plans are created, you may want to mark plans as favorites so they can be quickly accessed without the need to scrolls through numerous plans on the Planner Dashboard. By clicking on the ellipsis (…) to the right of the Charts link, you can select "Add to favorites." This will add the plan to the Favorites heading in the left hand side of Planner.

Editing a Plan

To edit a plan, click the ellipsis (…) in the top bar of the plan and select Plan settings. A modal window named "EPlan settings" will open and you can edit the name and the description by clicking "Edit group." You can also make a plan public or private depending on how the plan was originally created. Marking a plan as private or public does not hide the plan but limits who can access the plan. On the Plan Settings screen you can also change the email settings to send an email when a task is assigned or completed to the group.

Deleting a Plan

Deleting a plan is as simple as choosing "Delete this plan" (Figure 8-7) in the ellipsis menu as described above.

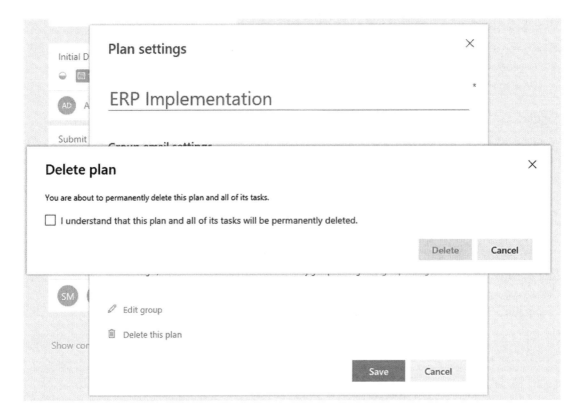

Figure 8-7. *Delete Plan confirmation screen*

Deleting a plan will permanently delete the plan as well as all of the tasks. Currently a deleted plan is non-recoverable.

Plan Notifications and Communications

Planner offers little in the way of notifications but as the service progresses I can definitely see more control over the notifications received. Part of this isn't that Microsoft isn't able to accomplish it; it's more of not overloading your inbox with countless notifications about when tasks are completed or new plans are created.

To access the current notification settings available, access the cog/gear in the upper right corner of Planner. You can toggle the checkbox to alert you when someone assigns a task to you. You also can toggle the notification when a task is late, due today, or due in the next seven days. Click "Save" when you have made your choice. The default setting that is that both options are selected.

Task Management

Being able to manage tasks is a cornerstone of Planner and is what makes Planner an effective application. Tasks can be added, edited, and deleted. Planner also presents dashboards to manage the number of tasks and to quickly gain an understanding of their statuses.

Adding Tasks

Create your first task in the ERP Implementation plan by adding a task to the Internal Tasks bucket; see Figure 8-8. Clicking the + sign makes an Add Task window appear.

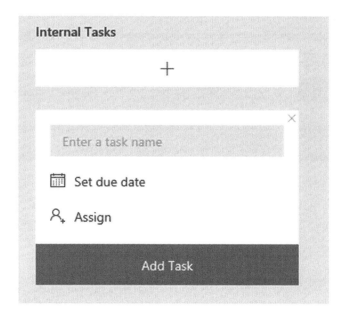

Figure 8-8. *Adding a task to a bucket*

The Add Task window allows you to simply create a task name, set a due date, and assign it to a user. Once the task is added, you can further edit the task. For this scenario, I created a task with the following settings:

- **Title**: Submit RFP for Review

- **Set a due date**: 12/31/17

- **Assign**: Sarah Merrill

Note   The values for "Assign" and "Set a due date" will be different because the users will be different in your environment. Also, the dates will be different.

Adding more tasks is as simple as following the above steps of adding tasks to the buckets. One interesting feature about adding tasks is the ability to assign a task to more than one person. This is a great way to assign tasks to multiple users. To assign a task to multiple users, simply add those members during task creation; see Figure 8-9.

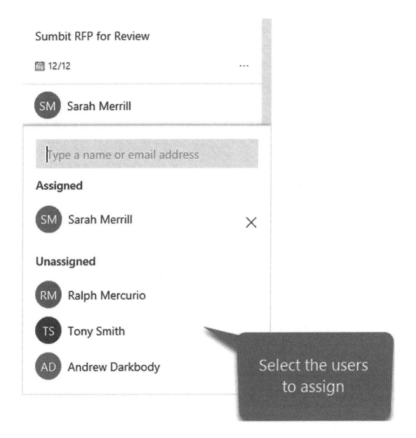

Figure 8-9. *Adding multiple members to a task*

Open the task you created before and click the "Assign to" field. A list of members will be displayed; click the user to whom you want to assign the task. You can select a single user or as many users you want by clicking their name.

Note   To remove a user from a task, open the task and hover over the "Assign to" field. Once the list of users appears, select the X to the right of their name.

Because Microsoft Planner is part of the Office 365 suite, there is tight integration with other Microsoft Office 365 applications. When a user is added to a plan or when a task gets assigned to a user, the user will receive an email in their Outlook inbox. This is great because most of us work out of our inbox and cannot be expected to check a Planner plan for tasks. Figure 8-10 shows the email that is sent to the user. Currently the email is not customizable in Microsoft Planner.

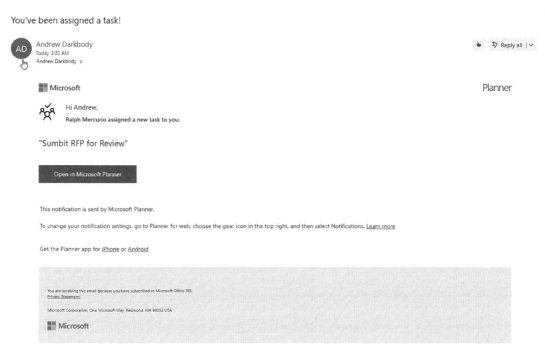

Figure 8-10. *Task assignment email from Planner*

Editing a Task

Now that you have a solid understanding of creating and assigning tasks, let's begin to edit tasks. As the creator of the task, the fields are limited to only three pertinent pieces of task information: "Task name," "Assign," and "Set a due date."

Click the task. In this case, the task is titled "Submit RFP for Review." Clicking the task opens a modal window with the ability to add more context to the task. See Figure 8-11 for the task detail window.

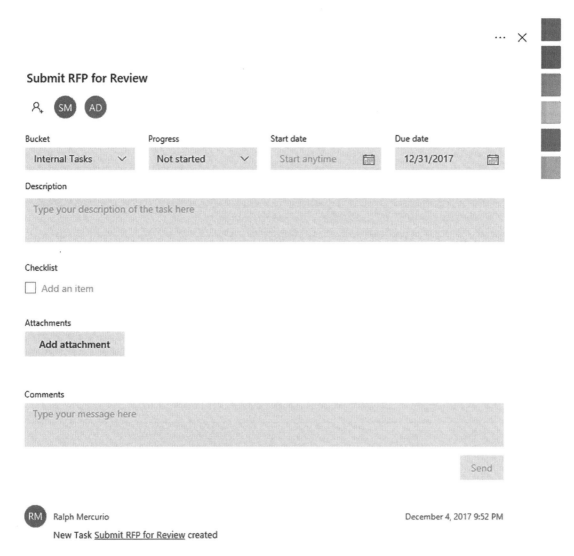

Figure 8-11. *Task detail window*

This now probably looks a lot more familiar when adding a task. Now that the task detail window is open, let's explore the areas further. The first thing you will notice is the title of the task. The members assigned are located in the upper left corner. One thing to be aware is that Office 365 displays users as initials, but you can always hover over the image of the initials and it will display the user name. If two users have the same initial,

Office 365 will use different colors for the user image. You can also remove users by clicking the image of the initials and selecting the X.

Note   By default, Office 365 will display a users' intials as their profile image. You have the ability to customize your profile picture by clicking your intitials in the upper right corner and uploading your image. The newly uploaded image will popualte across the Office 365 applications.

The first row of the Edit Task window contains four fields: Bucket, Progress, Start date, and Due date. With buckets, the task can be moved to any other bucket within the plan. It cannot be currently moved to other plans. The Progress drop-down contains three statuses: Not started, In progress, and Completed. You may have noticed that you cannot add percent complete like you can do in SharePoint or Outlook tasks. This was always one of my pet peeves with tasks; I am relieved that they decided to remove it (but it may show up in a future update). You also cannot add more statuses because these are the main three statuses that are tracked. With regards to dates, a start date can be added for when the user begins the task, and the due date can be modified as well.

Attention   Users who have access to the plan also have modify rights, including delete. These users can change due dates and any task information.

The remaining fields include Description, Checklist, Attachments, and Comments. The Description text box is used to hold the description as well as any details you feel are pertinent to the task.

The Checklist area allows the creation of checklist items. To add items to the checklist, begin typing the items where it says "Add an item." Be aware that each item added to the checklist can only be 100 characters long and cannot be assigned to other users. The checklist items and tasks are assigned to the same user(s). Once one item is added to the checklist, the "Show on card" and Checklist checkbox become active. The "Show on card" (see Figure 8-11) checkbox shows all the checklist items on the main task card while the checkbox to the left of the subtask strikes through it (completed) or not.

To further build out the exercise, I added four subtasks to the main task, "Submit RFP for Review." These subtasks are "Create RFP Team," "Meet and Draft First Version of RFP," "Meet and Compile Final Version of RFP," and finally "Submit RFP to Management Team for Review and Sign Off." Checking "Show on card" (Figure 8-12) displays the checklist items on the main task card.

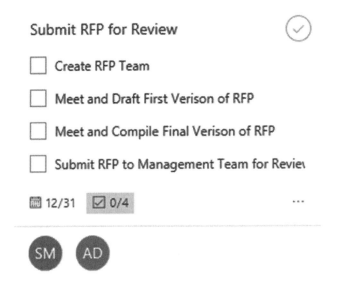

Figure 8-12. *Task with checklist items added*

When the checklist items are shown on the card, you'll see a counter (highlighted in yellow in Figure 8-12) regarding how many checklist items are completed and the total. Checklist items can also be promoted or removed completely. When hovering the mouse pointer over a checklist item, two icons will appear to the right of the item (see Figure 8-13). These icons are the garbage can and the promoted arrow. Promotion in Planner means that the checklist item becomes an actual task and is removed from the current task. You need to fill out the task details because those properties are not carried over during the promotion.

Figure 8-13. *Promoted arrow and Trash icons*

The final two fields on the task detail window are Attachments and Comments. Attachments can be a file, a link, or a SharePoint attachment. For file attachments, an Open File dialog box appears, and you simply select the file from your local computer.

A link attachment contains both an address field and text to display. For example, the link could be www.capelesssolutions.com and the text to display would be Capeless Solutions. The next attachment I find to be very clever on Microsoft's part.

When creating a plan, Microsoft creates a SharePoint site and an Office 365 Group to gather and serve as a repository for content that lives outside of Planner. I discussed SharePoint Online in Chapter 2 and Office 365 Groups in Chapter 4. SharePoint attachments point to the SharePoint document library where the content is stored. This tie into other Office 365 services allows you to leverage the document management capabilities of SharePoint Online without the headache of having to create a site for each plan.

As with checklist items, the attachments can also be shown on the main task card. However, only one attachment or the checklist can be shown. You can't currently show both checklist items and attachments. To remove or edit an attachment, hover over the attachment in the task detail view and click the ellipsis (…). You can then delete the item or edit the item as desired.

The last option in the task detail window is labels (see Figure 8-11). Planner offers six different label colors (violet, red, orange, yellow-green, green, and blue). You can add text to the label colors to denote severity or importance, but you can't change the actual color of task label.

Note   These text labels will apply to all tasks in each plan.

To edit a label, open any task in detail mode. You will notice the six label colors to the right of the task detail window (Figure 8-11). Hover over the label you want to add text to and type the specific text.

Viewing Tasks

Planner offers a quick way to view the tasks assigned to you. On the Planner dashboard, the My tasks link (see Figure 8-3) available to the left of the main dashboard will show you tasks assigned to you either grouped by plan (Figure 8-14) or grouped by progress (Figure 8-15).

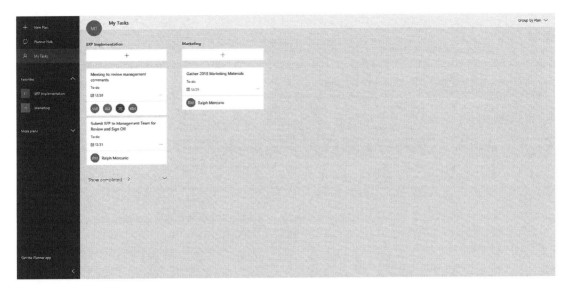

Figure 8-14. *My Tasks grouped by plan*

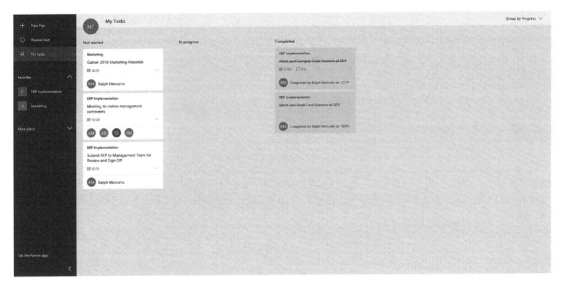

Figure 8-15. *My Tasks grouped by progress*

Another way to view tasks, not just your tasks but tasks within a plan, is to click "Planner Hub" in the leftmost menu (Figure 8-3). Now that you have created a plan, added tasks, and added it as a favorite, it will show the remaining tasks within your favorite plans; see Figure 8-16.

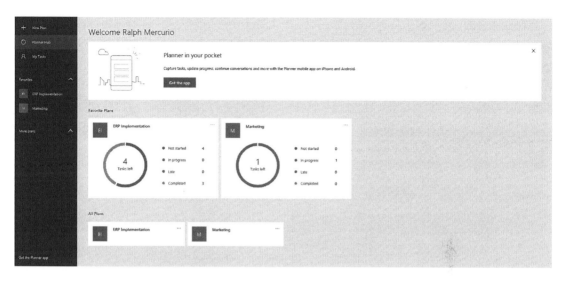

Figure 8-16. *Planner Hub with favorite plans*

As you can see, the remaining tasks inside each plan are shown in a donut chart with the appropriate status. The view does not show the tasks assigned to you but simply a count of all the tasks.

Viewing the tasks assigned to a user can be achieved in two ways. The first way is to use "Group by Assigned to" in a plan. "Group by Assigned to" will group the tasks within a plan into individual silos for each user. If a task is assigned to multiple users, the same task will be displayed in each silo.

Note   You can quickly see which tasks are assigned by clicking the use initial icon within the plan. This will shade the task box, which is assigned to a user. You can also toggle multiple user initial icons to show tasks assigned to multiple users.

Task Labels, Copy Tasks, and Delete Tasks

Planner includes three options to manage tasks within a plan. Hover over the ellipsis (...) on the main task you want to manage. Three options appear: Label, Copy task, and Delete.

You can quickly apply a label to a task. In this view, you can't edit the text label but you can do so in the task detail window, as described in the previous section.

"Copy task" allows you to copy the task. It can duplicate the task and it will allow you to copy over portions of the task. These portions include Assignment, Progress, Dates, Description, Checklist, Attachments, and Labels. It will also allow you to copy the task using a different task name. This is useful if you want to duplicate a task but change the title of the task.

The next option available via the ellipsis (…) is the Delete action. Selecting the Delete option deletes the item. Presently, Planner does not include a recycle bin or a way to recover a deleted task.

The final available option for task management is the ability to move tasks between buckets. Simply drag and drop the task into another bucket. To move a task between buckets, left-click the task and move it to the desired bucket.

Task Ordering

Planner does not automatically sort tasks in a bucket by due date, assigned to, or any other criteria. As tasks are created in a bucket, they are simply added as the first item regardless of the due date or any criteria. The tasks can be manually ordered by simply dragging the task into the correct spot.

Task Completion

You have explored creating a plan, adding buckets and tasks, and editing those tasks, but what I have not talked about is completing tasks. Tasks can be completed in a number of ways, either directly on the plan or within the task detail view. To complete a task when looking at a plan, simply hover over the task and a checkmark will appear in the upper right corner of the task; see Figure 8-17. Clicking it marks the task complete by setting the status to "Completed." Another way to complete a task is to set the Progress drop-down to Complete within the task detail.

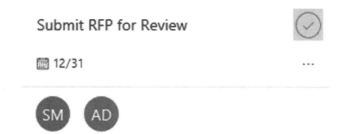

Figure 8-17. *Completing a task*

Once the task is marked complete, it will be collapsed into a completed view. You can expand the view and see all the tasks that have been completed. Figure 8-18 shows the effect of marking a task complete.

Figure 8-18. *Completed Task view*

If a task is marked complete but should not have been, anyone can set the status back to "Not started" or "In progress" in the task detail view or by viewing the completed tasks and hovering over the task. A Reactivate Task icon will become available, and the task will be marked as "Not started."

Planner Dashboards and Reporting

For the most part, you have been working in the Board view of Planner. Planner offers a Charts dashboard (Figure 8-19) to view task status, members, and group tasks by bucket, Assigned to, Progress, and Due Date.

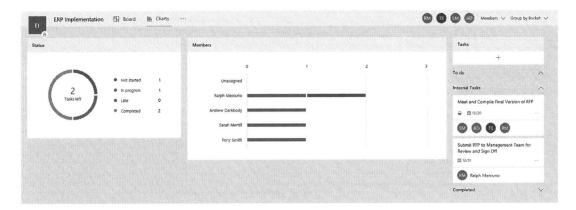

Figure 8-19. *Charts dashboard for a Planner plan*

The Charts dashboard is accessible by selecting Charts in about the center of the screen of any plan; see Figure 8-20.

Figure 8-20. *Planner Charts view*

Continuing with this example, the Charts view of the ERP plan shows a doughnut chart of task statuses and the number of tasks left in the plan. Each status is color-coded: gray for not started, blue for in progress, red for late, and green for completed. The Members line chart shows the number of tasks assigned to a member and the status of those assigned tasks. The right-most column of the Charts dashboard for the ERP plan allows for grouping by Bucket, Assigned to, Progress, Due date, and Labels.

Note   For the other tasks, I promoted the checklist items I added earlier to tasks and assigned them to members of the ERP plan.

Planner also has a calendar view called Schedule (Figure 8-21). This view displays the tasks in a calendar view based on the task details.

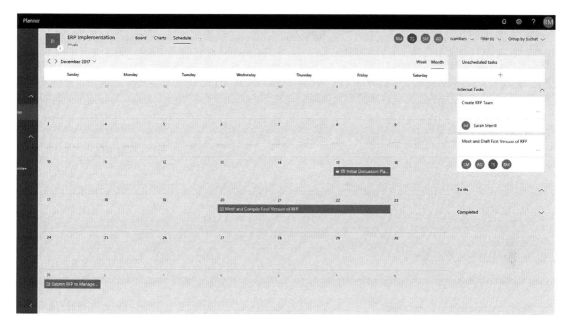

Figure 8-21. *Monthly schedule view of Planner*

This view uses the start date and due date to calculate the duration. For example, if only the start date is populated, the Schedule view will use that value and place the task on the corresponding date. If the due date is the only populated value, the task will be placed on the due date of the task. If both the start date and due date are populated, the task will appear as a duration (days in between) in the Schedule view.

Planner Integrations

As you may have noticed while reading this book, Microsoft has done a great job of building separate applications that can entirely function on their own but also can be utilized within other applications to form a cohesive collaboration toolset.

Planner is no different. As you saw at the beginning of the chapter, Planner integrates with Office 365 Groups as well as SharePoint Online. You explored both Office 365 Groups in Chapter 4 and SharePoint Online in Chapter 2; and in the later chapters you will see the integration with Microsft Flow (Chapter 11).

There is a one-to-one relationship between Office 365 Groups and Planner. Each group has a Planner plan; each time a plan is created, a correpsonding Office 365 group is created.

Exploring the Planner App

The Microsoft Planner app runs on both IOS and Android devices. The app allows you to view plans, tasks, and almost everything else you can do in the web version.

Getting the App

To get the Planner app, click the link in the lower left corner in the Planner menu; see Figure 8-3.

Upon clicking the link, a modal window opens, asking for your mobile number. Microsoft will send a download link via SMS. The apps are also available in either the Google or Apple app store.

Once the Planner app is installed, it will ask you to sign in; see Figure 8-22.

Welcome to Planner

Sign in using your work or school account

Sign in

Office

Figure 8-22. *The Sign in screen*

Signing into the Planner App

Sign in with your credentials. Once the app loads, you will be directed to the Planner Hub. Keep in mind that the experience doesn't translate fully from the web version to a mobile device. There just is not enough room to show everything on the smaller screen sizes of mobile devices.

Creating a Plan

The Planner hub on a mobile device shows the current plans. You also have the ability to create a new plan by clicking the + located in the upper right corner. The experience of creating a plan in the app is very similar to the web version; the only option not available is to "Subscribe new members to notifications emails." Once you input the plan title, privacy settings, and a description if needed, you will be directed to add members to the plan. Choose the members as you did earlier in this chapter. Once that is completed, the plan will sync with Office 365 and in moments will show up in the Planner Hub in the web version.

To explore a little deeper, go ahead and click a plan. The experience is similar, and the Planner app will render the plan that you clicked almost the same way as the web version. If you swipe left in the app, you will see the buckets and any tasks in them. By clicking and holding on the task, you can move it to another bucket.

Task Management

As with the web version, the app also allows for adding, editing, and deleting tasks. The experience is similar to the web version without any lack of capabilities.

Adding Tasks

In the Planner app, open the ERP Implementation plan you created earlier in this chapter. To open the plan, click ERP Implementation in the Planner Hub. When the plan opens, you will see the task buckets: To do and Internal Tasks. You can view the buckets by swiping left or right.

In the Internal Tasks bucket, click "Add a task…" surrounded by a red rectangle; see Figure 8-23.

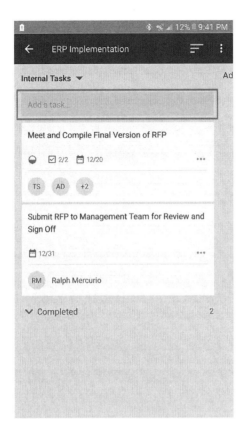

Figure 8-23. *Adding a task through the Planner app*

Clicking into "Add a task…" allows you to type the task name, set a due date, and assign to a team member of the plan; see Figure 8-24. Go ahead and add a task.

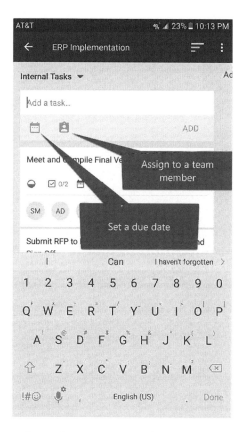

Figure 8-24. *Adding a task and its associated properties*

The task is added to the plan and in near real time is available in the web version as well.

Editing Tasks

Editing tasks are like editing tasks in the web version with near one-to-one functionality. Clicking the task in the Planner app brings up the Edit Task view; see Figure 8-25.

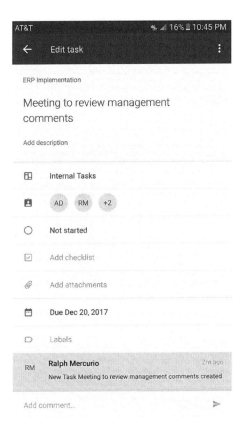

Figure 8-25. *The Edit Task window in the Planner app*

As you can see, you can do almost everything in the web version. The big difference is the experience on the mobile device vs. the desktop/laptop.

Deleting Tasks

Deleting a task can be done when the task is in edit mode. It's available via the vertical ellipsis in the upper right corner of the window.

Summary

Microsoft Planner is like the big brother to the way we have been managing tasks currently in the Microsoft ecosystem; Excel spreadsheets, Microsoft Project, Microsoft SharePoint, and Microsoft Outlook. The ability to easily create plans and group tasks together allows users everywhere to have a formidable task management system. In my opinion, what sets this apart from the other ways we have managed tasks is the Charts dashboard. The ability to report graphically without heavy customization or manipulating the data in Excel is well worth the use of Planner.

The integration with Office 365 Groups and SharePoint Online provides a cohesive set of services that can be used to support collaboration in any business environment. Instead of trying to force an application into unorthodox situations, Microsoft is utilizing all the apps to do what they do best and integrate them. Gone are the days of having super-rich feature sets with product overlap and the ensuing confusion over how to use an application.

Not only is the integration into existing services great but so is the cross-platform functionality. Whether you are using the web versions of the products in a variety of browsers (IE, Chrome, Firefox, etc.) or an array of devices utilizing the Planner app, the experience is strikingly similar. This new Microsoft is getting back to its core: building apps that accomplish a goal, not overextending apps to be overly complex.

In the next chapter, I will discuss Microsoft Stream, which allows companies to create video libraries in Office 365. This new application is built to be an enterprise video platform and improve video capabilities and delivery.

CHAPTER 9

Stream

In Chapter 8, I reviewed Planner, a new application to manage tasks within Office 365. In this chapter, I will discuss Microsoft Steam, a new application to upload and consume video. Over the past few years, video content has exploded and arguably has invaded both our personal and business life.

Video can now be produced with a smartphone, uploaded to the Web, and consumed quickly by anyone. No longer is expensive camera equipment, well-lit studio, or top-of-the-line editing equipment needed to produce video content and distribute it. Video content can be created and edited to quickly disseminate information in a new, accepted format that is consumable by almost everyone.

If you happen to be an existing subscriber to Office 365 Video, Stream is the replacement application as designated by Microsoft. Stream does have some limits, and it is essential to be aware of them prior to using Stream in a production scenario. Video files in Stream can be no larger than 50GB as of the publication of this book. I doubt that most video files you create will ever be that large, but if they are, Microsoft Stream can't support them.

There are three available plans for Stream. I will focus on Stream Plan 2 because it has a few innovative features that I will discuss in detail in this chapter.

Microsoft Stream attempts to bridge the divide for video content in a business environment by creating an innovative platform for video content. With Stream, you can search for the title of video file and you can search within a video because every video is transcribed. As I progress through the chapter, I will highlight all that Stream has to offer and how it can provide a new communication platform for any organization.

© Ralph Mercurio 2018
R. Mercurio, *Beginning Office 365 Collaboration Apps*, https://doi.org/10.1007/978-1-4842-3849-3_9

Using Microsoft Stream

In the Office 365 tenant, click the app launcher in the upper right corner and select Stream; see Figure 9-1. If you do not see Microsoft Stream, click the "All apps" link and select it from there.

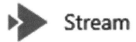

Figure 9-1. *Launching Microsoft Stream from the app launcher*

After clicking the application link, Microsoft Stream will launch as depicted in Figure 9-2.

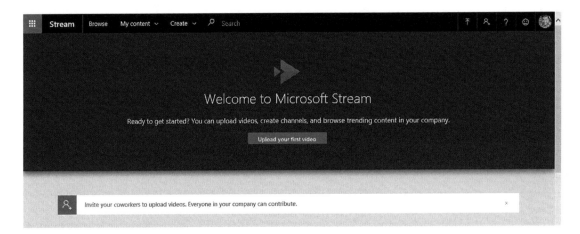

Figure 9-2. *The Microsoft Stream application*

Looking at the interface of Stream, let's review the navigation and essential elements. At first glance, there is not much happening with the application, but that is part of the simplicity of the Stream platform. Figure 9-3 depicts the primary navigation elements.

Figure 9-3. *Microsoft Stream navigation elements*

- **Browse**: Allows you to search Stream by specifying keywords and then you can sort by a variety of attributes, such as "Relevance," "Trending," "Publish date," "Views," and "Likes."

- **My content**

  - **My videos**

    This portal allows you to see the videos you have uploaded to Microsoft Stream, as shown in Figure 9-4.

Figure 9-4. *My Videos page of Microsoft Stream*

> You can also view the videos in a variety of way: "Upload date," Relevance," "Views," and "Likes." The "State" drop-down refers to if a video file is still in draft or published. If a video is marked as published, it is fully viewable and searchable by the users who have permission. Draft is the opposite state, and videos marked as draft will not be viewable by anyone except the uploader.
>
> The final available drop-down choice is Privacy. It filters the videos based on if they are viewable by everyone (company), limited, or both.

  - **My channels**

    > Channels are another foundational element of Office 365, which I discussed in Microsoft Teams. Channels in Microsoft Stream are similar and so have similar properties. In Stream, channels can be created and scoped to either the entire company, meaning that everyone has access, or scoped to an Office 365 group.

- **My watchlist**

  A watchlist is a list where video content that you want to see has been tagged for further viewing. This watchlist is also searchable and sortable via "Relevance," "Trending," "Added date," "Views," and "Likes."

- **My groups**

  Groups in Microsoft Stream are the same as Office 365 groups. Making a group via Microsoft Stream is similar to making an Office 365 group via Outlook. You will notice that every Office 365 group also has a Microsoft Stream component. Unfortunately, at the time of writing this book, the integration between the Outlook and Stream appears to be quite limited.

  I discussed Office 365 Groups in Chapter 4. I will also discuss channel management later in this chapter.

  Be aware that deleting a group via Microsoft Stream will also delete the corresponding Office 365 group. This includes deletion of conversations, files, sites, etc.

- **Followed channels**

  Followed channels are channels that you have selected to follow and get notifications from. The followed channel list can be searched and sorted by "Number of Followers," "Number of videos," and "Relevance."

- **Create**

  - **Upload a video**

    Allows you to upload a video to Microsoft Stream. This will be discussed later in this chapter.

- **Create a channel**

  Creating a channel allows similar content to be classified together. This makes it easy to find content on a specific topic. Creating channels is also discussed later in the chapter.

- **Create a group**

    This link allows you to create an Office 365 group via Microsoft Stream. This group retains all the properties of an Office 365 group but can also leverage Stream to upload and play video content.

- **Search**

    Allows you to search Stream by specifying keywords and then you can also sort by a variety of attributes. You can sort the result set by "Relevance," "Trending," "Publish date," "Views," and "Likes."

Walking Through Stream

Even though Stream is centered around video content through a simple, clean interface, let's go through the process of uploading a video, creating a channel, and navigating around Stream.

Uploading Your First Video

To upload a video to Stream, either select the "Upload video" link located within the "Create navigational element" area, as discussed, or drag the file onto the My videos pages. Instead of the traditional upload form with a variety of fields, Microsoft presents just a page (Figure 9-5) where a file can be dragged onto, or you can choose to upload files through a Window Explorer-like interface.

Figure 9-5. *Uploading a video file to Microsoft Stream*

Once a file is uploaded by either dragging the file or uploading a selected file, you must populate the details of the video file, as shown in Figure 9-6.

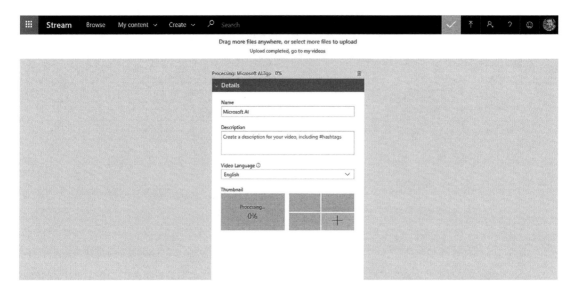

Figure 9-6. *Populating the details of an uploaded video*

Provide the name, description, video language, and thumbnail. The thumbnails auto-generate, but you can also specify your own. You also need to set the appropriate permissions. By default, videos are viewable to the entire organization, but you can share the video with a specific group, channel, or set of people.

Note   You can share with a combination of channels, groups, and people so that you can upload and post to specific areas of Microsoft Stream instead of the traditional method of sharing with users.

There are three options available under the Options heading. By default, Comments and Captions are enabled. These settings allow others to post comments, thus creating another way users can collaborate and post feedback throughout Stream.

Creating a Channel

As discussed, channels are a way to group videos that have a similar context, department, or theme. To create a new channel, click the "Create a channel" link under the Create navigational element. Once you click the link, you will be presented with the Create a Channel interface depicted in Figure 9-7.

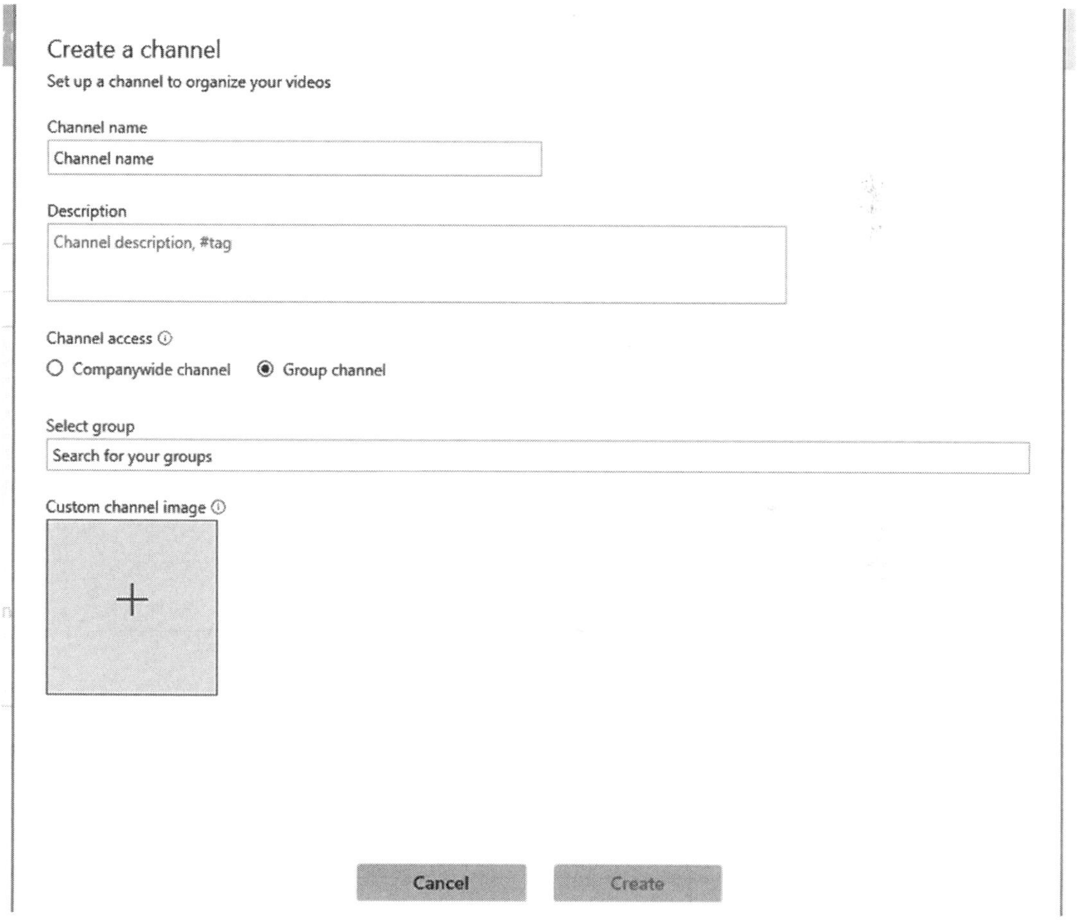

Figure 9-7. *Creating a new channel in Microsoft Stream*

When creating the channel, you need to specify a channel name and, if desired, a description. Select either "Companywide channel" or "Group channel" under Channel access. A companywide channel allows anyone in the organization who has access to Stream to upload and watch videos. This option might be preferable in some circumstances, but I would venture to say that corporate communications would like to check for content and message. With that, you can also select Group channel, which

241

allows a group to manage videos; this option limits who can view or post and only users who have access to the group also have access to the channel.

You also have the option to choose a channel image. Once you are satisfied with your settings, press the Create button. You can also access your channels by selecting the "My channels" link under the My content heading.

Creating a Group

Group creation in Microsoft Stream is similar to creating an Office 365 group in that it shares some of the familiar settings but because this group is being created in Stream, it also presents you with some Stream-only options, as I will discuss shortly.

To create a group within Microsoft Stream, click "Create a group" from the Create navigational heading. The "Create a group" interface looks like Figure 9-8.

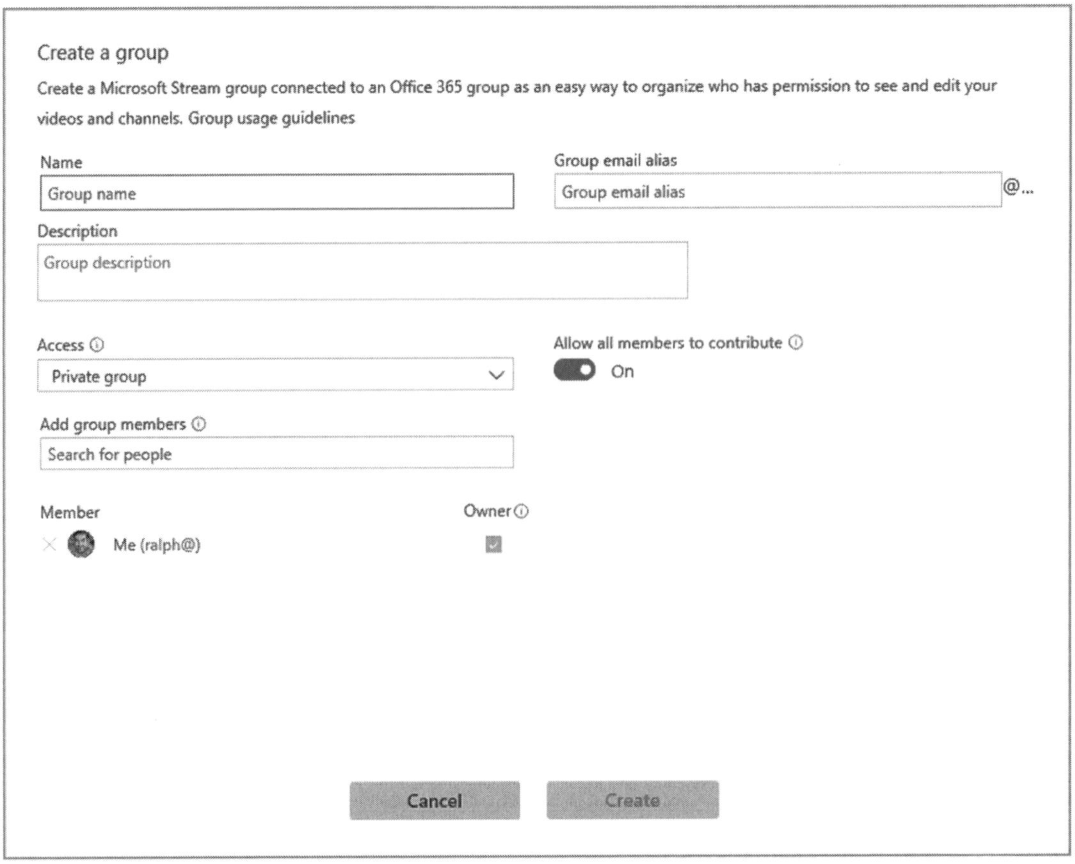

Figure 9-8. *Creating a group in Microsoft Stream*

242

To create the group, you need to specify a name and a group email alias, making sure that the alias is a unique email address. Also, you may include a description of the group if desired. As with creating an Office 365 Group, you need to choose either a private or public group, which is available from the Access drop-down. To recap, a public group is a group that is searchable and anyone can join. In a private group, the members must be invited to participate.

The "Allow all members to contribute" toggle button is only available when creating a group within Microsoft Stream. This group setting by default (On) gives all members of the group the ability to upload videos, delete videos, create and delete channels, and edit the membership of the group; if that is not a desired scenario, set the toggle to Off.

Interacting with Videos

Uploading and categorizing content is just one part of Microsoft Stream. The other part is interacting with content and finding the relevant content. As you saw with Microsoft teams and chats, liking, following, and commenting on comments provides a rich collaboration environment, and Stream aims to do the same for videos.

Commenting on a Video

Commenting on a video is similar to commenting in the other Microsoft Office 365 products. In order to comment on a video, select any video in Microsoft Stream. Once the video is loaded, click "Comment," as shown in Figure 9-9.

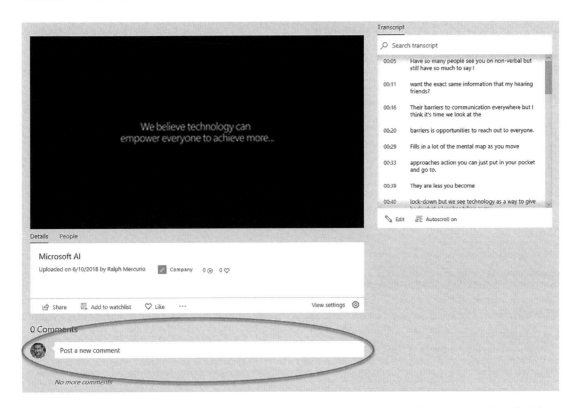

Figure 9-9. *Commenting on a video, as seen in a screenshot from the video "AI for Accessibility" recorded by Microsoft for Build 2019*

At the time of writing this book, Microsoft Stream only supports comments in plain text. Plain text refers strictly to text without the ability to embellish, such as using bold or italics, changing the font, or embedding documents or links to other content. Once you have typed your comment, select "Post" in the lower right corner.

Your comment will be posted, and if needed you will be able to edit or delete the comment.

Liking a Video

Liking a video in Stream increases its relevancy and also gives a user the ability to refine when searching because likes is one of the search refiners. By liking videos, it shows that the content is relevant and that it might be useful to others. In order to like a video, browse for the video you want to like, and choose "Like," as shown in Figure 9-10.

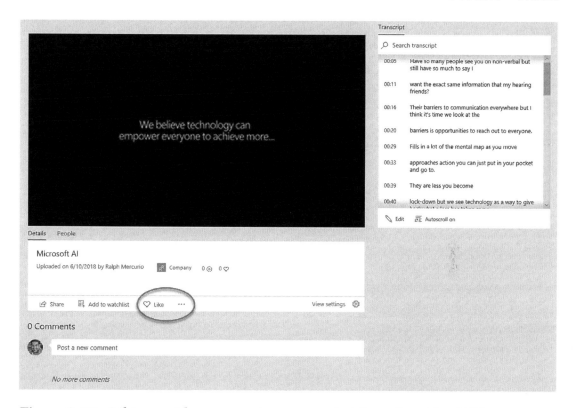

Figure 9-10. *Liking a video, as seen in a screenshot from the video "AI for Accessibility" recorded by Microsoft for Build 2019*

Choosing "Like" will toggle the like button to "Liked." If needed, you can also unlike a previously liked video.

Adding a Video to Your Watchlist

Watchlists are a great feature because they allow you to save videos to watch at a later date. As discussed, the watchlist can be sorted by a variety of refiners as well as full index searching. In order to save a video to your watchlist, select "Add to watchlist," as shown in Figure 9-11.

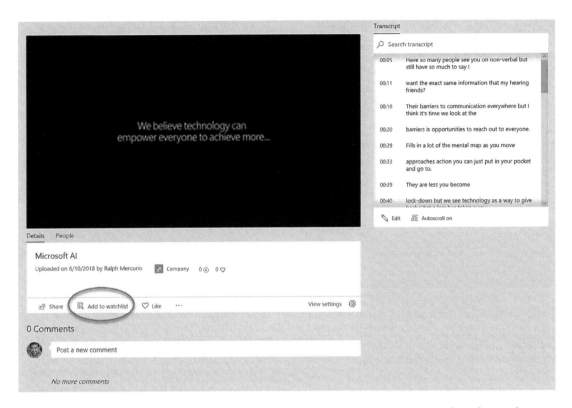

Figure 9-11. *Adding a video to your watchlist, as seen in a screenshot from the video "AI for Accessibility" recorded by Microsoft for Build 2019*

Similar to liking a video, you can also remove a video from your watchlist by selecting "Remove from watchlist." Videos can also be removed from your watchlist by selecting the "Remove from watchlist" icon when viewing the watchlist.

Transcript

Microsoft Stream introduces the ability for videos to be transcribed. A searchable transcript is generated automatically without any user interaction. The transcript is also searchable so any search terms in the transcript will be found and shown in the specific time location. In order to view the transcript if it is not being shown, enable it via the cog in the lower right corner, as shown in Figure 9-12.

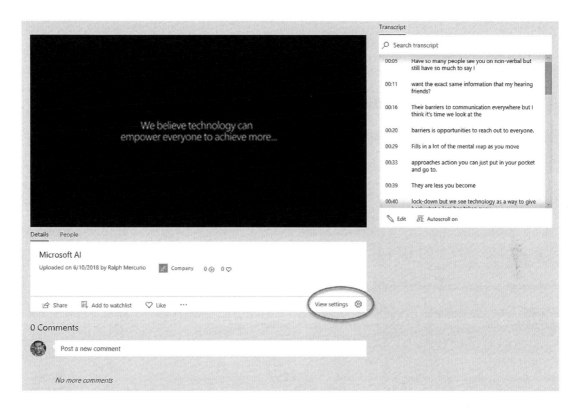

Figure 9-12. *Showing the transcription for a video, as seen in a screenshot from the video "AI for Accessibility" recorded by Microsoft for Build 2019*

The transcript autoscrolls as the video is playing so it can be consumed. Microsoft Stream gives you the option to disable the auto scroll so you can scroll to any point of the transcription whether the video is currently playing or not.

As with any transcription service, the success rate varies, and a number of factors play a role in how well it is transcribed. At this point, technology still can't replace a person, but as innovations occur, the service will ultimately get better. Because of this, Microsoft Stream allows you to edit the transcription of any video by selecting the text in the transcription and choosing "Edit."

When the transcription is in Edit mode and a specific section is highlighted, two icons will appear to the right of the selected text, as shown in Figure 9-13.

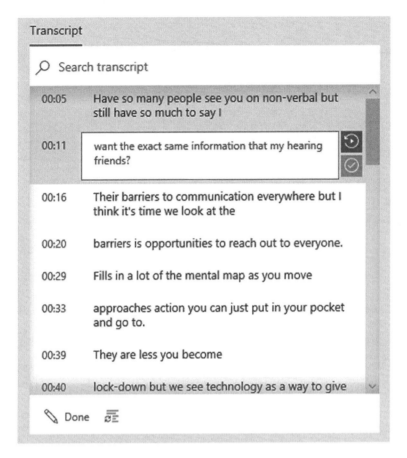

Figure 9-13. *Editing a transcription*

The top icon plays the video at the specific point of the transcription. The bottom icon acknowledges the transcription is correct and verified. Edit the text as needed; when complete, select "Done" in the bottom left corner of the transcript.

Note   This feature is not perfect. I have noticed that it struggles a little bit to transcribe each word correctly when there is background music or accents.

People

Microsoft also introduced a new feature into Stream called People. This new feature analyzes the video and detects the people in the video using face-detection algorithms. At this point, it cannot tell who the person in the video is but will show you the periods of time when the person's face is shown in the video and length of time, as shown in Figure 9-14.

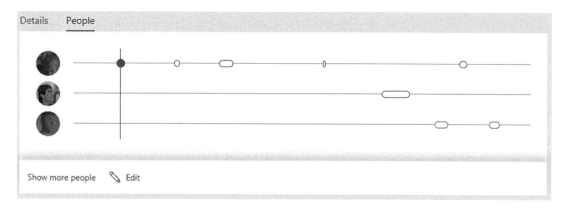

Figure 9-14. *Face detection in a video in Microsoft Stream*

To view this feature, click "People" located directly below the video, as shown in Figure 9-14. By default, it only shows a few people, but it does detect every face occurrence and catalogs them all. To see the entire list of people that were recognized, click "Show more people."

Since this feature is still relatively new, it isn't perfect yet. Because of this, you can edit the dataset and merge multiple face recognitions into one person if the service miscategorized them by clicking Edit.

Accessibility in Stream

Ensuring that all users can create and consume content is the main priority for not only organizations but also Office 365. Microsoft introduced features that make accessibility a priority and allow all users to be part of the experience.

Closed Captioning

Closed captioning, which has been around since the 1970s, aims to transcribe the speech portion of a broadcast or video and display it on the screen for people who have hearing limitations. With Microsoft Stream, closed captioning is available for any video uploaded.

To enable closed captioning for a video, click the Closed Captioning icon displayed in Figure 9-15. Likewise, to disable closed captioning for the video, click the same icon.

Figure 9-15. *Enable/disable closed captioning for a video*

Note   By default, closed captioning is not enabled for a video, but the user can select it to show.

By accessing the cog next to the Closed Captioning button, you can also change the look and feel of the captions. You have control over the size of text, color, and background transparency setting.

Screen Readers

Many users around the world use screen readers to aid them in their day-to-day tasks. Screen readers allow the text displayed in Windows, a web page, etc. to be read aloud to the user. Microsoft Stream supports many screen readers to aid the user in both consuming video content and navigating around the application.

High Contrast

Microsoft Stream supports high contrast scenarios set at the operating system level. For example, in Windows 10 you can access the High Contrast settings shown in Figure 9-16 by searching for "High Contrast" in the Windows 10 search bar located next to the Windows Start menu.

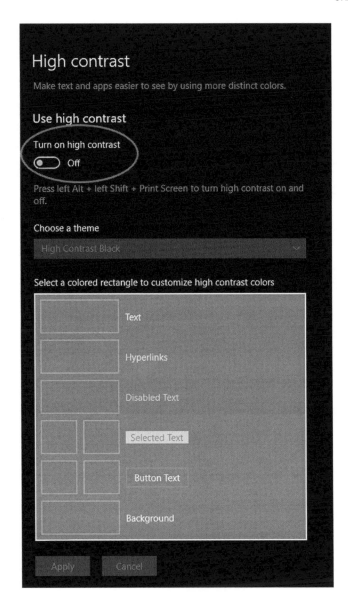

Figure 9-16. *High contrast settings in Windows 10*

After enabling the high contrast settings, Stream will adjust and display in high contrast mode, as shown in Figure 9-17.

Figure 9-17. *Viewing Stream in high contrast mode*

Keyboard Navigations

Microsoft Stream supports keyboard navigations and hotkeys to control the video or choose a specific element of Microsoft Stream. For instance, while a video is playing, the hotkeys in Table 9-1 become active.

Table 9-1. *Microsoft Stream Hotkeys*

Hotkey	Hot Key Action
F	Exits full-screen mode
M	Mutes the video
Up arrow/down arrow	Increases/decreases volume
Left arrow/right arrow	Rewind/Fast-forward
Numbers (0,1,2,3,4,5,6,7,8,9)	Quick jump to the percentage of the video. For example, pressing 4 jumps the video to the 40% played mark and begins to play from there.
Spacebar	Pauses/plays the current video

With keyboard navigation, pressing Tab advances the cursor to the next element on the page; pressing Shift+Tab moves the cursor to the previous element. This is like pressing Tab in other applications. Clicking the space bar resembles a left-mouse click.

Integrations with Other Office 365 Apps

Other Office 365 applications are making guest appearances in other apps. You saw that Planner is a supporting app in Office 365 Groups and that Planner is also available within Microsoft Teams. Stream is no different; it is a stand-alone enterprise video platform, but it can be integrated into other applications to provide a video platform and capabilities.

The first integration is with SharePoint. As you saw in Chapter 2, SharePoint has many web parts that can be added to a site to provide some context. SharePoint Online has a Stream web part that can be configured to show a single video or videos from a specific channel. To add the Stream web part, put the SharePoint page in edit mode and add a web part. Select the Stream web part; upon adding it to the page, the web part properties will appear as shown in Figure 9-18.

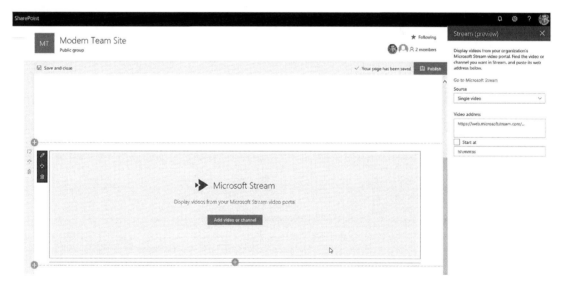

Figure 9-18. *Adding Stream to a SharePoint site*

Select "Single video" or "Channel" from the Source drop-down. You must also specify the video or channel URL in the Video address text box. Hopefully, in a future update, you will not have to specify the URL and will be able to select it directly.

With Microsoft Teams, Stream is available to add as a tab within a team; I discussed teams in Chapter 5. Navigate to any of your teams and select the + sign next to Wiki. Select Stream from the available options. After selecting Stream, you will be presented with a modal window titled Stream; you need to provide the tab name and the URL, as shown in Figure 9-19.

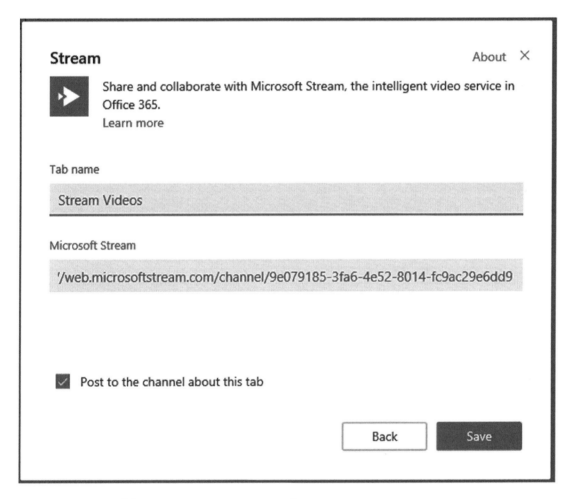

Figure 9-19. *Adding Stream to a Microsoft team*

Once you specify the appropriate values and press the Save button in the lower right corner, a new tab is added and displayed as shown in Figure 9-20.

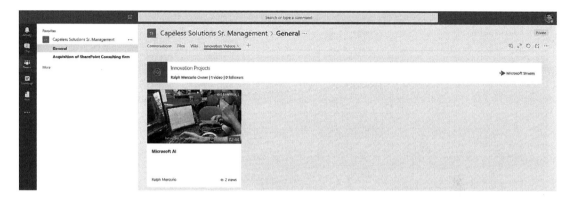

Figure 9-20. *Stream integrated with Mircosoft Teams*

As videos are uploaded to Stream and tagged with the appropriate channel, teams will be able to update itself with the current videos. Part of the allure of this integration is that video files are stored on the appropriate enterprise product and not stored and uploaded to Microsoft teams or stored in a document library.

Summary

Microsoft Stream is the next-level video platform that enterprises need. Gone are the days of storing videos on YouTube or buying expensive video platforms. Stream provides needed capabilities such as transcription, facial recognition, and ways to group videos together through channels.

Even though Stream is still relatively new, it is based on the current Office 365 video product titled Video. Microsoft learned its lessons with Video, responded to customer feedback, and crafted a powerful application that is more than suited to handle the video needs of an enterprise moving forward.

In the next chapter, I will discuss Microsoft Forms, which is also relatively new to Office 365 and is designed to provide an interface (forms) to collect information from users.

CHAPTER 10

Forms

In Chapter 9, I discussed Stream, which provides video capabilities and a platform for enterprises. Microsoft Forms is a new application from Microsoft that is used to create forms and surveys to collect information and quizzes that can be shared and graded. Forms is built to with a mobile-first approach, ensuring that it works not only on the mobile platform but also on many other devices.

A distinction needs to be made before we start and that is that Microsoft Forms is not an InfoPath replacement. There are similarities between the two, but the intended purpose of Microsoft Forms is for quizzes, surveys, and polls. Microsoft is moving in the direction of using PowerApps to be the replacement for InfoPath, the last released version of which was included in Office 2013.

In this chapter, you will create a form to collect responses from employees about the annual company picnic, exploring the available data types you can use to create the questions. You will also create a quiz to demonstrate how quizzes can be created and graded. Finally, you will look at the reporting features so you can view metrics about the forms.

Using Microsoft Forms

In the Office 365 tenant, click the app launcher in the upper right corner and select Microsoft Forms; see Figure 10-1.

Figure 10-1. *Microsoft Forms application*

© Ralph Mercurio 2018

R. Mercurio, *Beginning Office 365 Collaboration Apps*, https://doi.org/10.1007/978-1-4842-3849-3_10

Once you click the application, you will be presented with the Forms dashboard (see Figure 10-2). This dashboard allows you to create a new form, search for existing forms, or create a new quiz.

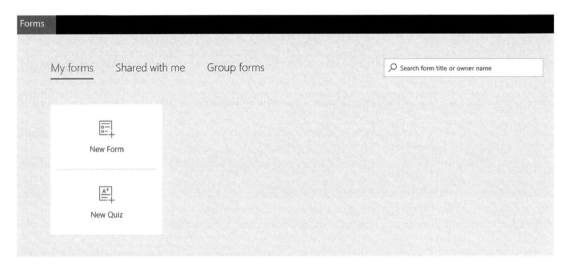

Figure 10-2. *Microsoft Forms application dashboard*

You can also review forms that someone has shared with you by clicking "Other Forms." The third option, Group forms, shows any forms that exisit in Office 365 Groups.

Editing Mode

When editing or creating a form or quiz, the Preview, Theme, Share, and ellipsis (...) options (Figure 10-3) become available.

Figure 10-3. *Microsoft Forms dashboard menu*

The Preview button allows you to preview the form to see how your form or quiz renders. The Preview mode offers an interesting function: it allows you to preview the form on both a typical mobile device and a computer.

The Theme button allows you to change the look and feel of the form. You can select from an available theme or upload your own image to use as a background image. If you choose to add an image, you can connect to the Bing search engine for pictures, One Drive, or your local computer. Currently, you can only upload one picture to create a custom theme.

The Share button allows you to share your completed form or quiz in various ways (Figure 10-4) with any user. The form or quiz can be shared internally or externally because the object is hosted within Office 365, so the object can be filled out from anywhere. The form can also be sent via email with a link, embedded in a web page, accessed via QR code (barcode), or the link can be shared.

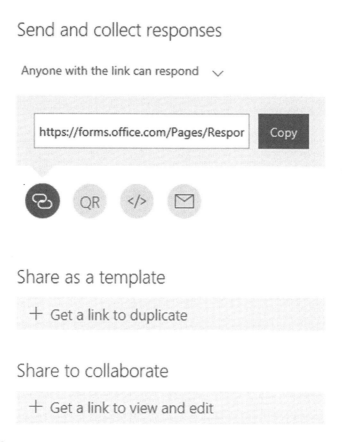

Figure 10-4. *Sharing menu*

Part of collaboration is the ability to share your data with others. By sending the "Share as a template" link, other users can duplicate your form and use it as a base for their own form. By selecting the "Share to collaborate" link, you can send the form to others to edit the questions and/or add values to the questions.

The ellipsis (…) (Figure 10-3) offers some additional functionality when the form in edit mode. The first advanced option is called branching. This allows you to configure the form so that after a question is answered you can direct the user to another question, meaning that the form does not need to be completed in sequential order. For example, if the form contains a question that asks the user if they are in favor of working remotely, a yes or no answer could direct them to a different set of questions or end the form completely.

The second advanced feature is the Settings menu. These options let you allow anyone to fill out the form (anonymous) or restrict it to just internal company users. This setting isn't permanent; when you go to share the form you can change the option. This simply sets the default for the form.

The options for responses mean you can accept responses, the Start date and End date of when the form can be filled out, whether to shuffle or lock the questions, and if you want to receive a notification of each response. These advanced settings are useful if you need the form filled out prior to a deadline.

Creating Your First Form

Click the New Form (Figure 10-5) button to create your first form. Give your form a title by clicking "Untitled form" and changing the text to "Annual Company Picnic." It's also a wise choice to give the form a description, so edit the description to "Basic Survey Form." See Figure 10-6.

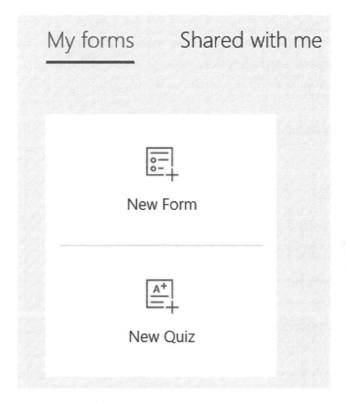

Figure 10-5. *Creating a new form*

Questions	Responses

Untitled form

Enter a description

+ Add question

Figure 10-6. *Editing the title and description*

Clicking the new form creates an empty form that you will add your questions to. Note that there are two tabs: Questions and Responses. Within the Questions tabs, you add your questions to create the form. The Responses tab, discussed later in this chapter, shows the responses to the form in a graphical format.

Before you get involved crafting the form, let's add a title and description to the form. This is done by editing the first textbox and entering a description below it. You can also add an image to the area by clicking the image icon in the title textbox.

In the next section, I will discuss the available data types and how they can be used to craft forms and quizzes.

Data Types

On the form, select "+ Add question." In the resulting menu (Figure 10-7), each button represents a different data type that can be used in your form. These data types control the way a user can respond.

Figure 10-7. *Microsoft Forms data types*

Choice

Choice is the basic multiple-choice data type we all know. A predetermined set of choices is presented and a user selects one of them (or multiple selections, if allowed). These details are controlled in the interface (Figure 10-8).

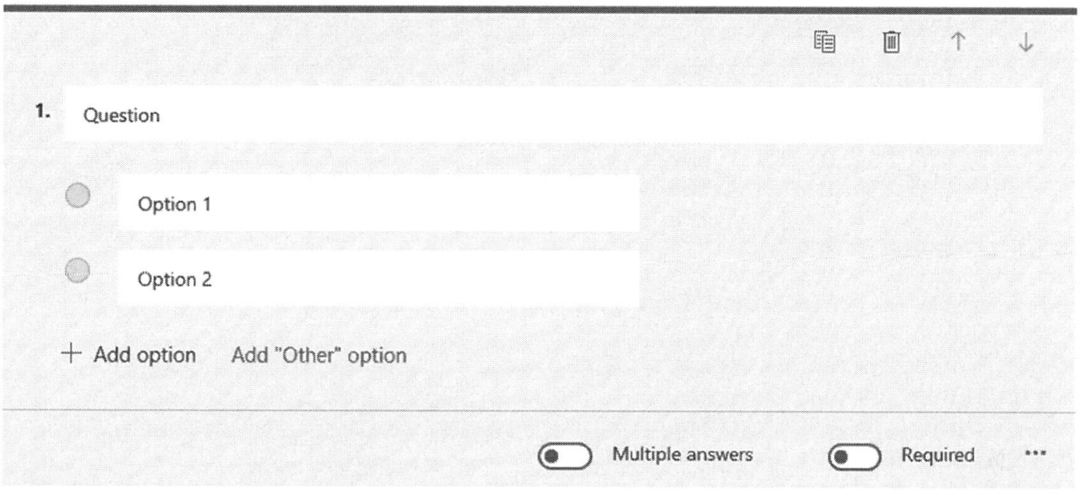

Figure 10-8. *The choice data type*

With this data type, Microsoft Forms allows two options: "Multiple answers" and "Required." Selecting "Multiple answers" allows the submitter to select more than one choice. You will notice that the radio buttons turn into checkboxes when "Multiple answers" is selected.

Multiple answers are useful when there is more than one choice that could be selected or a submitter can select multiple correct answers to a question. Selecting the "Required" toggle forces the user to answer the question; the form can't be submitted if the question is not answered. Selecting the ellipsis (…) shows the options to add a subtitle and set the questions to shuffle, which presents the options in a different order to individuals.

For this exercise, let's create a survey to gather information from employees about the annual company picnic. For the choice datatype, add two choice questions:

Question 1: Are you likely to attend this year's company picnic?

- **Choice Options**: Yes, No

- **Allow Multiple Choices**: No

- **Required**: No

Question 2: Please select an activity which you will like to participate in?

- **Choice Options**: Basketball, Bocce, Horseshoes

    - **Select "Add "Other" Option" to add a freeform field**

- **Allow Multiple Choices**: No

- **Required**: Yes

Once you are satisfied with the entering of the question and choices, select "Add question" and add another question using the date data type.

Questions also contain three other functions: copying a question, deleting a question via the Trashcan icon, and moving the question up or down in the form; see Figure 10-9.

Figure 10-9. *Question options*

Note   When creating questions, you can also insert a video or image into the question. This is done by selecting the Image icon to the right of the text box.

Date

The date data type allows a user to answer the question with a date (Figure 10-10). Unlike the other data types, the configuration is quite limited to a question field and a date field. This data type also has the Required switch.

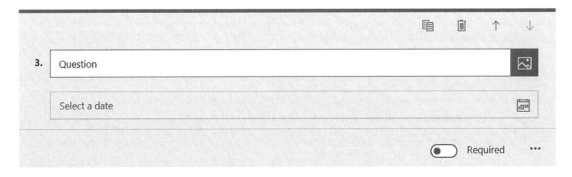

Figure 10-10. *The date data type*

Question 3: Select the date that would be best for the company picnic.

- **Required**: Yes

- **Subtitle**: Please select a date in June 2018, July 2018, or August 2018

Rating

The rating data type (Figure 10-11) asks users to rate using either the familiar stars or numbers. The form creator has the option to display 5 or 10 stars or numbers. Utilizing 10 stars is effectivity a scale of 1 to 10.

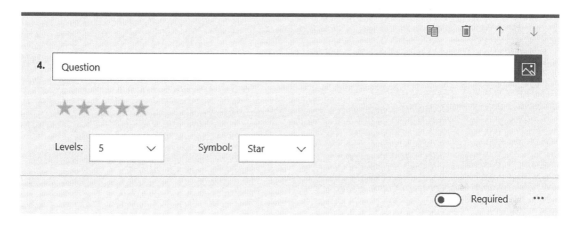

Figure 10-11. *The rating data type*

Selecting the ellipsis (...) presents the opportunity to add labels to your rating. Labels help define what a single star/number is in terms of the lowest and highest.

Question 4: How would you rate last year's company picnic activities?

- **Required**: Yes

- **Symbol**: Star

- **Labels**:

  - **1 Star**: Bad

  - **10 Stars**: Excellent

Text

The text data type allows free entry of data and doesn't have preset options like the choice data type. This data type has similar options to the choice data type (Figure 10-12).

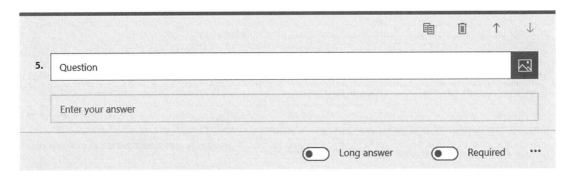

Figure 10-12. *The text data type*

The text data type does contain a "Long answer" toggle. Selecting this toggle increases the number of lines available for the user to fill out. This is preferred because you do not want to abruptly cut off an answer unless there is absolute certainty that the answer will be short.

Selecting the ellipsis (…) presents the option to restrict the data entered to a restriction value. The restrictions are limited to numbers only and cannot be used to restrict text.

Question 5: Please describe the best part of last year's annual outing.

Long answer: Yes

Required: Yes

Ranking

The ranking data type (Figure 10-13) allows the options to be sorted or ranked in an order. This is useful if you are trying to schedule a team meeting. Submitters can sort the available times from best to worst time slots.

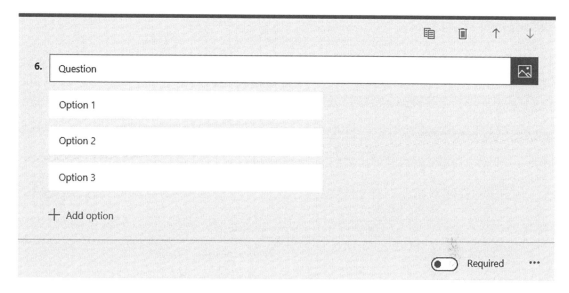

Figure 10-13. *The ranking data type*

The ranking data type does not contain any other configurable properties besides Required and Subtitle.

Note   One issue with the ranking data type is that if the field is set to Required, the order must be changed and set back to the default if the submitter agrees to that ranking.

To complete the form, use the following values for Question 6:

Question 6: Please rank the following food options from most desirable to least.

- **Required**: Yes

- **Options**: Seafood, Barbeque, Vegan, Italian, Sandwiches

Likert

Microsoft Forms also includes the Likert (Figure 10-14) data type. This datatype is available by clicking the ellipsis when adding a question. This data type strives to gauge a response by having the user select one of the corresponding options.

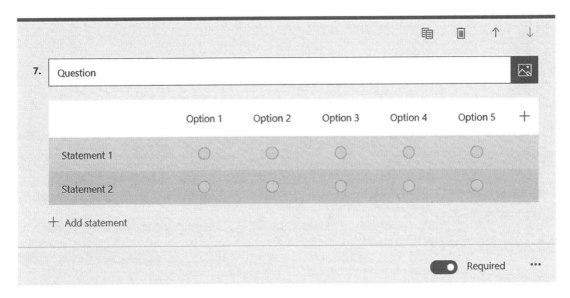

Figure 10-14.   *The Likert data type*

You aren't going to use the Likert data type in your survey but let's review the configuration of it. The keys to this data type are both the options and statements. The options are the gauge and are most commonly "Strongly Disagree," "Disagree," "Neutral," "Agree," and "Strongly Agree." You can have more but I think five is the perfect level of granularity and offers clear definitive lines between the options. The statements of the Linkrt data type are the statements that are gauges by the user.

Once all the questions have been entered, your form should like Figure 10-15.

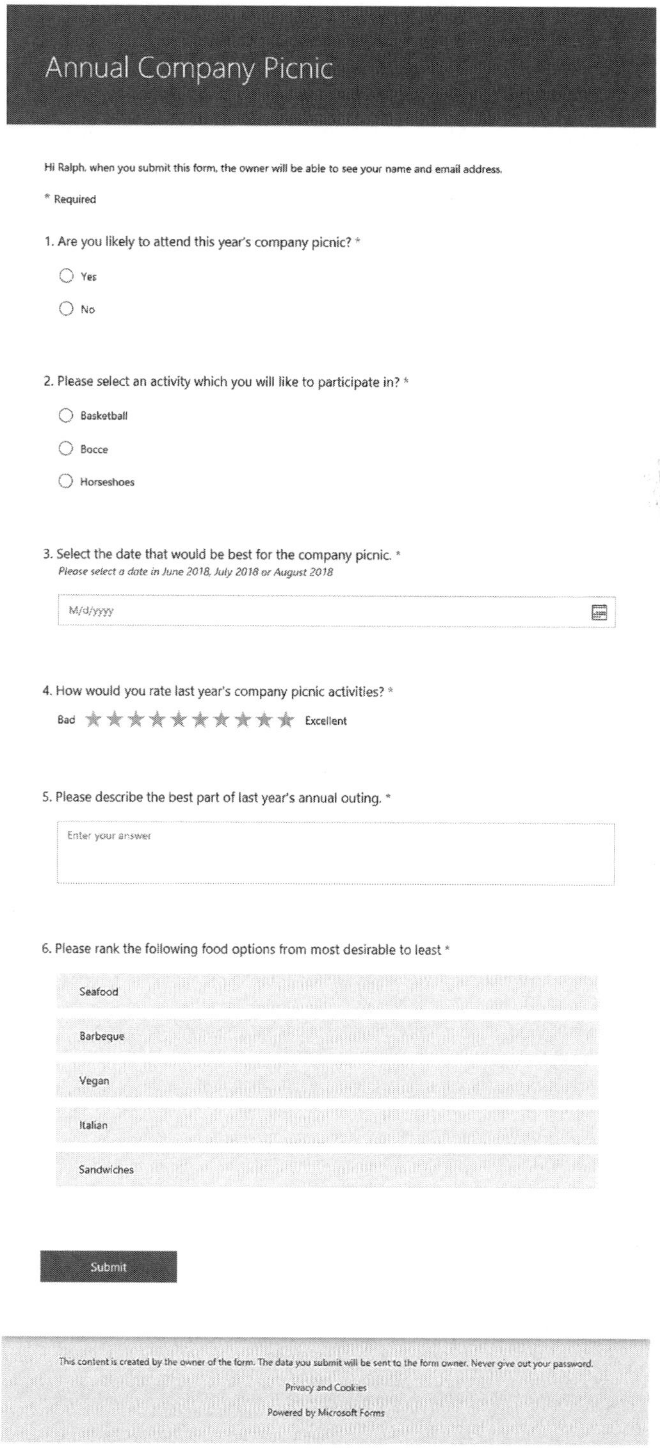

Annual Company Picnic

Hi Ralph, when you submit this form, the owner will be able to see your name and email address.

* Required

1. Are you likely to attend this year's company picnic? *

○ Yes

○ No

2. Please select an activity which you will like to participate in? *

○ Basketball

○ Bocce

○ Horseshoes

3. Select the date that would be best for the company picnic. *
Please select a date in June 2018, July 2018 or August 2018

| M/d/yyyy | 📅 |

4. How would you rate last year's company picnic activities? *

Bad ☆ ☆ ☆ ☆ ☆ ☆ ☆ ☆ ☆ ☆ Excellent

5. Please describe the best part of last year's annual outing. *

| Enter your answer |

6. Please rank the following food options from most desirable to least *

| Seafood |
| Barbeque |
| Vegan |
| Italian |
| Sandwiches |

Submit

This content is created by the owner of the form. The data you submit will be sent to the form owner. Never give out your password.

Privacy and Cookies

Powered by Microsoft Forms

Figure 10-15. *The completed Annual Company Picnic form*

Branching

Microsoft Forms contains a feature called branching. This feature allows you to tailor the questions asked or to end the form based on an answer to a question. This feature can be used in forms, surveys, or quizzes.

In this example, let's create a new form titled "Company Picnic Survey." Create the following questions with the following details:

Question 1: Did you attend the company picnic last year?

- **Data Type**: Choice

- **Choice Options**: Yes, No

- **Allow Multiple Choices**: No

- **Required**: No

Question 2: Why did you not attend the company picnic last year?

- **Data type**: Text

- **Long Answer**: Yes

Your finished form should look like Figure 10-16.

Figure 10-16. *Company Picnic Survey with branching*

Now that the form is created, let's add branching logic to the form to end the survey for users who answer "Yes" to the first question. By doing so, users will not have to worry about answering the second question, which in this context means nothing to them.

To add branching to the form, click the settings (...) located in the upper right corner when the form is in edit mode. Clicking the Branching option reveals the interface in Figure 10-17.

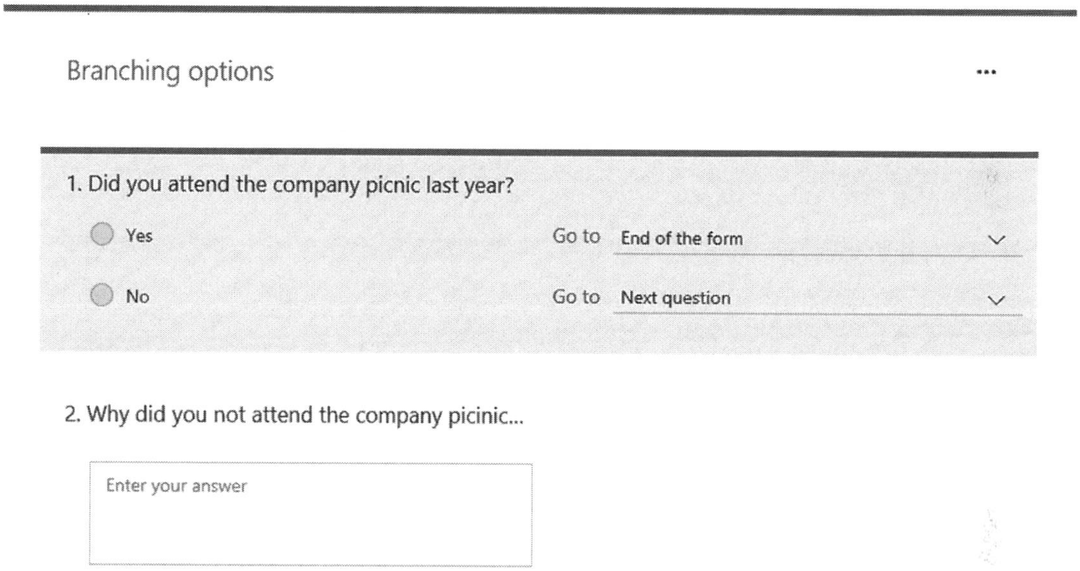

Figure 10-17. *The Branching interface*

Based on your example, when a user answers Yes to question 1, you want to skip the next question and end the form for the user. In Question 1 of the form, select "End of the form" from the "Go to" drop-down on the Yes row. The branching logic should now look like Figure 10-18.

Branching options   •••

1. Did you attend the company picnic last year?

○ Yes   Go to   End of the form   ⌄

○ No   Go to   2. Why did you not attend the company pic... ⌄

2. Why did you not attend the company picnic l...

```
Enter your answer



```

Figure 10-18. *Branching logic added to a form*

Once the logic is added, click the Back button in the interface and it will reload the form in edit mode. Go ahead and preview the form; if done correctly, Question 2 will be hidden unless you select "No" for the first question.

Note   If you make a mistake in the branching logic, you can reset all the branching logic by selecting the ellipsis (…) in the Branching Options interface and select "Reset."

Quizzes

Quizzes and forms are quite similar and share the corresponding Microsoft Forms platform. A big difference between a quiz and form is that the quiz can be auto-graded (provided you specify the answers) and the results can be shown automatically at the end of the quiz or after the author has marked them. The settings for the quiz can be selected from the ellipsis (…) when the quiz is being created. The default setting is that responders will see their results upon completion. See Figure 10-19.

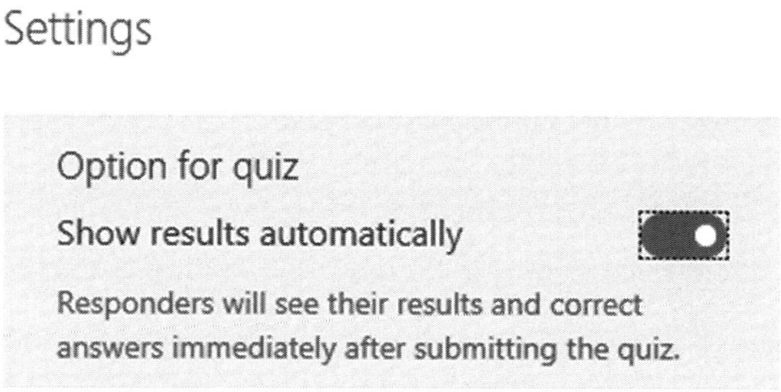

Settings

Figure 10-19. *Grading options for a quiz*

Quizzes are extremely useful in the workplace or classroom. One excellent use of them is to test the knowledge of an employee after human resources or safety training. Obtaining a certain percentage shows understanding of a concept. The quiz can even be restricted so it can be filled out only once by a person once their quiz is graded. You will explore more of quizzes when you build a sample quiz shortly. See Figure 10-20.

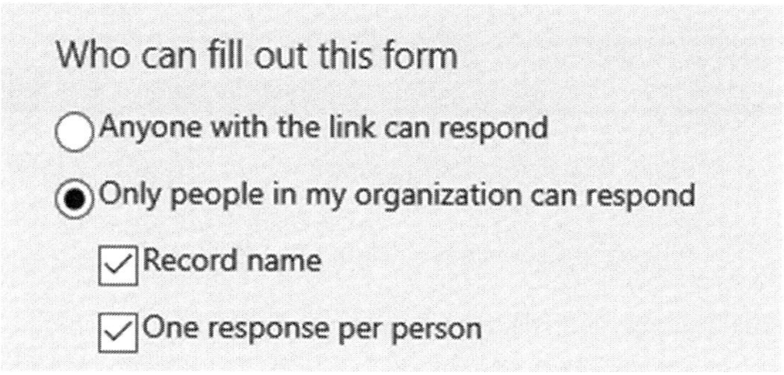

Figure 10-20. *Who can take the quiz*

The data types are the same as when creating a form: choice, text, rating, date, ranking, and Likert. However, quizzes contain some special elements that you will explore further. To explore the full feature set of quizzes, you will construct a quiz that will be used in an educational setting.

Creating Your First Quiz

On the Microsoft Forms dashboard, select "New Quiz." This creates an empty quiz where you can enter the questions and answers. Start by changing the title of "Untitled Quiz" to "Weekly Quiz" by clicking "Untitled Quiz" and entering the new title.

Add your first question. Click "Add Question" and select the choice data type. Use the following data for the question:

Question 1: Which numbers are divisible by 3?

- **Answers**: 3,5,7,9,23

- **Required**: Yes

- **Multiple answers**: Yes

If you hover over the answers 3 and 9, three options appear to the right of the answer. See Figure 10-21.

Figure 10-21. *Answer options*

The Trashcan, Message Box, and Correct Answer icons appear. If you click the Trashcan icon, the answer will be deleted. The next two options separate forms from quizzes. The message box allows the quiz author to display a message when the answer is selected, and the Correct Answer icon marks the answer correct if chosen. At the end of the quiz, the correct answers are tallied and a score is displayed.

Mark answers 3 and 9 correct using the Correct Answer icon when hovering over each value. On answer values 5, 7, and 23, add a message box to each one informing the user that "The answer selected is incorrect." Add a points value of 10 points in the points box in the lower left corner. The question should now look like Figure 10-22.

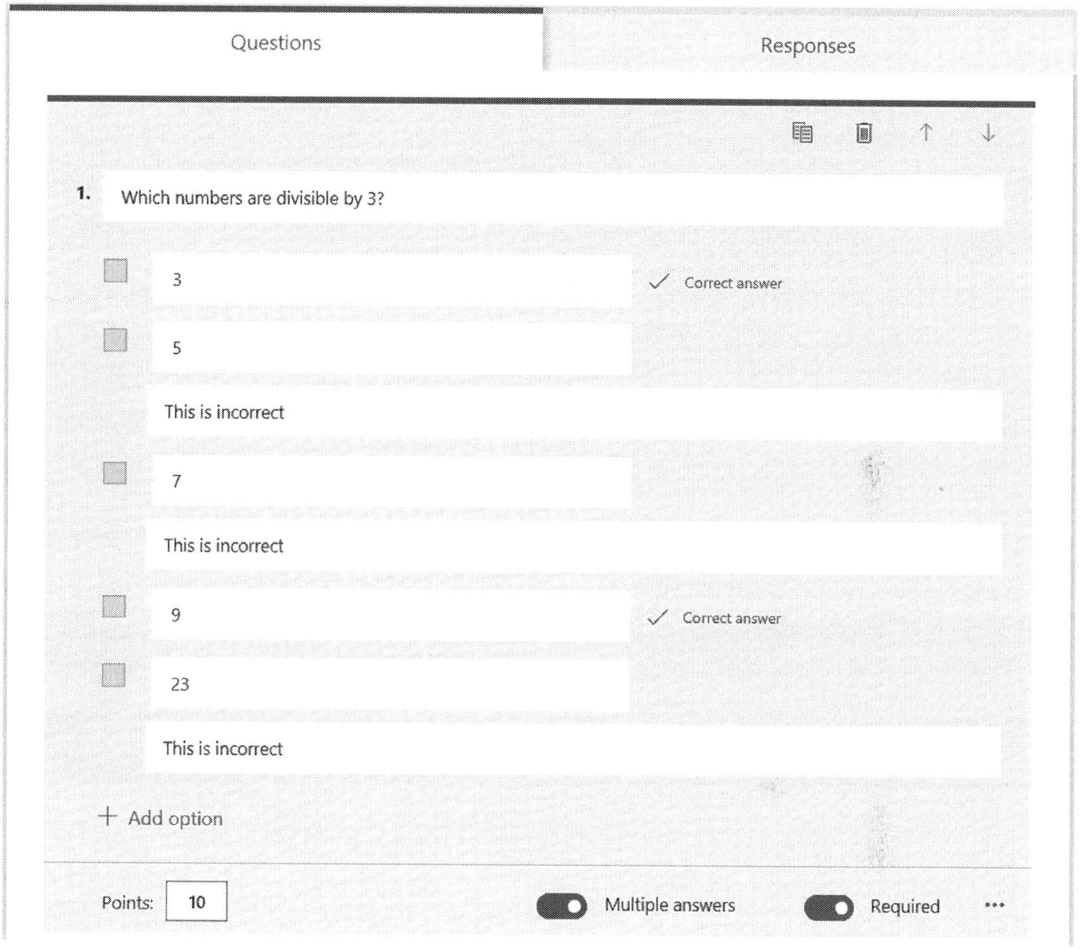

Figure 10-22. *The finished quiz*

Add a second-choice question by selecting the "Add question" box and choosing the choice data type. Use the following info to build the question:

Question 1: Solve the following equation:

- **Answers**: 7, 14, 18

  - **Correct answer**: 7

- **Required**: Yes

- **Multiple answers**: Yes

Click the ellipsis (…) in the lower right of Question 2. Select the "Math" and "Subtitle" options and an equation editor will appear where you can enter a math equation in the subtitle box. This formula editor offers a wide range of complex mathematical formulas. Currently you are only able to add mathematical formulas that are visible, but I could see where this could be extended to include chemistry, computer science, or physics formulas. For now, add the square root symbol with a value of 49.

Note   Microsoft Forms contains a handy formula solver as well. If no answers are entered, Forms will suggest an appropriate answer. Perfect for late night quiz building!

Assign a point value of 10 points to the question and mark the question required. The question should look like Figure 10-23.

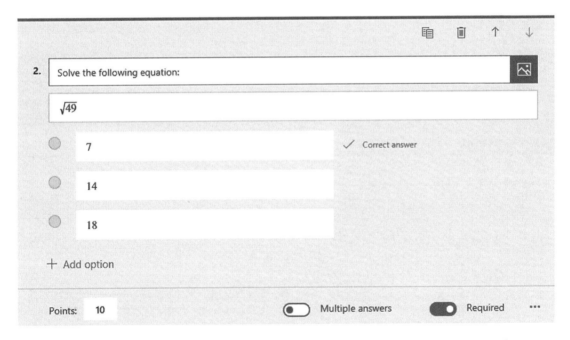

Figure 10-23. *Question 2 with the correct answer marked and a point total assessed*

The completed quiz should now look like Figure 10-24. Feel free to add more questions.

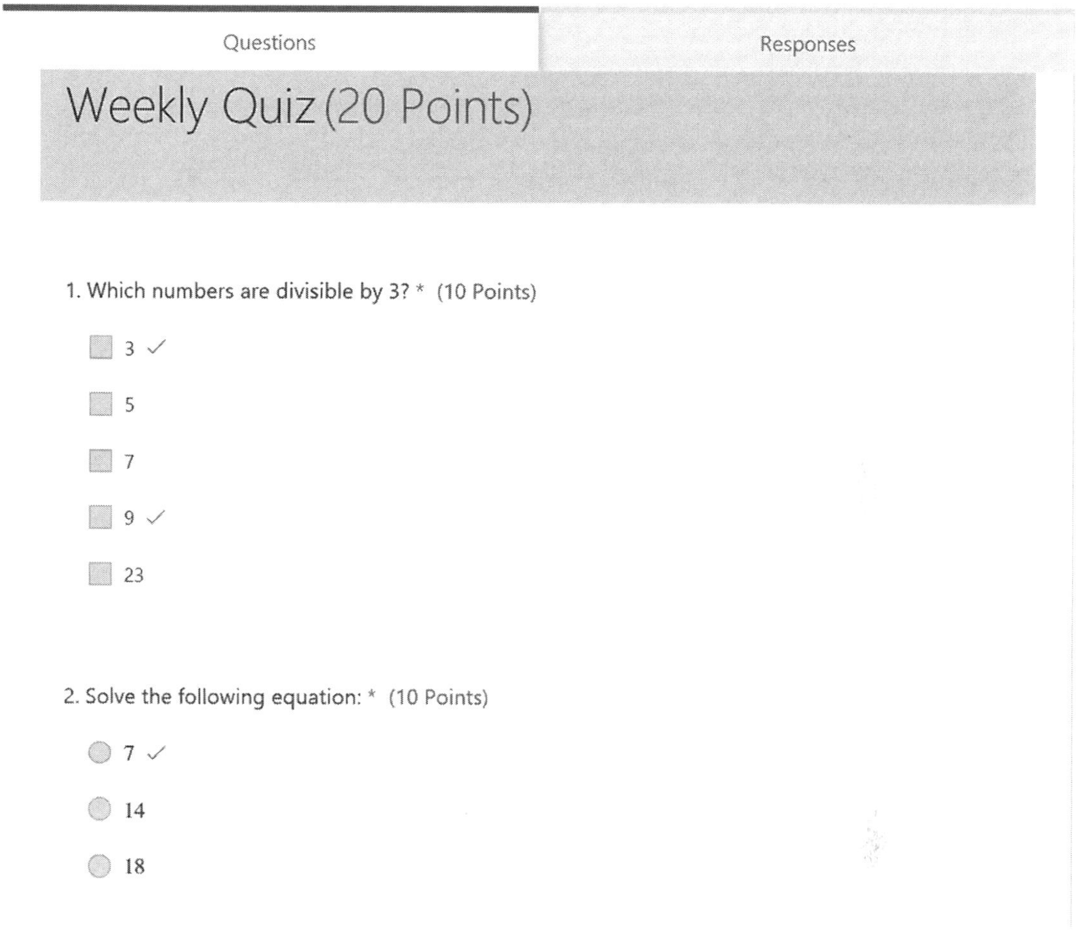

Figure 10-24. *The completed quiz*

Select the Preview button and go ahead and complete your first quiz. Once completed, you will see your score and you can view the responses.

Note   Only choice data types can be auto-graded. All other data types need to be graded by reviewing the answers, which is discussed in the next section.

Viewing Responses

In the previous sections, you explored forms and quizzes and the available data types that are allowed within Microsoft Forms. The second part is viewing and acting on the data collected or the quiz graded.

Forms

After creating your first form and distributing it through one of the share methods, it's time to view the responses to your form. Microsoft has made this process extremely simple and consolidates the responses in an easy-to-read graphical dashboard.

To view the responses to the form, navigate back to Microsoft Forms, if you are in another Office 365 application, by utilizing the app launcher. Once in Microsoft Forms, simply select your form from the Forms dashboard (Figure 10-2). When the form opens, select Responses from the top of the form (Figure 10-25).

> **Note**   In this example, you will view the responses for the Annual Company Picnic form. You need to fill out the form or share the link with your colleagues.

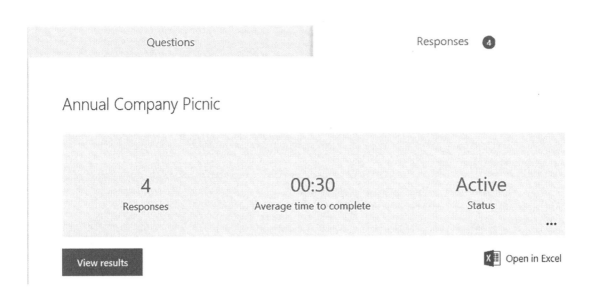

Figure 10-25. *Questions and Reponses tabs*

Click the Responses tab (Figure 10-25) to see the responses displayed in a graphical format; see Figure 10-26. The summary includes the number of responders, the average time to complete the form, and whether the form is active or not. Clicking "View results" shows the individual responses for each submitter. If the form is set for anonymous or you chose not to record the name in the settings of the form, you will not know who filled out the form.

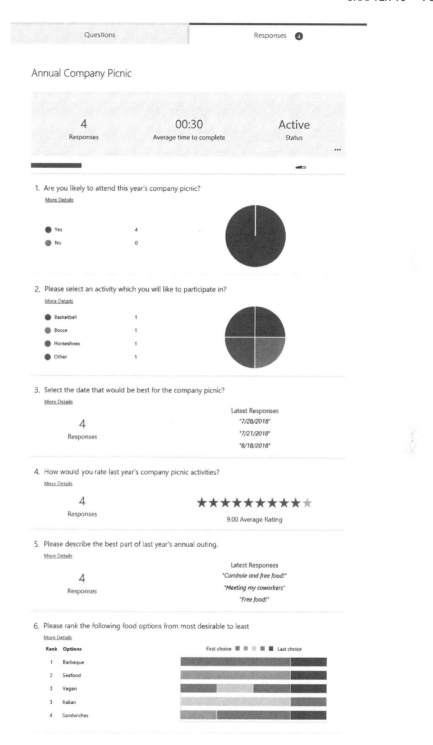

Figure 10-26. *Quiz responses*

You can also export the results to Excel for further data analysis or if you want to create different charts from the dataset. In most cases, the displayed results are sufficient. Take, for example, Question 2 (Figure 10-27); the data is displayed in an interactive pie chart totaling the sports activities that have been selected. As you hover over each segment of the pie chart, the chart renders the total responses for the answer chosen.

2. Please select an activity which you will like to participate in?

More Details

● Basketball	1	
● Bocce	1	
● Horseshoes	1	
● Other	1	

Figure 10-27. *Interactive pie chart for Question 2*

Clicking the ellipsis (…) in the form summary gives you the following options: "Delete all responses," "Print summary," and "Create a Summary Link."

Quizzes

Quizzes share a lot of the same functionality as the forms but offer a few different options. When viewing the responses for a quiz, you can review answers and post scores.

The "Review answers" option is located underneath the responses for the quiz and shows the answers chosen, time to complete the quiz, and the score by quiz taker. You can adjust the point values given. This can be done by editing the "Auto-graded" total. You can also give feedback on a question by selecting the Message icon and adding feedback. See Figure 10-28.

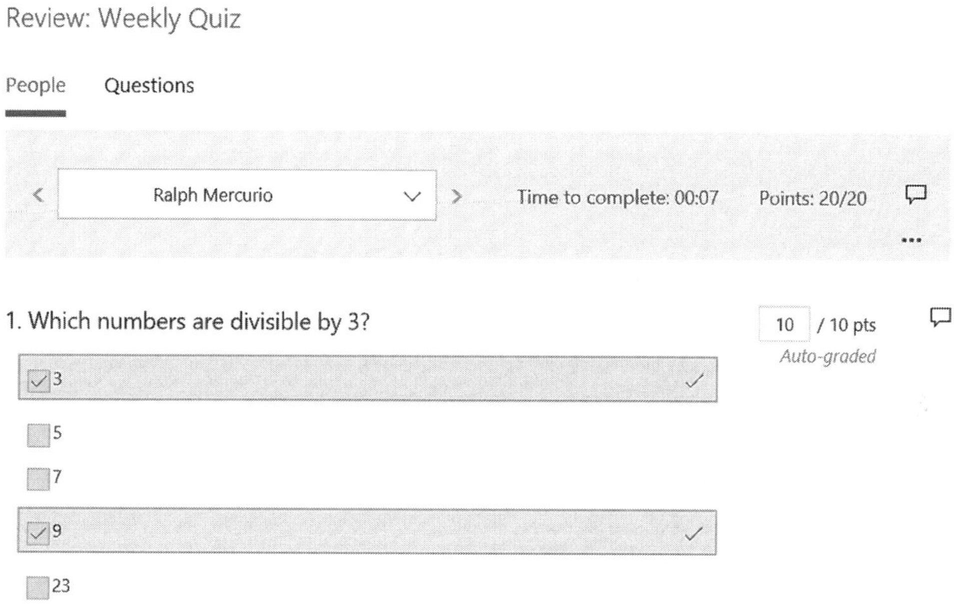

Review: Weekly Quiz

People   Questions

1. Which numbers are divisible by 3?   10 / 10 pts

Auto-graded

✓ 3 ✓

☐ 5

☐ 7

✓ 9 ✓

☐ 23

Figure 10-28. *Review options by quiz taker*

Under the Questions tab, the form author can review the questions or print all the answers for each question.

Back on the Responses tab of the quiz, select "Post scores." Posting scores allows you to view the feedback, if any, and the correct questions. There currently is no portal, so you need to use the same link to view the completed graded quiz. To provide immediate feedback, set the "Option for quiz" to show results automatically. This option is located in the Settings menu of the quiz.

Deleting Responses

There may come a time when you want to delete all the responses or a singular response from a form or a quiz. Perhaps you want to remove incorrectly filled-out forms so they don't skew the dataset or delete quizzes that are not filled out.

To delete all responses, click the ellipsis (…) in the Responses tab. Simply select "Delete all responses" and the responses will be deleted. To delete a single response, click "View results" on the Responses tab. Choose which response to delete by navigating with the left or right arrows. To delete a single response, select the ellipsis (…) and click "Delete response." Agree with the deletion and Forms will remove the response from the form.

Printing Form Responses

Printing the form responses is straightforward. On the Responses tab, select the ellipsis (…) and select the "Print summary" link. This will render the summary of the results in a printable format.

To print just a single response from all the responses, select the "View results" link. Navigate to the response you would like to print either with the left or right arrows. On the desired response to be printed, select the ellipsis (…) and chose "Print response."

Creating a Summary Link

A summary link allows anyone to view the responses to the form. This link can be posted on an internal intranet (SharePoint), sent through email, or shared in Microsoft Teams. The summary link is created by Microsoft forms and can be created by selecting the ellipsis (…) and choosing "Get a summary link."

Summary

Microsoft Forms has the potential to be an innovative product in the Office 365 application suite. In this chapter, you reviewed the Forms interfaces, available options, created your first form, shared the form with others, and viewed the responses.

This application can also be used to create online quizzes and have them graded automatically. This type of application can be used to streamline quiz taking in education environments, moving away from Scantron tests and moving to an interactive online experience for students.

This is a powerful application and future updates should add more functionality, provide more data types, and add more equations. I am excited to see what Microsoft does with this product and how it can streamline surveys and quizzes and provide the analytical data we crave without using other Microsoft application such as Excel.

In the next chapter, you will explore Microsoft Flow, which is designed to automate reparative actions in not only Office 365 but also third-party services.

CHAPTER 11

Flow

In Chapter 10, I discussed Microsoft Forms, which allows for the creation of web-based forms for data collection, surveys or quizzes. In this chapter, I will focus on Microsoft Flow, which is a new application from Microsoft centered on automation and integration between many services.

Microsoft Flow aims to automate tasks or repetitive actions and create a "flow" that will run automatically. These flows are similar to IFTTT, which is an open source protocol to link multiple third-party services together. For example, using IFTTT and the appropriate hardware/software, you can create an IFTTT that will turn on your house lights as you approach the front door carrying your mobile phone.

Microsoft aims to deliver a similar service in Office 365 that links not only the Office 365 collaborative applications I have discussed but also connects with third-party services such as Twitter, Instagram, and Adobe.

Before you dive into Flow, I do want to discuss the currently available plans for Flow. Microsoft Flow is available in three different tiers. The first tier, which is included with the Office 365 subscription, is the Free tier; it allows for 2,000 executions or runs per month and is currently set to execute every 5 minutes. The second tier, Flow Plan 1, allows for 4,500 executions, premium connectors, and 3-minute execution. The third tier, Flow Plan 2, allows for 15,000 executions a month, 1-minute execution checks, premium connectors, and organization policy settings. These plans are aimed at the user, not the tenant. It is possible that some users who use Flow more than others might need to upgrade their specific license.

Overview of the Flow Interface

To launch Microsoft Flow, click the app launcher in the upper right corner of Office 365 and select Flow, as shown in Figure 11-1. If it is not visible, select the "All apps" link under Yammer in the app launcher. Flow is available from OneDrive and SharePoint as well.

© Ralph Mercurio 2018
R. Mercurio, *Beginning Office 365 Collaboration Apps*, https://doi.org/10.1007/978-1-4842-3849-3_11

Flow

Figure 11-1. *Launching Microsoft Flow from the app launcher of Office 365*

Upon clicking the icon, you will be presented with the Microsoft Flow initial screen, as shown in Figure 11-2.

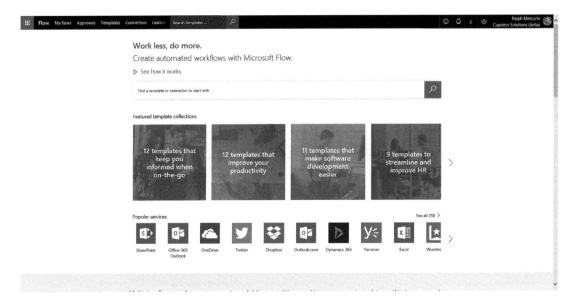

Figure 11-2. *Microsoft Flow introductory screen*

Before you create your first flow, let's review the interface and where to find the right resources with Flow. As shown in Figure 11-2, the global navigation contains the following headings:

- **My flows**: All the flows you create, both personal and team.

- **Approvals**: Specific approval flows, which request approval from a user.

- **Templates**: Preconfigured Flow templates to use. Some of the flows do require subscription outside of Office 365 and may contain premium connectors. In order to use premium connectors, you must subscribe to a plan that includes them.

- **Connectors**: The building blocks to connect not only to Office 365 but also a variety of third-party services. Some connectors are marked "Premium," meaning you must subscribe to the correct Flow plan. There may be a cost associated with subscribing to a third-party connector/service.

- **Learn**: Resources such as training, support, and documentation.

In the upper right corner of Flow, you will also find specific Flow settings as designated by the cog next to your initials or profile image.

Connectors

Before you create your first flow, let's look at the available connectors by clicking "Connectors" in the global navigation. The page will refresh, and all the available connectors will load. You will notice that some connectors are tagged with a green "Premium" label, meaning you need to subscribe to at least Flow Plan 1 to access them; see Figure 11-3.

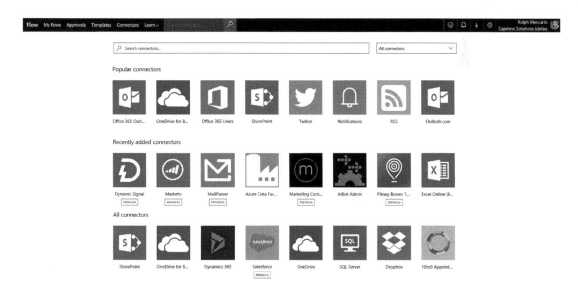

Figure 11-3. *Microsoft Flow Connector library*

Let's explore a connector a little further by clicking into one of the available connectors. For this example, click the SharePoint connector. It will show the available configurations for that connector; see Figure 11-4.

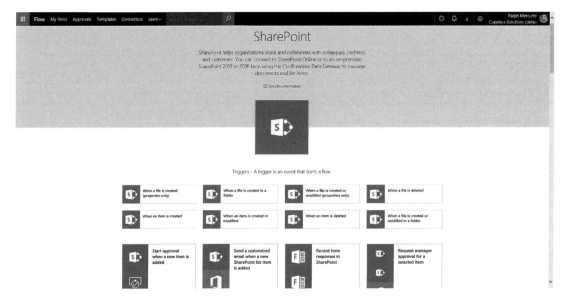

Figure 11-4. *SharePoint Flow Connector configuration settings*

On the SharePoint connector page, below the SharePoint logo, you will notice that eight triggers are available. A trigger is defined as a starting event that begins a flow. Currently the eight triggers for SharePoint center around document and item management. When a user creates/modifies/deletes a document or item, a flow can then be created to perform some action.

Note   Connectors are configured and use the credentials of the creator of the flow. The Microsoft Flow team will be releasing updates to the application to overcome this limitation in the future.

Templates

On the same page, there are also preconfigured flow templates where the SharePoint connector is used. Many of the templates are created and published by Microsoft, but some are published by the community.

Connectors power Flow by connecting with services, and when combined with logic operators they create a flow. To view the available templates, click "Templates" in the global navigation. The Templates page (Figure 11-5) contains all the available templates, categorized into specific categories such as Approval, Data Collection, Email, Productivity, and Social Media.

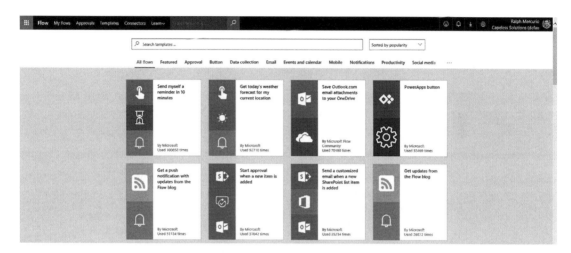

Figure 11-5. *Available templates*

You can also search for a specific template by specifying a connector or a service. The search resultset can also be refined further by popularity, name, and published time.

As you can see, flows are not complicated and rely on the foundational building block of connectors and logic actions. Microsoft has also done a great job of creating templates that you might find useful and can use to automate a basic task or repetitive action.

Creating Flows

For the remainder of this chapter, you will focus on creating flows to approve an item, report software bugs, and apply an electronic signature to a document. These flows will be based on preconfigured templates so you can easily become familiar with flows and the related interfaces.

Approval Flow

The first flow you are going to create is a flow to start an approval on an item in a SharePoint library. To create your first flow, click "Approvals" in the global navigation and select the "Start approval when a new item is added" template shown in Figure 11-6.

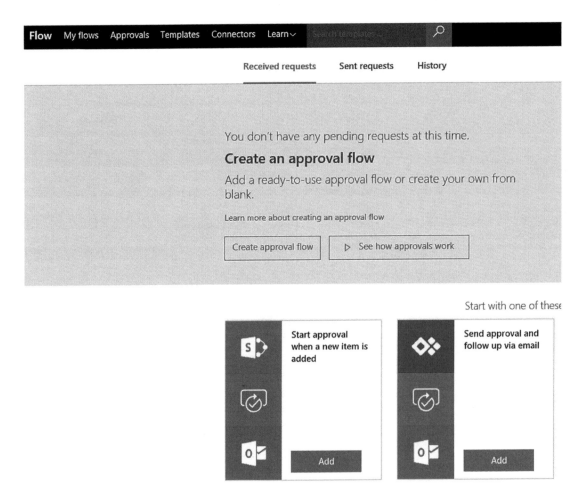

Figure 11-6. *Adding the "Start approval when a new item is added" template*

Go ahead and click "Add." The page will refresh, and you will be presented with the template configuration screen depicted in Figure 11-7.

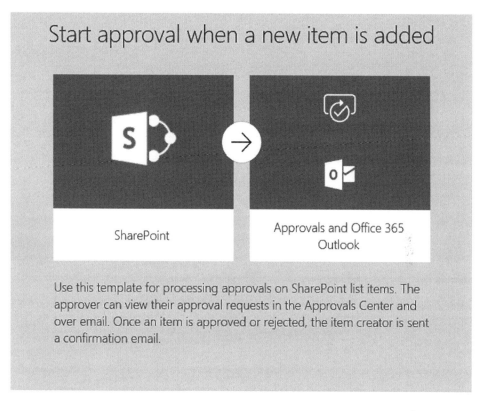

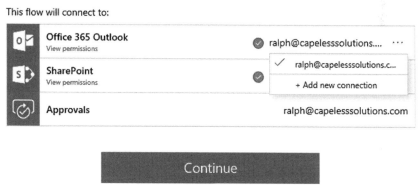

Figure 11-7. *Template configuration settings*

On this page, you will notice a few items. The first item is that this flow will use SharePoint, Outlook, and the Flow Approval engine. It also provides a definition of the flow, so you can be sure that this is the correct flow you want to use. Click "Continue" to configure the flow.

The Flow design page shows the associated actions and needed logic for the flow; see Figure 11-8.

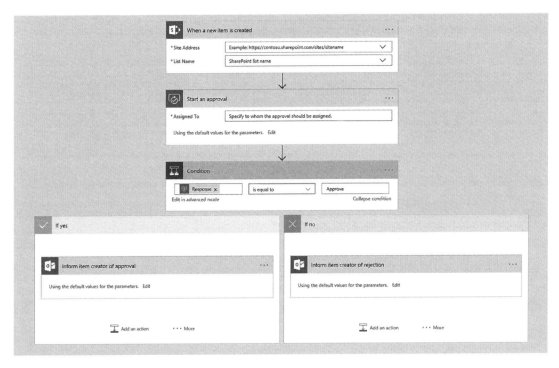

Figure 11-8. *Configuring flow actions and logic*

Starting from the top and working your way down, configure each box with the appropriate values. As mentioned, this flow uses a SharePoint library to store the item and begin the flow. Before you can configure the flow further, let's switch gears and open SharePoint from the app launcher. If you need a refresher, see Chapter 2.

Create a new site called "Procurement" to configure for this flow. The goal of this flow is to allow users to add items to a SharePoint list so the purchase can be approved in as little time as possible and to ensuring the appropriate information is provided before the request approval flow is started.

Note   When an Office 365 Group is created, a corresponding SharePoint site is also created.

On the newly created Procurement site, create a new library to store the items needing approvals. To create a list, select "List" from the "+ New" button located directly below the title of the site and title the list "Procurement Items." As discussed in Chapter 2, you need to add appropriate metadata to the list so that you can capture the information that is relevant. Create the columns shown in Table 11-1.

Table 11-1. *Procurement Items Columns*

Column Name	Type	Values
Description	Multiple lines of text	
Vendor	Choice	Amazon; OfficeMax; Staples; Target
Cost	Currency	
Notes	Multiple lines of text	
Approval	Single line of text	

Upon completion, the SharePoint list should look exactly like Figure 11-9.

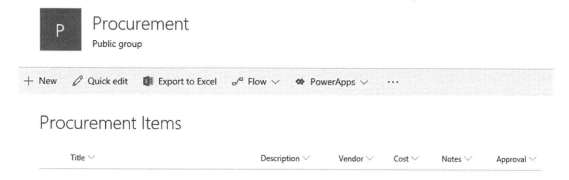

Figure 11-9. *Configured Procurement Items list with added columns*

Now that the SharePoint list is configured correctly, switch back to Microsoft Flow. In the first action, "When a new item is created," specify the SharePoint site and associated library. If it does not appear in the drop-down list, choose "Enter custom value" and add the Procurement site URL. Select the "Procurement Items" library from the List Name drop-down. The completed action should look like Figure 11-10.

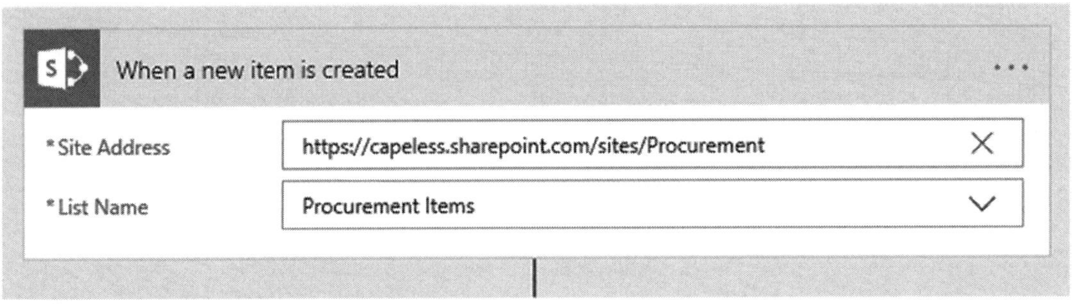

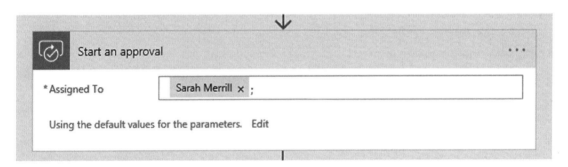

Figure 11-10. *Configured action with Procurement site URL and associated library*

Moving on to the next action, "Start an approval," specify the "Assigned to" value. In this case, you'll send all approvals to a single user; in a true production scenario, it would be ideal to send to multiple approvers because a single approver could be out of the office or not available, and the requests could queue waiting for approval. In my case, I added Sarah Merrill as the approver; see Figure 11-11.

Figure 11-11. *Adding an approver to the flow*

Note   Remember that the approver and other variables will be specific to your own instance of Office 365.

The final change you will make the flow is to set the "Approval" field in the Procurement list with an appropriate status of Approved or Rejected. In the "If yes" action box shown in Figure 11-12, click "Add an action."

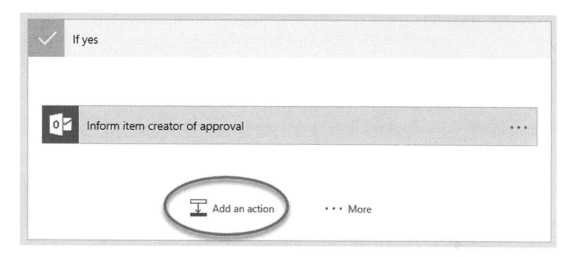

Figure 11-12. *Adding an action in Microsoft Flow*

In the "Add an action" box, click SharePoint and then select the Update item action. Once the action is added, it needs to be configured to update the item. Specify the site address, list name, ID, title, and approval, as shown in Figure 11-13.

Update item	
*Site Address	https://capeless.sharepoint.com/sites/Procurement ✕
*List Name	Procurement Items ∨
*Id	ID ✕
*Title	Title ✕
	Add dynamic content ⊞
Vendor Value	∨
Cost	
Description	
Notes	
Approval	Approved

Figure 11-13. *Configuring the Update item action to update a SharePoint list column*

293

To set both the ID and Title fields, place the cursor inside the corresponding text box. For instance, to set the ID to the current item you are approving, select ID, as shown in Figure 11-14.

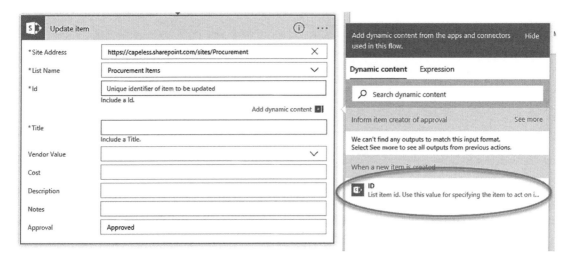

Figure 11-14. *Set the ID of an item within a flow*

Perform the same action for the Title field, selecting Title from the available choices. Repeat the same steps to set the Approval field to Rejected if the approver rejects the procurement request. The completed flow should be similar to Figure 11-15.

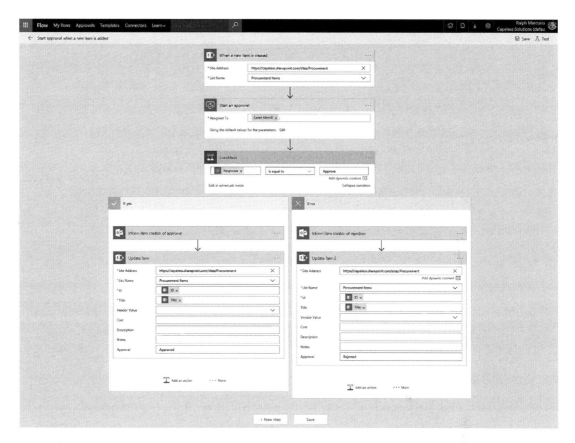

Figure 11-15. *Completed approval flow*

Each action also has a set of options that are available to configure the action further. Clicking the ellipsis in the upper right corner of each action reveals a context menu. For the purposes of this book, I will discuss the "Add a comment" and "Rename" menu options. Clicking "Add a comment" allows a comment to be made to describe what the action is doing or a specific configurations setting. This is a good practice in the event that someone else needs to debug your flow, make changes, or if you need to make changes down the road but don't entirely remember why you created specific actions. The second context menu of importance is the Rename link. It allows you to rename an action to a friendlier name and give some context to the flow.

Saving and Testing

Once the actions are appropriately named, and you added comments as you see fit, the next step is to save the flow and test it. In the upper right corner underneath your profile picture or initials, click Save. After the save is performed, click Test to execute a test of the flow and see if there are any errors or issues. Clicking Test opens a modal dialog with two options: "I'll perform the trigger action" or "Using data from previous runs." The first option requires you to add an item to the list in SharePoint while the second option uses data already on the list from a previous flow to execute the flow. For the purposes of this book, let's use the first radio button: "I'll perform the trigger action." Select the radio button and press "Test." In the SharePoint list you created earlier, add a list item, updating the fields as needed. This includes title, vendor, cost, and description. Once an item is added, return back to the flow to see the progress; see Figure 11-16.

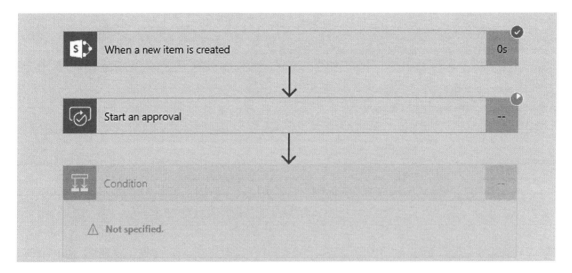

Figure 11-16. *Viewing the status of the approval flow*

By looking at the flow, you can tell that the first step was successful, as designated by a green circle with a white checkmark. You can also infer that you are on the "Start an approval action" as designated by the orange processing icon. The actions following "Start an approval" have not executed yet because they are greyed out. In this flow, Sarah Merrill is the approver, and in her inbox, she did receive an email from Microsoft Flow concerning the approval request, as shown in Figure 11-17.

Please review: Paper

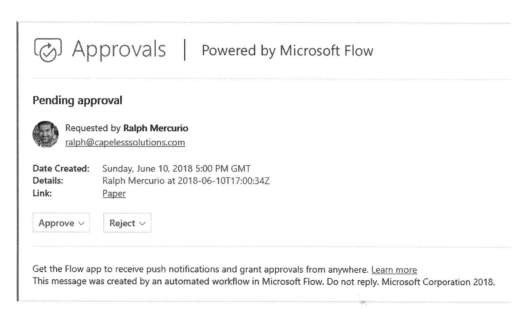

Figure 11-17. *Approval email sent to the approver in a flow*

As the approver, Sarah as two choices. She can either approve or reject the item. Upon her clicking "Approve," specify any notes and click "Submit" in the email; the flow will take her response and execute the corresponding branch in the flow.

Looking at the flow test, you can now see that all the steps have executed, as designated by the green circles, and the flow is finished; see Figure 11-18.

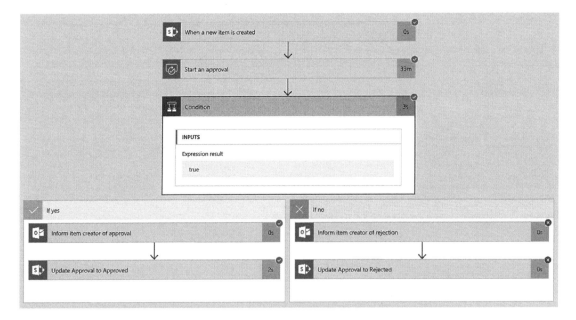

Figure 11-18. *Completed flow diagram*

As specified in the flow, you also set the Approval column to either Approved or Rejected. Examining the SharePoint list, you can see the Approval column is set to the correct value; see Figure 11-19.

Procurement Items

Title ∨	Vendor ∨	Cost ∨	Description ∨	Approval ∨
Paper	Staples	$45.00	Copier paper for 2nd Floor printer, 3 reams.	Approved

Figure 11-19. *SharePoint column value set from Microsoft Flow*

The submitter will also receive a notification in their respective inbox when the flow is complete about whether the item was approved or rejected.

Creating a Flow Between Office 365 Applications

In this example, you will link Microsoft Forms and Planner together to create a software bug submission flow. When a user finds a bug, they can fill out the form located within a SharePoint site, and upon submission, a Planner task will be created for software debug lead to perform. The lead can also reassign the task to one of the available developers. Before you create the flow, you need to configure the form, SharePoint Site, and Planner.

In Microsoft Forms, which was discussed in Chapter 10, create a simple form like the one in Figure 11-20.

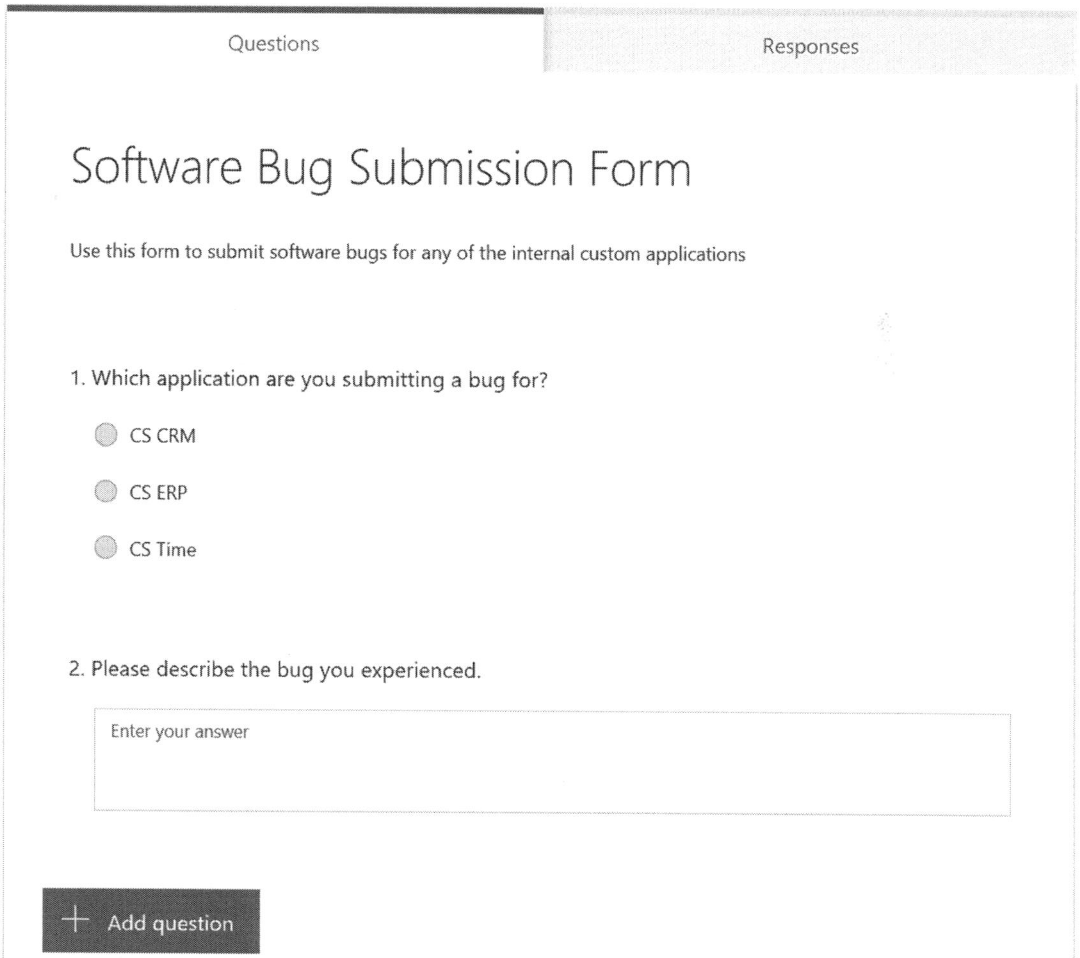

Figure 11-20.   *Form for submission of software bugs*

Now that you have the form, let's configure Planner to support this solution. Planner was discussed in Chapter 8.

In Planner, create a new plan by selecting "+ New plan" in the left-hand navigation of Planner. In the New Plan modal window, title your plan and set the privacy to private, as shown in Figure 11-21.

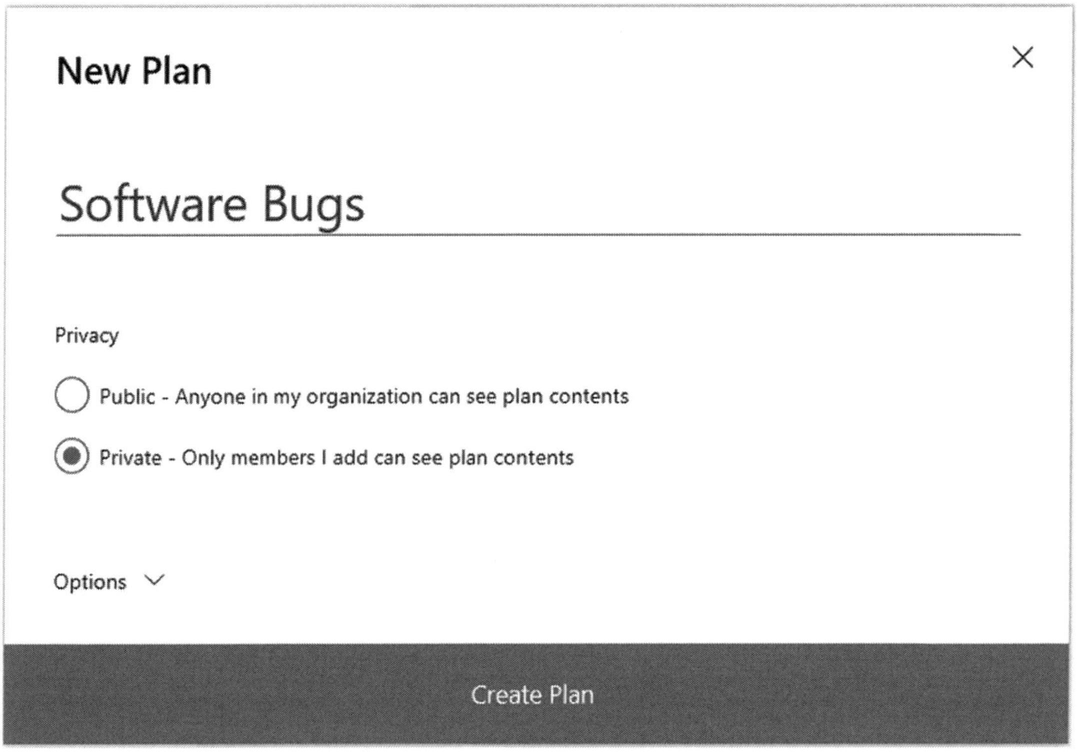

Figure 11-21. *Planner plan to support software bug tasks*

For the final setup step, let's embed the Microsoft form you created into a SharePoint site so that it is easily accessible to the users.

In a SharePoint site (which was discussed in Chapter 2), put the page into Edit mode. Select a section of the page and add the Forms web part. Once the web part is added, paste the link of the form into the configuration settings and click "Ok" and then "Publish." To get the form link, click "Share" in Microsoft Forms and copy the available link. If done correctly, it will look like Figure 11-22.

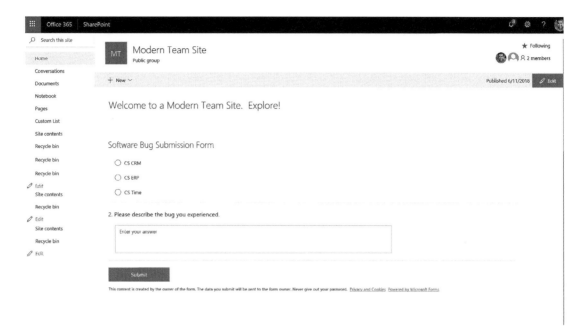

Figure 11-22. *Software Bug Submission form embedded in a modern SharePoint site*

Now that you have configured the supporting applications in this Flow example, configure a flow to accomplish your goal.

In Microsoft Flow, click "My flows" in the global navigation and then click "Create from blank." The first step is to find the Form triggers so the flow can execute an action. In the search box, type "Forms" and choose "Microsoft Forms – When a new response is submitted." Once the trigger is added, click "New step" and then "Add an action." In the search box, search for Planner and add the "Planner – Create a task" action to the flow. If done correctly, your flow should resemble Figure 11-23.

Figure 11-23. *Microsoft Flow with Forms and Planner*

Configure the trigger by choosing the name of the form from the drop-down box for Form Id. In the "Create a task" action, configure the Plan Id and add a title to the Title text box. Leave all other fields blank for now. The trigger and the action should resemble Figure 11-24.

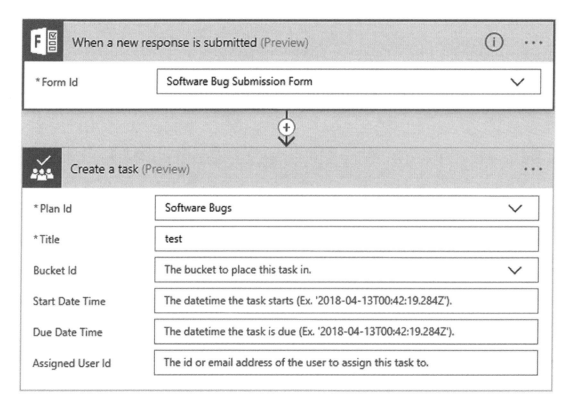

Figure 11-24. *Configuring the trigger and action to create a Planner task via a form*

At this point, you added a trigger and an action to create a flow. If you were to run the flow, a user would fill out the form, and a task would be created in Planner with very little detail. Let's add a little bit of logic so that you can use the form responses to update the task details.

Between the two current actions, click the + sign and choose to add an action. Within the search box, search for Microsoft Forms and select "Microsoft Forms – Get response details" under the Actions tab. This action requires two pieces of information: the Form Id and Response Id. For the Form Id, choose the "Software bug Submission Form" from the drop-down. For the Response ID, click into the "Response Id" field and click "See more" within the Dynamic Content window. The window will refresh and a single value will be displayed: Response Id. Click "Response Id," as shown in Figure 11-25.

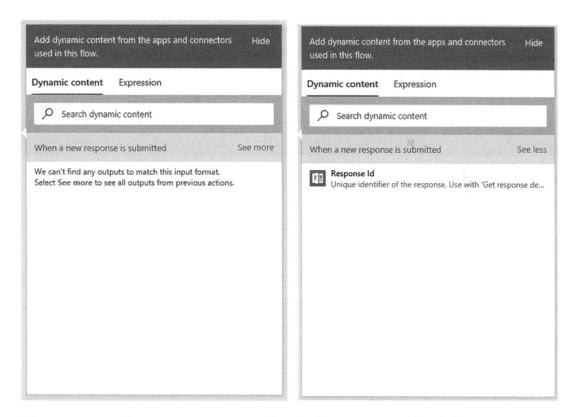

Figure 11-25. *Choosing Response ID for the "Get response details" action*

Once the field is added, the "Get response details" action is enveloped within an "Apply to each" for loop. This loop will iterate through the responses and expose the form data. In this case, the response set is a single item.

The next step is to move the "Create a task" action into the "Apply to each" action. This is done by clicking the header of the "Create a task" action and dragging it onto the "Apply to each" action. If done correctly, the "Create a task" action should be below the "Get response details" action.

Open the "Create a task action" and click the Title field. Delete the existing text and type "New Bug for: " Clicking into the Title field allows you to insert dynamic content after your text; click the "Which application are you submitting for?" detail shown in Figure 11-26.

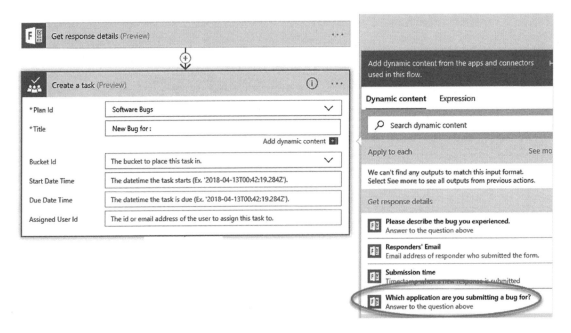

Figure 11-26. *Adding the title field of the filled-out form to the Planner task*

Leave the other fields empty for now because you will update the details via a different action because you can't update the details of the task in the current action.

At this point, you can take data entered into Microsoft Forms and use it to create a task in Planner. You have only set the Title field and the Plan Id for tasks to be created; now let's set the other fields to add context.

To accomplish this, you need to add two actions: Delay and "Planner – Update task details." To add the Delay action, click "Add an Action" below the "Create a task" action. Using the search box, search for "Delay" and select it. Set the count to 20 and the unit to second. This delay is needed to allow Planner to create the task before you attempt to update it.

Repeat the adding action sequence and search for "Planner – Update task details" and add it to the flow you are working on below the Delay action. In this action, you provide two values: a Task Id to tell Planner what to update and a Description to add context to the newly created task. Clicking into the Task Id textbox opens the Dynamic Content window, as mentioned. Select "ID" located in the "Create a task" section. The second update is to the Description field. Click into the field and select the "Please describe the bug you experienced" tag located in the "Get response details" section. The entire flow will look like Figure 11-27.

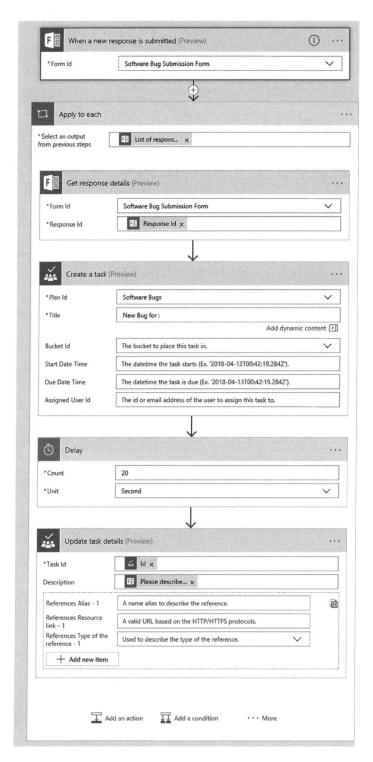

Figure 11-27. *Completed flow for software bug collection*

In this example, you connected three separate applications (Forms, SharePoint, and Planner) using Flow to create a cohesive work scenario without any heavy coding or custom work. This example can be further refined in numerous ways, such as adding a notification action, emailing a user, or even potentially integrating with a third-party software bug tracking system.

The final step is to test the flow, as you did earlier in this chapter, and ensure the task gets created with the correct metadata and bucket. In Figure 11-28, you can see that based on the form data submitted, the appropriate task is created in Planner.

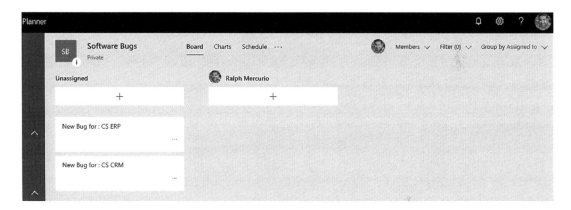

Figure 11-28. *Newly created tasks from data entered in Microsoft Forms*

At this point, you have seen Flow cross Office 365 application boundaries, but Flow also has the ability via actions to connect to third-party services.

Creating an Advance Flow to Interact with a Third-Party Service

In this section, you will configure a flow to step outside the bounds of Office 365 and integrate with an entirely separate third-party service.

In this example, when a document is saved to a particular folder in OneDrive, you will route the document for electronic signature using Adobe Sign. This app does require separate licensing since it is a service offered strictly from Adobe. Electronic signatures are becoming more common in enterprises because they are legal timestamp signatures that can be integrated into workflows to automate requests, similar to this example.

In order to create the flow, navigate to "My flows" in the global navigation. Note that the "Start approval when a new item is added" flow appears here; if needed, you can disable the flow, edit, add an owner, view analytics, or delete it. Before you create a new flow, check if a template has already been created which you can utilize and modify to fit your needs. As discussed, Flow has a wide variety of templates that can be used as is or modified.

In this example, you are interested in having a document electronically signed by Adobe whenever a file is added to a specific folder in OneDrive. Click "Create from template" on the My flows page. Clicking the link opens the template library and searchs for Adobe Sign. Flow will return 12 flows that in some part use Adobe Sign; see Figure 11-29.

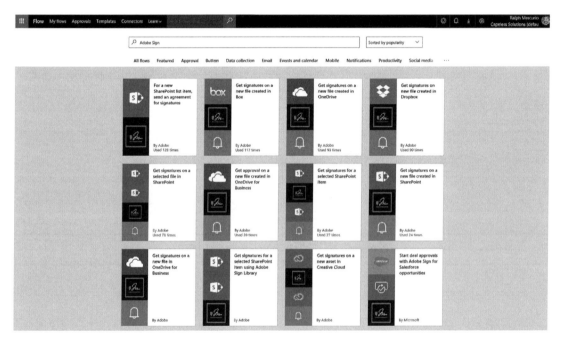

Figure 11-29. *Available Adobe Sign template flows*

The flow you want is "Get signatures on a new file created in OneDrive." Selecting this flow requires an account to connect to Adobe Sign. Since this is not a Microsoft product, you will need to create an account with Adobe Sign to proceed.

Once you have authenticated to Adobe Sign with valid credentials, you can begin customizing the actions to meet your intended goal. The flow is quite simple and is comprised of four actions, shown in Figure 11-30.

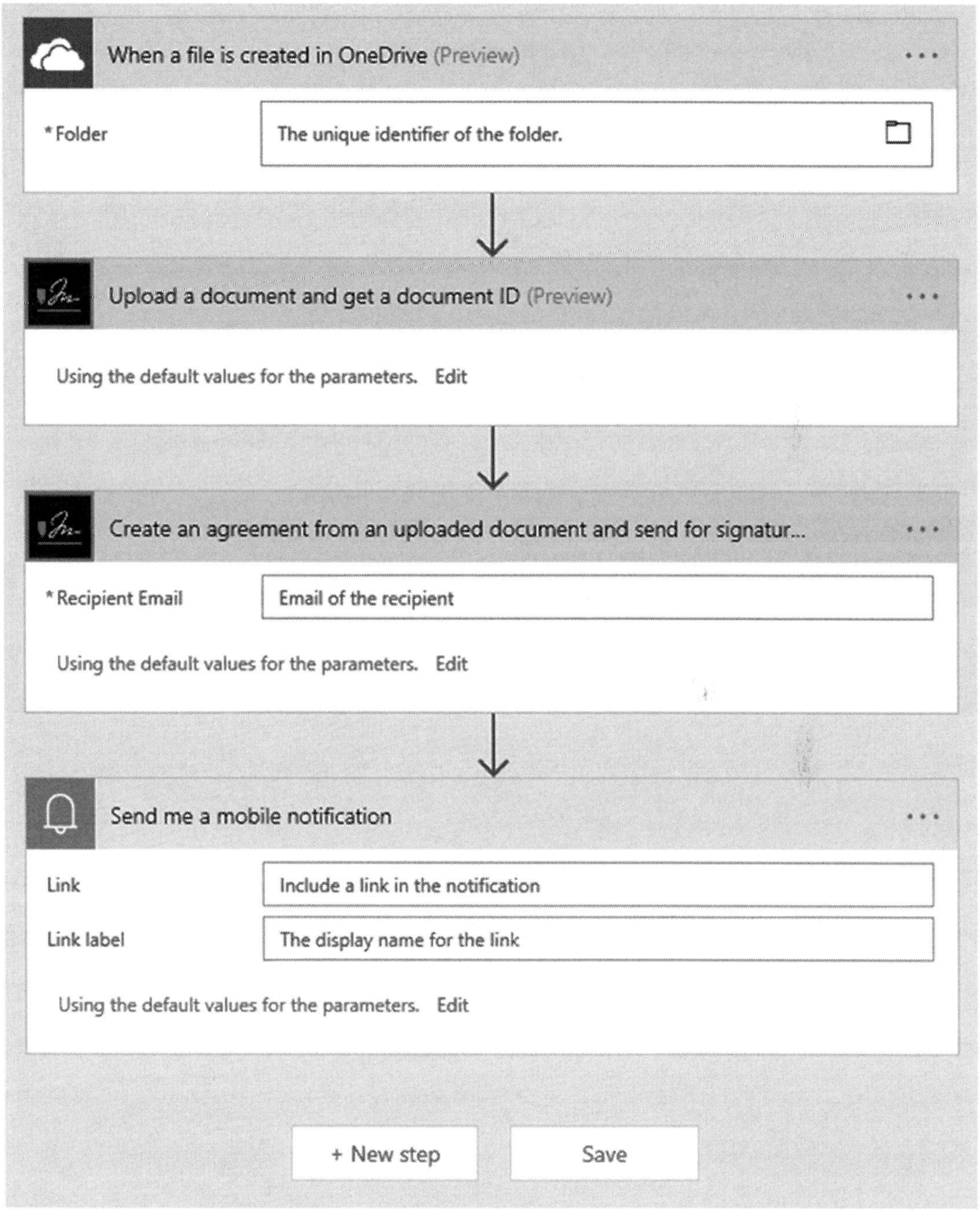

Figure 11-30. *Microsoft Flow - Get signatures on a new file created in OneDrive*

The first action, "When a file is created in OneDrive," requires a unique identifier of the OneDrive folder. In order to select the folder (create the folder prior in your OneDrive), click the Folder icon within the action. Clicking the Folder icon allows you to navigate to the folder you would like to use. The third action, "Create an agreement from an uploaded document and send for signature," requires the email of the signer (recipient). In your case, provide a static signer (smerrill@capelesssolutions.com), but in a production scenario, a metadata column can be created to hold the email addresses of the signers to populate this value.

The final step in this flow is to set the notification properties. Click into "Link" and choose "Agreement ID" and set the "Link Label" to "Signed Agreement." Now that the flow is configured, test the flow by selecting "Test" in the upper right corner. Because you have never executed this flow, the "Using data from previous runs" option is disabled. Go ahead and click "I'll perform the trigger action" and upload a document to the OneDrive folder specified in the first action.

Note   In this flow, Sarah Merrill also has an Adobe Sign account.

As the flow progresses through the actions, it will send emails to the parties involved: Sarah and me. I will receive an email informing me that the document I uploaded is out for signature and Sarah will receive an email asking her to sign, as shown in Figure 11-31.

Please sign SendforSign.docx

Figure 11-31. *Email sent to Sarah from Adobe Sign*

Once Sarah clicks the link within the email and signs the document, we all will receive a PDF in our inboxes with her signature applied. As a future exercise, the signed document can be deposited into another folder or even a SharePoint library.

Summary

Microsoft Flow is an innovative application that has the ability to connect the services we use, whether they are Office 365 applications or external third-party services. Flow takes workflow to another level by providing an easy and intuitive way to create flows. I was not able to cover the advanced logic and conditions available in Flow, but this chapter should have provided you with the foundation and understanding of Flow.

With Flow, triggers are the key to starting a flow while actions are the building blocks that connect the actions to perform an approval, simple process, or even a complicated process involving third-party services.

Flows are aimed at the user executing the flow and are not technically the same as workflows. As Flow evolves, the possibility if not the opportunity is available to have Flow become the de facto workflow engine for Office 365.

You created a basic approval flow that sent a document for electronic signature and a flow to ease the tedious process of software bug tracking. I am excited for what Microsoft has in store for Flow in the upcoming update cycles.

If you made this far, thank you! I hope the information I provided in both text and images has allowed you to conquer the beginning aspects of the Office 365 collaboration apps and has piqued your interest and excitement to continue using Office 365 and build on the foundation this book has given you.

In the next and final chapter, I will highlight some key points of each application and offer scenarios or guidance that will help you to choose the best application for your need.

CHAPTER 12

Making Sense of It All

As you saw throughout this book, Office 365 provides a comprehensive suite of apps to foster collaboration in the workplace. Collaboration is not just working on a document together but sharing information, working on a team, and managing aspects and artifacts in the workplace.

Office 365 is Software as a Service (SaaS), for which a monthly license can be purchased. That license allows you to use the service. Because of this, Microsoft continually updates the applications and provides disaster recovery and continual uptime so that any downtime is mitigated.

Before I summarize each app and its intended use, remember that there is some overlap between the applications. Because of this, it can be challenging to choose the right application for the intended scenario, and at times it will feel like you made the wrong decision. Learning Office 365 and using it are two different things, so my advice to you is to use Office 365 as much as you can and just know that over time you will come to understand the nuances and be able to choose the right application.

SharePoint, OneDrive, Stream

This group of applications provide document, item, and video sharing and storage. These application allow content to be easily shared with others, ability to assign metadata, and allow for complex video sharing.

SharePoint is strongest when there is a need for structure and very organized data in a team environment. With SharePoint, a site can hold libraries, and those libraries can be defined with metadata columns. These columns in conjunction with document libraries and lists provide the structure that some teams require.

> **Best for: Structured sharing of documents/items in a team/ project setting**

© Ralph Mercurio 2018
R. Mercurio, *Beginning Office 365 Collaboration Apps*, https://doi.org/10.1007/978-1-4842-3849-3_12

OneDrive, which is very similar in terms of function to SharePoint, is geared at personal storage of documents and sharing those items with people. In OneDrive, all content is stored in a single location and can be segmented via folders. Content in OneDrive can be shared with colleagues or external parties so that items can be part of a collaborative process.

Best for: Personal storage and sharing as needed with one or a few users

Microsoft Stream, which provides intelligent video storage in Office 365, replaces the Office 365 Video application. Videos can be organized into channels and shared throughout the enterprise or within specific groups. Stream introduces some new features generally absent from video platforms, such as facial recognition and video transcription in the premium license level. Facial recognition creates a People Map, which catalogs when a person's face is shown throughout the video. Transcription, while not perfect at all times, allows for the audio portion of the video to be transcribed into an editable transcript. These features happen automatically and do not require any intervention or execution from the uploader of the video.

Best for: Video management within the enterprise

Office

Microsoft Office, a cornerstone application of the computing world, is tightly integrated with Office 365. With Office 365 not only do you have access to the transitional Office install but you also have access to Office Online, which is the web-based versions of Office. Office includes Outlook, Word, PowerPoint, Excel, OneNote, and Sway. These applications allow information workers to create and edit content.

Best for: Document creation and editing

Teams and Office 365 Groups

Microsoft Teams provides a new and innovative way to work in the Microsoft suite. It is based on the concept of chat and does away with email. Members post to a channel and interact with other members via chat or video calls.

Best for: Group collaboration not centered on documents. Also allows for fluid communication (chat or video) with members.

Office 365 Groups is an application mashup of an Outlook inbox and calendar, SharePoint site, and OneNote notebook to provide a familiar toolset to its members. Office 365 Groups are part of Outlook and currently only associable via Outlook.

Best for: Group collaboration centered on email and calendaring with the ability to store documents

Yammer

Yammer, an enterprise-level communication platform, allows news and updates to be posted to a single site for consumption. With Yammer, users can subscribe to Yammer groups, either public or private, and collaborate with them.

Best for: Social media-like tool to foster communication within an organization at any level

Planner, Forms, Flow

Microsoft Planner is a new way to assign and report on tasks. The application provides a central location for task management outside the typical task management apps (Outlook and SharePoint).

Best for: Assigning tasks and reporting on progress

Microsoft Forms allows for forms, quizzes, or surveys to be created to collect responses. Forms can be embedded within a SharePoint site or a link to the form can be posted to be filled out.

Best for: Collecting data and tracking responses

Flow provides a workflow-like experience based on triggers and actions. Flow connects to a multitude of services, both Office 365 and external third-party services.

Best for: Performing a repetitive task or getting approval based on a document or item

Conclusion

Thank you for both purchasing and reading my first book, *Beginning Office 365 Collaboration Apps*. I hope that it has answered many of your questions surrounding the collaboration applications and have provided a solit understanding of the Office 365 platform. I also hope you feel confident with the platform and continue to explore the ever-changing Office 365 platform.

I will maintain a "Beginning Office 365 Collaboration Apps" blog where I will post updates to accompany this book; go to `www.capelesssolutions.com`. If you encounter any issues, comments, or questions, please feel free to reach out to `ralph@ capelesssolutions.com` and I will respond as soon I can.

Index

A

Actions
    adding an action, 292–293, 301, 303
    approval flow, 288–292, 294–295
    electronic signature flow, Adobe Sign,
        307–308
    software bug flow
        forms, 298–304, 307
        planner, 298–305, 307

B

Branching, 270–272
Browse, 237, 244

C

Channels
    add a tab, 137
    channel options, 133–134
    creating, 131–133, 237
    Microsoft Stream, 237
    settings, 135–136
Closed captioning, 250
Co authoring, 197
    office online
        Excel Online, 198–202
        PowerPoint Online, 204
        Word Online, 203

Collaboration apps
    flow, 16
    forms, 16
    Office, 14–15
    Office 365 Groups, 14
    OneDrive, 15
    Outlook, 14
    planner, 16
    PowerApps, 16
    SharePoint, 15
    stream, 17
    teams, 15
    Yammer, 16
Columns, 43–45, 47
Components of Office 365 Groups
    calendar, 112–113
    conversations, 111–112
    files, 114–115
    notebook, 116
    planner, 115–116
    site, 113–114
Content, Microsoft Stream, 242
Context menu, 73–75, 83–85

D

Dashboards and reporting, 225–227
Datatypes
    choice, 262–264, 266, 270, 273, 275, 277
    date, 264, 273